Library of
Davidson College

Georg Lukács
translated by
Susanne Bernhardt
and Norman Levine

THE PROCESS
OF DEMOCRATIZATION

*The Process
of Democratization*

SUNY Series in Contemporary Continental Philosophy
Dennis J. Schmidt, Editor

THE PROCESS OF DEMOCRATIZATION

Georg Lukács

*Translated by Susanne Bernhardt and Norman Levine
with an Introduction by Norman Levine*

State University of New York Press

First published in Hungary in 1988, © Ferenc JÁNOSSY,
by the Publishers Akadémia

Published by
State University of New York Press, Albany

© 1991 State University of New York

All rights reserved

Printed in the United States of America

No part of this book may be used or reproduced
in any manner whatsoever without written permission
except in the case of brief quotations embodied in
critical articles and reviews.

For information, address State University of New York
Press, State University Plaza, Albany, N.Y., 12246

Production by Dana Foote
Marketing by Dana E. Yanulavich

Library of Congress Cataloging in Publication Data

Lukács, György, 1885–1971.
    [Demokratisierung heute und morgen. English]
    The process of democratization / Georg Lukács ; translated by
Susanne Bernhardt and Norman Levine ; with an introduction by Norman
Levine
       p.   cm.—(SUNY series in contemporary continental
philosophy)
    Translation of: Demokratisierung heute und morgen.
    Includes bibliographical references and index.
    ISBN 0-7914-0761-6 (alk. paper).—ISBN 0-7914-0762-4 (pbk. :
alk. paper)
    1. Socialism—History—20th century. 2. Capitalism—History—20th
century. 3. Democracy—History—20th century. I. Title.
II. Series
HX.L7913   1991
320.5'31'90—dc20   90-47554
                                                                          CIP

10 9 8 7 6 5 4 3 2 1

*To My Wife,
Rose Levine*

Contents

Acknowledgments ix

Introduction

On the Transcendence of *State and Revolution*   3
    Norman Levine

The Process of Democratization

Notes on the Translation   65

Preliminary Methodological Remarks   67

Part I. Bourgeois Democracy as a False Alternative for the Reform of Socialism

1. Democracy and Its Various Economic Formations   71

2. The Necessary Developmental Tendencies of Bourgeois Democratization   77

3. Bourgeois Democracy Today   81

Part II. The Pure Alternative: Stalinism or Socialist Democracy

4. Theoretic and Historic Presuppositions of a Concrete Problem   93

5. Stalin's Victory Over His Rivals *107*

6. Stalin's Method *117*

7. The Twentieth Congress and Its Consequences *137*

Index *173*

Acknowledgments

I came across *DEMOKRATIZIERUNG HEUTE UND MORGEN* on the first day of my first visit to the Lukács Archiv in Budapest. The idea of journeying to Budapest was initially suggested to me by Eva Karadi and Georgy Mesterhazy whom I met while delivering a paper at a symposium in Paris in April, 1985 commemorating the hundredth anniversary of the births of Georg Lukács and Ernst Bloch. It was Karadi and Mesterhazy who convinced me to come to Budapest that summer for I would be in West Berlin on a fellowship from the Historische Kommission. Taking the train from East Berlin to Budapest that August, I made the pilgrimage to the Lukács Archiv. After familiarizing myself with the apartment of the master, glancing over his library and catching the work of Nicolai Hartmann, Mesterhazy handed me a copy of Lukács's *DEMOKRATIZIERUNG* that the Archiv had recently published. To my question of whether or not I could publish an English translation of this book, both he and the Director of the Archiv László Sziklai answered in the positive. My long marriage with the Lukács text began.

My dedication to this project was reciprocated by Professor Dennis Schmidt, Department of Philosophy, State University of New York at Binghamton. As the editor of the series under which this book appears, Schmidt was also attracted to the idea of publishing Lukács's last will and testament on the necessity of an overthrow of Stalinism. Schmidt recommended the book to the State University of New York Press and I am grateful to the Director, William D. Eastman, for his patience during the protracted completion of this work.

From September, 1988 until February, 1989 I was a Fulbright Senior Research Scholar at the Free University, West Berlin, and this generous support allowed me to complete most of the work on this manuscript. Ulrich Littman and Reiner Rohr of the German Fulbright Commission, Bonn, were particularly helpful to me.

It was a pleasure working with my co-translator Susanne Bernhardt. The text the reader has is the result of a true division of labor. Bernhardt carried the responsibility of doing the initial translation into English. I brought the expertise regarding Marxism to the work and refined the text so it was an accurate English statement of the history and philosophy of Lukacs's thought.

The presence of my children, Todd and Melissa, are in the pages. Their sacrifices are not silences, but part of the substance of the text.

Norman Levine
Columbia, Maryland
June, 1990

Introduction

On the Transcendence of *State and Revolution*

Norman Levine

Georg Lukács's book *The Process of Democratization*[1] introduced a new era in the history of Marxist political theory. This book is a prolegomena to a contemporary revival of a Marxist theory of politics. After the death of Stalin, Lukács devoted himself to a renaissance of Marxist thought, and *The Process of Democratization*[2] shows him reformulating Marxist principles in the area of a theory of politics. However, Lukács's desire in the last two decades of his life to contribute to a rebirth of Marxist speculation led him first to the realms of aesthetics and social phenomenology.

In his *Die Eigenart des Asthetischen*,[3] completed in 1963, Lukács demonstrates that art was the objectification of the sociohistorical development of humankind. Offering a Marxist response to the ontological views of Martin Heidegger and Nicolai Hartmann,[4] Lukács counters their idealist phenomenology with a social phenomenology. The ever-changing substratum of society is the ground out of which art and all objectifications of human labor emerge. Art defetishizes everyday thought; it is critical, because it reveals to the spectator the true forces which operate behind the seeming certainty of everyday reality. Lukács attempted to pass beyond the "art-as-reflection" debates within Marxist aesthetics of the 1930s, and move Marxist aesthetics in the 1960s to the ground of social ontology.

Lukács continued his speculations on the social origins of human objectification in his *Zur Ontologie des gesellschaftlichen Seins*.[5] This work was begun in earnest in 1964, the entire manuscript was typed in 1968, but it was not rewritten or refined and bears the marks of incompleteness. *Zur Ontologie des gesellschaftlichen Seins* is an extended commentary on the constitutive nature of human *praxis*, of teleological action. This book is speculative sociology, an attempt to offer a phenomenological interpretation of how human labor is the generative force in social evolution.

These phenomenological investigations are broadened to the realm of politics in his *The Process of Democratization*. In Lukács's excursion into social ontology, the aesthetic, social being and politics must be seen as three ex-

pressions of an ambitious enterprise to offer a unitary view of human social existence. In *The Process of Democratization,* Lukács tries to found the presuppositions of a Marxist political theory in the concepts of civil society, species being, and human teleological action. On a more political level, Lukács's book is his final statement that Stalinist bolshevism[6] is a deformation of Marxism. *The Process of Democratization* is an effort to distinguish a Marxist theory of politics from Stalinist bolshevism. It is a dissident work, an expression of the "Leninist opposition," a statement that Marxism cannot be reduced to Stalinism, and that Marxism is a refutation of Stalinism.

In this book, Lukács transcends the orthodox Marxist definition of politics, offering a critique of the Engels-Lenin idea of the state as presented in Lenin's *State and Revolution.* If *State and Revolution* represents the utopian expectations of revolutionary bolshevism in 1917, so Lukács's *The Process of Democratization* renders *State and Revolution* obsolete and instances the reformulation of Marxism which begins after Stalin's death. The *Process of Democratization* must be read essentially as an anti-*State and Revolution.* Whereas Lenin sought to subsume politics into administration, Lukács liberates politics in the Marxist tradition from both administration and economics. Lukács's book begins the repoliticization of a Marxist theory of politics.

The Process of Democratization is an incomplete work, and should be considered as a prolepsis to a Marxist theory of politics. It is a draft of some of the fundamental principles of Marxist political theory. It was written in great haste and under great pressure, following the Soviet repression of the Czechoslovakian reform movement of Alexander Dubcek in August, 1968. Lukács wrote the text between September and December, 1968,[7] but he was not happy with the text, thinking it too much of a summary for a true scientific work and too scientific for a good summary. He planned to enlarge the manuscript into a chapter of his projected book on ethics.[8] The complete manuscript was published in 1985 in German by Dr. László Sziklai, Director of the Lukács Archiv in Budapest. This edition is the first English translation.

In terms of its political context, *The Process of Democratization* must be seen as a statement of support for Dubcek's Czech reformation of Marxism. Lukács took an active role in the Hungarian Revolution of 1956, and was Minister of Culture in the government of Imre Nagy. Lukács was arrested when he fled to the Yugoslav Embassy by the Soviets as they repressed the Hungarian Revolution. He was exiled to Rumania for about six months. He was a supporter of the reform movement in Eastern Europe and the ideas of 1956 in Hungary and 1968 in Czechoslovakia fill these pages. *The Process of Democratization* is an embrace of the reform movement which continued from Budapest to Prague: it is a philosophical apology for this dissent against the Stalinist imperium. Although the Soviets extinguished this progressive renaissance of socialism in 1956 and 1968, it erupted again in Poland in 1981,

in Hungary in 1987–1988, and has surfaced also in Moscow under Gorbachev. When Lukács wrote *The Process of Democratization* in 1968 he looked back at Dubcek's aborted rebirth of Marxism, wrote a partisan assessment of defeat, but today the book stands as a prophecy to the events in Poland, Hungary and contemporary Moscow. A consistency of idea sustained the reform movement from the Petöfi Circle to Moscow. Today *The Process of Democratization* represents a prophetic blueprint by which to judge the policies of Gorbachev.

Ferenc Fehér and Agnes Heller offer an insightful analysis of the various currents of reform which flowed into the Hungarian Revolution in their book, *Hungary 1956 Revisited*.[9] Fehér and Heller write of their teacher, Georg Lukács: "oppositional 'reform' Marxism, whose greatest personality was beyond any doubt George Lukács, formulated this constellation with an even more merciless diagnosis. It was Lukács again (and perhaps not by chance within the Petöfi circle, that forum of preparation of the Hungarian Revolution of 1956) who formulated the programme: the renaissance of Marxism."[10] But a reform movement has many branches and in order to understand Lukács's position in this reform movement it is necessary to situate him with greater exactitude. Fehér and Heller again come to our aid when they write of the various camps of the Hungarian Revolution: "The second was Lukács; the inconsistent Bolshevik; the man with the sincere conviction of being 'the authentic Bolshevik;' the man, who precisely because of his inconsistency, could become the defender of the revolution of 1956. . . . an indefensible cause when viewed from strictly Bolshevik premises."[11] In my interpretation, Lukács was part of the Leninist opposition to Stalinism, which was a centrist position in the 1956 revolution in Hungary. By the phrase "Leninist opposition" I mean a political reform movement which did not want political pluralism, or a market economy, or to have Hungary withdraw from the Warsaw Pact, but which saw the Leninist tradition itself as offering possibilities for the reform of Stalinism and specifically looked upon the New Economic Policy of 1921 in the Soviet Union as the basis of such a communist reformation. To the left of Lukács was the more radical democratic wing of the Hungarian Revolution, which did advocate political pluralism, a market economy, withdrawal from the Warsaw Pact in return for the "Finlandization" of Hungary, and whose representative was Imre Nagy. The axial theoretic difference between the centrist Leninist opposition and the radical democratic left (Liberals), was that Lukács never sought to step outside Leninist bolshevism, indeed wished to resurrect it, while Nagy "had transcended bolshevism."[12] Although Lukács transcends *State and Revolution,* he never transcends Lenin himself, and Agnes Heller felt that his dedication to Lenin was a fatal flaw.[13] In his autobiographical sketch,[14] Lukács distances himself from the radical democracy of Nagy, stating that he joins the government "in order to help"[15] but not out of

deep commitment to its policies. Lukács did not want Hungary to withdraw from the Warsaw Pact, voted against that measure while in the government,[16] and was opposed to the full introduction of a market economy because "it would be an illusion to believe that such elements of the market could lead socialist production along the right democratic path."[17]

All parties agreed on the rejuvenation of the Soviets, the labor movement and worker self-management (the Yugoslav model) and these three demands formed the great stream which has propelled the reform movement in Eastern Europe and the Soviet Union forward, regardless of the other differences which separate the Leninist opposition and the radical democrats. Based upon the idea that the Communist party was a hegemonic apparatus for the expropriation of the laboring classes, an idea first put forward in Milan Djilas's *The New Class*, all the reform camps agreed that the working class must be politically empowered and the control of the party-state over the life of society must be smashed.

In discussing the significance of Lukács's text to a Marxist theory of politics, I use the phrase theory of politics rather than a theory of the state because theory of politics is a more inclusive term.[18] I use theory of politics as commensurate with political theory and mean a study of the origin, constituents, institutions and nature of governance. A theory of the state is a subdivision of a theory of politics for it essentially relates to the institutions of governance. A theory of politics is antecedent to the problem of the state, because it establishes those conditions which call the state into being. A theory of politics cannot be reduced to the problem of the state, for to make the intellectual equation that politics is equal to the state is to maim the definition of politics because it is to define politics as only institution and to omit the whole question as to the manner in which society will make decisions. The problem of the state was posterior to the issue of the protocols of the decision-making process necessary to society.

A theory of politics was the black hole of the Marxist *weltanschauung* in the nineteenth and twentieth centuries. This is not the place to discuss the history of a theory of politics in the thought of Karl Marx himself, or in the period of the Second International in general. When Marx moved to England in 1850 he became absorbed in the question of economics and that remained the center of his interest until his death. Marx's immersion first into classical economics and then into economic anthropology left him no time to fulfill a desire he expressed in 1844 to write a philosophy of the state.[19] The core of Marx's political theory, as distinct from a theory of revolutionary tactics, is essentially located in seven texts: *Critique of Hegel's 'Philosophy of Right'*, *On the Jewish Question*, *The Eighteenth Brumaire of Louis Bonaparte*, *The Class Struggles in France*, *The Civil War in France*, *The Critique of the Gotha Program*, *and On Bakunin's Statism and Anarchy* but these do not set forth a de-

tailed description of what he means by politics or state or a communist society. Marx bequeathed to following generations a fateful absence of specificity on these fundamental questions of political philosophy and a theory of politics as well as a theory of the state. This absence of a theory of politics is a crippling loss, because after the founding of communist societies following the Russian Revolution of 1917 no canonical guideline existed to assist in the establishing of communist states. The tactics of revolution are easily substituted for a theory of politics. This vacancy of political theory is a black hole in the evolution of socialist thought in the nineteenth and twentieth centuries.

Marxist political theory suffered from a linguistic collapse, for in the absence of a theory of politics it conflated the ideas state and politics. The Second International in general, and *State and Revolution* in particular, equated three terms: state, anarchy and politics. In the age of the Second International down to 1917, the political logic of Marxism took the following form: Marx called for the "withering away of the state" and this meant that communism was synonymous with anarchism. Communism was a society in which the state did not exist and in which politics was unnecessary. The terminological confusion between state and politics,[20] the identification of politics with the state created a linguistic logic in which "statelessness" was immediately translated into politicslessness.[21]

I use the terms Leninism and the Marxism of the Second International as synonyms. I am, of course, aware of the significant differences which existed between Lenin and the Second International, differences which ultimately exploded the Second International and led Lenin to establish the Third International. I am not concerned with the divergences which separated Lenin and the Marxism of the Second International, but rather with the ideas they shared in common, and one of these ideas concerned a Marxist theory of politics. When I assume the unity between Lenin and the Second International I do so on a restricted basis, on the question of a Marxist theory of politics only. However, when I refer to Marx himself I assume that his political theory is opposed to that of Lenin and the Second International. I use the terms Marxism and Marxism of the Second International as opposites. In the period of transition from Marx to the Second International the Marxism of Marx was lost. The Marxism of the Second International which Lenin absorbed offered a distorted version of the political theory of the Marxism of Marx.

The Marxism of the Second International held to a class-property reductionist view of the state. Revealing an anarchist tendency in Marxist thought, Second International theory defined the state simply as an instrument of class oppression. The classic expression of the state-as-domination thesis was Engels's *The Origin of the Family, Private Property and the State*, which Lenin in *State and Revolution* says offered the clearest analysis of Marxist state theory. It is my belief that significant differences on a broad range of issues

separated Marx and Engels, and that Engels's theory of the state diverged in important ways from Marx's theory of the state. When Lenin concluded that Engels's book expressed Marx's thoughts on the state he was in error. *The Origin of the Family, Private Property and the State* was vintage Engels, but Lenin did not have the historical perspective to understand that Engels's point of view was at variance with Marx's opinion on this issue. Within the age of the Second International, the state was defined as a weapon in the hands of the dominant classes, which presented Marxists with the problem of distinguishing their political theory from that of anarchism. Both Marxism and anarchism agreed that ultimately the state would disappear, that freedom could only be claimed on the condition that the state was dissolved. Since both Marxism and anarchism agreed upon the ends of political theory, a stateless society, if they were not to be considered as identical they could only disagree as to means. For Lenin, the difference is one of means, is a question of the timing of the disappearance of the state. Bakunin saw the state dissolving immediately at the moment of the revolution, while Lenin saw the bourgeois state being abolished immediately by a proletarian revolution, but to be replaced by another state, the proletarian state, and this second state would then "wither away."[22]

Since the state was only a medium of force for class domination, the elimination of class was simultaneously the eradication of state, according to Second International theory. The logical grammar of the Second International extended from class reductionism to property reductionism.[23] Class was merely an economic category reduceable to the ownership of productive property, for if the abolition of class would remove the cause for the existence of the state then the abolition of private property would erase the cause for the existence of class. Communist society has no private property, therefore it has no classes, no state and no politics.

It is important to understand that Marx defines the word property in two senses, as personal property and as productive property. By personal property, Marx means objects people owned privately which did not produce social wealth, such as clothing, furniture, or cosmetics. By productive property, Marx means objects people owned privately which did produce social wealth, such as oil wells, coal mines or steel mills. The crucial aspect to Marx's approach to the question of private property relates to that property which contributes to total social value. From this frame of reference, when Marx calls for the abolition of property he does not call for the abolition of private property, clothing or cosmetics, but for the abolition of productive property: private possession of steel mills and coal mines.

According to Marxist historiography, a proletarian revolution would overthrow the bourgeois state and build a proletarian state, a stage in the revolutionary process designated as socialism, and ultimately the proletarian state would die off leading into the higher stage of communism which was proper-

tyless, classless, stateless and without politics. The conquest of communism still left the question of how this new society was to be managed, or governed. Two models were presented for the proper management of a communist society, the productivist and the egalitarian. In both these models politics was subsumed into economics and administration. The Marxist theory of politics ended in a tragic denouement: its success was its failure, for the victory of communism meant that economic production and social egalitarianism replaced politics, or democracy was considered expendable.

In addition to the idea of the state, the term politics also carried the meaning of a protocol for social decision making, a procedure to determine the allocation of social resources or power. In this sense, politics was a procedure which evolved out of social, individual or group interests and which aimed at the adjudication of these interests. This sense of the term political was a victim of the linguistic collapse of nineteenth century Marxist political theory. When the meaning of politics was confined to state, a Marxist theory of politics was excluded from thinking of politics as an agreed upon format for the negotiation of individual or group interests. Because of this terminological confinement, when communism was defined as without politics it meant that a communist society would have no need for established protocols by which to adjudicate a clash of interests.

The excising of politics-as-adjudication also arose because Second International Marxism thought communism to be a society without conflict. The Marxism of Friedrich Engels, Karl Kautsky and Nicolai Lenin rested upon the assumption that all social conflict stemmed from private property and from class warfare based upon private property. The property-reduction definition of class meant that the elimination of property removed the essential cause for all social antagonism. Communism was to inaugurate a new age of social harmony, and politics-as-adjudication would not be needed. Because communism witnessed the destruction of self-interest, it also transcended politics.

In the productivist model for the management of a communist society, interest was collapsed into need. The productivist model was based upon a vision of man as economic need and was capitalist in inspiration, for it saw man as driven to consume in order to satisfy need. Another aspect of the consumption-need equation was the idea that self-interest or dissatisfaction arose out of unfulfilled need. The nineteenth century idea of communism was built on a gratification formula: total gratification meant no self-interest, while incomplete gratification spelled the emergence of egoism and conflict.

These assumptions were capitalistic, because they pictured man as basically driven by the desire to gratify consumption needs. The nineteenth century Second International vision of communism was based upon a capitalist interpretation of man. Ironically, it was the claim of nineteenth century socialism that capitalist man could only be fulfilled in a communist society, that

communism was the fulfillment of the capitalist mission. Taking the consumption-need equation as basic to communism, there were two primary ways to gratify need and overcome self-interest: the productivist paradigm[24] and the egalitarian paradigm. The egalitarian paradigm is subdivided into economic egalitarianism and administrative-managerial egalitarianism.

The Productivist Paradigm and the Egalitarian Paradigm

Scarcity is the mother of self-interest. Marxist socialism was the product of the stage of economic development reached in the nineteenth century, when it was impossible to produce enough to satisfy most basic needs. Faced with the conditions of economic scarcity, Second International Marxism defined communism on the model of equal commodity distribution or need satisfaction. The change overtaking socialist thought in the second half of the twentieth century in the Western world arises out of the technological conquest of scarcity. Industrial productivity is sufficient to meet most basic needs, and so the problem of scarcity has been at least theoretically answered, and attention then shifted to other concerns.

In order to have communism it was necessary to overcome scarcity. The negation of scarcity could only come through the productivist paradigm: communism must be envisioned as unleashing the unused productive potential in society and creating economic abundance. Need gratification took place with economic abundance because there were sufficient commodities to distribute equally. The productivist model, based upon the science fiction idolization of technological marvels and a future economic cornucopia, was the precondition for a communist society.

The productivist theme also led to the capitalization of communism. The communist society was presented as superior to capitalism because it would prove to be more productive. Capitalism was shown to be unproductive because the desire of the capitalist class to maximize profits led it to curtail production, while communism was shown to be an economically liberating force because it would free modern technology into limitless productivity.

Economic Egalitarianism

The egalitarian formula rests upon the assumption that conflict arises from two sources: a) ungratified need which gives rise to self-interest; b) unequal distribution where disparities exist in private possession, giving rise to jealousy or envy, two forms of self-interest. In order to overcome these two sources of social conflict, the economic egalitarian paradigm offers two remedies: equalization of distribution and equalization of consumption.

The theory of equal distribution rests on the theory of the commensurability of need: if needs were equalized there would be no envy or jealousy. Want is the mother of aggression, and in good behavioralist fashion the economic paradigm believes that wants are quantifiable. The economic paradigm is mechanistic in theory, because if wants are quantifiable then it is possible to calculate the quantum of distribution needed to gratify wants. The problem of ungratified need could also be met by the equalization of consumption, for people gain equal consumption if they have equal incomes, or equal access to the commodities society produced. The overcoming of self-interest, the chief cause of social conflict, could be attained through the gratification of need. Economic egalitarianism is the condition for the emergence of social harmony, for the elimination of economic need is the condition for overcoming social disharmony.

Administrative-Managerial Egalitarianism

Whereas the productivist model addresses the problem of physical need, for the most part the administrative paradigm deals with the problem of human talent. The productivist paradigm confronts the problem of the physical requirements of man, while the administrative formula meets the issues surrounding skill and ability.

Without inventing the necessary vocabulary, Second International Marxism had located a source of social conflict outside the purely economic. In proposing an administrative model for the management of a communist society, Second International Marxism tacitly recognized that disparity of property was not the only source of class or social conflict. This new source was the inequality of human talents, an inequality which Marx enshrined in the phrase from *The Critique of the Gotha Program,* "from each according to his ability to each according to his needs." Because talents were stratified, social domination need not be solely economic because people of greater ability could find themselves in control of greater amounts of institutional power. While it was possible to think of an egalitarianism of need, it was impossible to think of an egalitarianism of talent. The administrative model was designed to confront those social conflicts which arose when highly talented people found themselves in positions of power because bourgeois society needed their skills and the bourgeoisie was willing to tolerate their domination of power. The administrative model addressed the issue of occupational hegemony.

Needs and talents differed because it was possible to equalize needs but impossible to equalize talents. Economic egalitarianism gratified needs, but no talent egalitarianism existed. The solution lay not in the equalization of tal-

ent, but in the equalization of jobs. Unequal people could perform equal jobs, and in this way the domination based on institutional or vocational authority would be erased. Although people were stratified in terms of skill, the jobs they performed were egalitarian so there would be no need for more institutional power to accrue to one vocational position in distinction to another. The lack of egalitarianism in talent did not mean there could be no egalitarianism in terms of function, depending upon the properties of the function itself. The stratification of talent did not necessarily entail the stratification of institutional or administrative power.

Lenin offers a solution to the stratification of talent in *State and Revolution,* and he refers to this solution as "accounting and control." His formula is: the stratification of talent cannot be overcome, but we must equalize the functions required by most jobs so that everyone, regardless of the talent hierarchy, could perform them. The phrase "accounting and control" is synonymous with the equalization of function, and in *State and Revolution,* Lenin indicates how this equalization could be reached. Influenced by the scientific management theories of Taylor, Lenin thought it possible to dissemble jobs into their simplest subfunctions so these subfunctions could be performed by the largest majority of people irrespective of talent stratification. In the dissemblement of complex jobs into simple subfunctions, Lenin adopts a mathematical-behavioral approach. Lenin uses the image of a post office when trying to describe the management of a communist economy in *State and Revolution,* and within this image the phrase "accounting and control" summons to the mind predominately secretarial and basic accounting skills. The managerial model assumes talent stratification, but is predicated upon function egalitarianism. The economic paradigm is based upon economic egalitarianism while the managerial paradigm is based upon a functional egalitarianism. Within the Marxism of the Second International, egalitarianism was the avenue to social harmony, and social harmony could only be predicated upon the absence of difference.

With job functions reduced to counting and matching skills, vocations would be democratized. A vocational elite based upon the stratification of talent ceases to exist. With the democratization of jobs, social conflict due to bureaucratic authoritarianism ends. When the job monopoly of the aristocracy of talent is broken, the administrative monopolization of power also falls. The world of work ceases to be a vocationally authoritarian domain, but rather an egalitarianism of function. When the world of work is authoritarian social conflict exists, but when the work place changes into a functional egalitarianism conflict ends: like economic egalitarianism, functional egalitarianism produces harmony.

The managerial paradigm is directed not to consumption, but to the area of social function, to the areas of educational competence. The managerial

paradigm is not aimed at the economic sphere, but rather at the institutional-bureaucratic sphere. Even in the institutional-bureaucratic sphere, the end of conflict and struggle means the end of politics. The end of conflict in the institutional-bureaucratic domain, through the medium of functional egalitarianism, spells the doom of politics.

The administrative model also supersedes politics. Within the Marxism of the Second International, the theory of politics was depoliticized. Communist society was not seen as a political society but as economic abundance and as social egalitarianism. The absence of conflict suspends the need for politics and the theory of communism is left without a political theory.

Marx himself did not advocate the preemption of politics by egalitarian economics and administration. All the sins of the Second International are not directly attributable to Marx, and the black hole of Marxist speculation is an absence of a theory of politics. He left scattered suggestions, and it is possible to elicit from these hints an outline for a Marxist political theory, and this reconstructed outline shows that he does not share the simplistic dreams of egalitarian economics and administration. A Marxist theory of politics is not the theory of politics of the Second International. Nevertheless, Marx did leave[5] a theoretic vacancy, and into this intellectual vacuum there poured all the misinterpretations of the Second International. Marx leaves a terminological vacancy, and the Second International filled this absence with all its own misconceptions.

In spite of his inability to complete a theory of the state, Marx bequeathed a group of ideas which are indispensable for any Marxist political speculation: the difference between civil society, species being and the state. Marx first discusses the idea of civil society in his *Economic-Philosophic Manuscripts of 1844*. This idea recurs again in a slightly altered form in the mature Marx, particularly in the *Grundrisse* of 1857–1858 and his *exzerpte* on anthropology from the 1870s, but in these works the divergence is not between civil society and state but between economic infrastructure and the state. Marx sees society and bourgeois state as antithetical, for the state has no independent existence, but is always an alienated reflection of the social structure of a society.

By the term civil society Marx means the assembly of human activities which can be categorized as social, economic, familial, educational and religious. Marx indicates that a group of activities exist which are independent of the activities of social power, and this complex of activities he calls civil society. The social state of humankind is inherently democratic, because it is a condition in which the everyday activities of all people find expression in the social decision-making process. Under capitalism, society is denuded of all political power; under bourgeois class rule, society is depoliticized.

The term "civil society" relates to the social life of humankind, while the term "species being" relates to the anthropological nature of humankind. The

terms civil society and species being differ because one concerns the customs and institutions used by society to reproduce itself, while the second concerns the psychobiological inheritance of the human species. Marx was familiarized with the ideas of civil society in the work of Adam Smith and Adam Ferguson, both leading members of the Scottish Enlightenment, and he learned of the notion of species being in the work of Ludwig Feuerbach and Hegel. The vision of man present in the *Economic-Philosophic Manuscripts of 1844* is a combination of the eighteenth century Enlightenment view of civil society and Feuerbachian humanist naturalism derived from the idea of species being. Regardless of the differences between these terms, Marx also uses them as though they have a common meaning, they are both polar opposites to state. In the remaining pages of this introduction I will use these words in their common meaning as an antithesis to state, while at the same time realizing the divergences between the sociological content of civil society as distinct from the anthropological content of species being.

The state is the domain of power. States reflect the social structures of a society, but have an existence independent of the society which they mirror. Society is the precondition of the state, while the state is only an effect of society. Under capitalism, the state monopolizes political power. Because the state is the executive committee of the ruling class, it is the repository of all political authority.

The Second International conflated state and all political authority. Since it had collapsed the meaning of politics into the rubric of the state, the call for the end of the state necessarily entails the end of politics as well. Marx himself does not fall victim to this linguistic collapse. When Marx calls for the overthrow of the state, he really means the depoliticization of the state and the repoliticization of society. Particularly in an advanced industrial society, Marx is aware that an agreed-upon procedure for reaching social decisions is indispensable. Marx is not an anarchist because he believes that procedures for the adjudication of social disputes, governance, are axiomatic. Marx does not call for the end of politics, but a change of location of the political. The project Marx sets for himself is to devise a way to politicize society, to invest social institutions with political power. For Marx, democracy means the correspondence between real social practice and desired social norms. Marx's enterprise is a redefinition of the term democracy, a repositioning of the infrastructures upon which political authority rests from propertied class to society. In this way there can be no distinction between the everyday activities of humankind and rules of behavior established by political power.

Written in July, 1917, Lenin's *State and Revolution* is a combination of the errors of the Second International and Marx's attempt to redirect political theory. *State and Revolution* is an amalgam of the economic and managerial egalitarianism of the Second International and Marx's project of redefining the

nature and social origins of democracy. Since Lukács's *The Process of Democratization* transcends *State and Revolution* a discussion of the Lenin text will provide the background against which to evaluate Lukács's only extended political monograph. I discuss *State and Revolution* under three general topics: 1) as an answer to anarchism and opportunism; 2) as a historiography of the state; bourgeois-as-class state and socialism and communism as "statelessness"; 3) the depoliticization of a theory of politics.

As an Answer to Anarchism and Opportunism

Marxist political theory always had an ambivalent relation to anarchism. In the stage of communism, Marxism embraces the anarchist idea that the state would cease to exist. If Marxism and anarchism share the vision of an ultimate goal, the differences between Marxism and anarchism must be asserted and explained. Since the ends were the same the differences could only arise over means. Anarchism believes that the state ceases at the moment the revolution was successful, while Marxism believes that the political revolution first destroys the bourgeois state and then substitutes the proletarian state. The end of the state occurs with the dying out of the proletarian state.

More importantly, anarchism believes in the inherent unity and organic harmony of the "people." Anarchism asserts that the natural condition of humankind is a state of cooperation. Authority, of which the state is the exemplary illustration, destroys the natural cooperation of humankind, and the uprooting of authority would mean the reemergence of a cooperative society. Since the major enemy of anarchism is authority, it does not assert that one authority (bourgeois) should be replaced by another (proletarian). Authority is evil *sui generis* and so it must be deracinated at one blow and in total.

Marxism believes in a society which is divided into classes. Rather than the organic harmony of the people, Marxism proposes the conflict interpretation of society based upon class warfare. Marxism is not anti-authoritarian per se, but antiproperty and anticlass. The uprooting of authority in itself does not eliminate social conflict, but the uprooting of classes eliminates class struggle. The primary goal of Marxism is not the state, but property and class because the state is only a function of property and class. The primary goal of anarchism is the state, which stands as the highest instantiation of authority. For Marxism, proletarian class rule must initially replace bourgeois class rule in order to repress a bourgeois counterrevolution. Only after the proletariat erases the bourgeoisie as a class, when it becomes the universal class would classes in general be superseded.

Just as *State and Revolution* attacks those who stood to the left of Marxism, so it also rebukes those who were located on its right, rejecting all as-

pects of what it refers to as opportunism. For Lenin, opportunism is a phrase which characterizes anyone who surrenders the hope of abolishing the capitalist class and the capitalist system and therefore ceases to be Marxist. *State and Revolution* is one of the opening salvos against Karl Kautsky, but the attack continues and with greater vehemence in the pamphlet *The Proletarian Revolution and the Renegade Kautsky.*[25]

Opportunism remains loyal to the parliamentarian system. In *The Dictatorship of the Proletariat,*[26] written in early 1919 soon after Lenin and the bolsheviks had disbanded the Constituent Assembly in December, 1918, Kautsky states his adherence to the parliamentarian system, to a system of indirect representation. For Kautsky, communism does not mean a search for alternative proletarian forms of government. Kautsky remains devoted to a form of government perfected by the bourgeoisie—parliamentarianism—and defines communism as a parliamentarian system in which the workers, because of the democratization of the voting system, would predominate. When Kautsky describes communism he does not think in terms of a stateless or anarchist society, rather he sees a society where universal suffrage was an actual practice and this suffrage, because a majority of the population would be proletariat, would express itself in parliament in which the majority of members would be industrial working class people.

For Lenin, any attempt to preserve bourgeois institutions is tantamount to a renunciation of the proletarian revolution. Lenin's quest in the area of a Marxist theory of politics is to discover alternatives to bourgeois thought and institutions. The Leninist project can be summarized as the search for an alternative form of state and an alternative form of democracy. Lenin's failure in this enterprise does not mean that the enterprise in itself is not necessary or significant. Lenin proceeds on the basis that a proletarian political theory must commence from proletarian principles. His project calls for the discovery of proletarian principles as distinct from all forms of previous bourgeois aristocratic or religious theories of politics. A revolution in society requires not only a revolutionary strategy, but a revolution in the axioms of a proletarian theory of politics.

As a Historiography of the State

According to the orthodox interpretation of Marxism, the pattern of a communist revolution would pass through the following three stages: 1) the overthrow of the bourgeois state; 2) the creation of a proletarian state; 3) the "withering away" of the proletarian state and the advent of communism. *State and Revolution* reaffirms the three-stage developmental process of a Marxist revolution: it restates the orthodox Marxist historiography of the state.

The Overthrow of the Bourgeois State

According to Lenin, the bourgeois state is merely an instrument of repression in the hands of the propertied classes. One of the most important sources for his definition of the state was Friedrich Engels's *The Origin of the Family, Private Property and the State,* and Lenin perpetuates a class-property reductionist view. Parliamentarianism is simply a disguise for bourgeois class rule, which places political power at the disposal of the propertied. The bourgeois state, like the aristocratic or clerical state, enshrines the class domination of wealth.

In *State and Revolution,* Lenin continues the linguistic collapse which characterizes the Marxist political theory of the Second International. Lenin collapses the words state and politics, understanding them as synonymous. When Lenin calls for the end of the state, because the word politics is totally subsumed in the word state, he simultaneously calls for an anarchist society.

State and Revolution also makes no mention of the distinction between state and civil society. Lenin's book makes no mention of Marx's *On the Jewish Question,* the book in which the separation between state and society is presented by Marx. The absence of *On the Jewish Question* from the thought of Lenin in July 1917 is interesting because he knew this Marx work and refers to it in his writing of the 1890s.[27] The early Lenin, the young revolutionary of the 1890s, was concerned with the coming of capitalism to Russia, with the uprooting of an agrarian society and its replacement with industrialism, as expressed in his book *The Development of Capitalism in Russia* (1899) and so the question of the separation of state and society was more visible to him at that time. The mature Lenin, the adult revolutionary calculating the insurrectionary moves of 1917, was more involved with questions of power and compulsion, and so in 1917 he was unconcerned with the state-society polarity, but was immersed in questions of tactics. *State and Revolution* made no mention of the state-civil society polarity, and this means that Lenin could not choose the logical option of politicizing society. Society as an independent entity did not exist for Lenin in 1917, and so it could not be politicized. The state became the sole center of the political, so its abolition was also a moment of depoliticization.

The Creation of the Proletarian State

In the course of the proletarian revolution, the bourgeois state would be abolished and replaced by a proletarian state. Feeling that he had captured the intent of Marx, Lenin looked upon the Paris Commune as the model of the proletarian state. Lenin looked outside of the history of the bourgeoisie, he looked inside revolutionary history for a model upon which to base the prole-

tarian state. The commune state was equal to the stage of socialism. The commune state was the middle point in the transition from capitalism to communism.

For Lenin, the Paris Commune represents proletarian democracy because in it political institutions based upon class (property) are abolished. Proletarian democracy carries the evolution of democracy beyond its bourgeois stage. The difference between bourgeois and proletarian democracy is the difference between representative democracy and direct democracy.

Bourgeois republics possess professional armies as well as professional police. Official armies and police are headed by an officer corps which is normally drawn from the propertied classes, and within bourgeois republics the same classes which govern the state also fill the governing posts in the army and police. Lenin wants to abolish both professional armies and police and to replace them with a militia and with a law enforcement agency based on an armed citizenry. For Lenin, the social functions of military defense and law enforcement should be carried out directly by the people themselves.[28]

The process of democratization which Lenin advocates for a commune-state, the proletarian state, extends beyond the eradication of a professional army and police to include the application of direct democracy to every branch of government. Lenin writes: "The commune, therefore, appears to have replaced the smashed state machine 'only' by a fuller democracy . . . all officials to be elected and subject to recall."[29] This means, for example, that the judiciary would no longer be appointed but elected on the basis of universal suffrage. Lenin is suspicious of bureaucracy because of his experience under Tzarism when the bureaucracy was simply a tool of Romanov oppression,[30] and in order to ensure that it would remain responsible to the people he wants to make certain that the principles of direct democracy, election and recall extend into the administrative branches of government. Another illustration of Lenin's democratic egalitarianism is his demand that people in government receive the same salaries as workers. Salary egalitarianism is simply another form of income egalitarianism. In the question of the relationship between bureaucratic and industrial labor, Lenin deals with the differences between mental and manual labor, skilled and unskilled labor, of vocational stratification, and he wants to surmount any hegemonic aspects that might lie in vocational stratification through the mechanism of wage egalitarianism.

Parliamentarianism would cease to exist under the proletarian state. During the period of the commune state, the dictatorship of the proletariat, representation would remain but the method of bourgeois representation, parliamentarianism, would be changed. The proletarian state form of representation is characterized by two features: 1) Commune state representation would not separate legislative and executive functions. Bourgeois parliamentarianism did separate these functions, and Lenin wants to surmount this

bourgeois compartmentalization by the "conversion of the representative institutions from talking shops into working bodies. The Commune was to be a working, not a parliamentary body, executive and legislative at the same time."[31] 2) The proletarian state is to be governed by the Soviets. In the proletarian state Lenin still retains the idea of representation, but the organ of representation changes, for it is no longer representation through parliament, but representation through the Soviets.

> Self-seeking defence of capitalism by the bourgeois ideologists ... consists in that they substitute disputes and discussions about the distant future for the essential imperative questions of present-day policy: the expropriation of the capitalists, the conversion of all citizens into workers and employees of one huge 'syndicate'—the whole state—and the complete subordination of the whole of the work of this 'syndicate' to the really democratic state of the Soviets of Workers' and Soldiers' Deputies.[32]

Lenin's search for an alternative form of state and democracy led him to transcend their bourgeois forms. Lenin invented a proletarian state and a proletarian form of democracy, and "the dictatorship of the proletariat" was to be the governance of the "Soviets of Workers' and Soldiers' Deputies," councils for direct democracy.[33]

The "Withering Away of the Proletarian State" and the Advent of Communism

Lenin's reaffirmation of Marx's three-stage view of the proletarian revolution completes itself when he describes the higher stage of communism. While parliamentarianism disappears in the second stage, in the era of the proletarian state, in the higher stage of communism both representation and democracy disappear. *State and Revolution* ends in anarchism and a Leninist theory of politics ceases to exist.

The term "withering away of the state" is meant to capture the sense of a slow habituation on the part of the population to "classlessness," "statelessness" and "politicslessness." The dictatorship of the proletariat[34] withers away because the people need to learn to do without politics. Rather than a revolutionary abolition, communism is the result of a slow process of behavior modification.

State and Revolution is not a blueprint for totalitarian government, for not only do state and Soviets wither away, but also the party. It accords with the democratic intent of *State and Revolution* that when Lenin describes communism in its higher stages he depicts a society without the Communist party.[35]

The Depoliticization of a Theory of Politics

State and Revolution is both catastrophe and promise. It is catastrophe because it ends Marxist political theory, stating that no need exists for a political theory under communism. *State and Revolution* legitimates the anarchist tradition of Marxism. It prevents Marxism from speculating on the question of the state, since communist society would have no state. Rather than a political theory, *State and Revolution* binds Marxism to a tactics of revolution. From the point of view of political thought, Marxism becomes fixed at the level of revolutionary tactics, at the level of state destruction rather than meditate upon state or political construction.

State and Revolution is promise because one of its essential themes is the history of democracy. *State and Revolution* is unfulfilled promise because it not only narrates the history of democracy but also gives a time period in which the need for democracy would come to an end. Lenin's book is not antidemocratic or totalitarian. Democracy as well as all forms of politics come to an end in the higher level of communism not because of Lenin's lack of appreciation of democracy, but because Lenin assumes that the social substructure which gives rise to the need of the political superstructure comes to an end.[36]

Applying the Marxist method of social analysis, Lenin assumes that every political form evidences an underlying social structure: politics is the superstructure to the social infrastructure. Class is the basic determinant of a social infrastructure prior to the withering away of the proletarian state. With the advent of capitalism, democracy became the political form by which class conflict is negotiated to the advantage of the bourgeoisie. The equation that conflict is reducible to class also carries within it the alternative equation that the elimination of class is simultaneously the elimination of conflict and the end of politics.[37]

Class struggle still exists in the proletarian stage of democratization. It is a class struggle as the majority seeks to uproot a minority, and the minority resists. It is the tyranny of the majority over the minority. Where there is class struggle, however, there is need for a state and democracy. The proletarian revolution ushers in the proletarian state, which is an instrument of class control in the hands of a majority. The continuity of social conflict also requires a proletarian democracy, a democracy in the interests of the majority. The superstructure of proletarian democracy is the commune-state or the Soviets. Politics still exists in the proletarian state because the conflict of the majority over the minority continues.

The higher stage of a communist society is a classless society. Lenin, following Engels on this matter, envisions the higher stage of a communist society as a form of social homogenization. It is the ending of all forms of social

stratification and social differentiation. If social conflict evolves out of class and social divisiveness, then the overcoming of social conflict means the transcendence of class and the creation of a socially homogeneous society. It means the equalization of all forms of social functioning.

In a society devoid of any form of social stratification social conflict ceases to exist. The end of social conflict means the end of the need of the state, and the supersession of democracy. Since democracy is a method of resolving social conflict, so the end of social conflict is also the end of the need of democracy. The higher stage of communism witnesses the cessation of class, state, and democracy, or any institution of governance.

In order to establish his scriptural justification for his theory of the supersession of democracy, Lenin does not quote Marx, but Engels:

> In the usual arguments about the state, the mistake is constantly made against which Engels warned and which we have in passing indicated above, namely, it is constantly forgotten that the abolition of the state means also the abolition of democracy: that the withering away of the state means the withering away of democracy. . . .
>
> In striving for socialism, however, we are convinced that it will develop into communism and, therefore, that the need for violence against people in general, for the subordination of one man to another, and of one section of the population to another, will vanish altogether since people will become accustomed to observing the elementary conditions of social life without violence and without subordination.
>
> In order to emphasize this element of habituation, Engels speaks of a new generation, 'reared in new, free social conditions which will be able to discard the entire lumber of the state' . . . of any state, including the democratic-republican state.[38]

The way to overcome the need for subordination is to reduce everyone to the same level. The way to overcome any need for authority is to erase any form of social stratification. Lenin contributed to the depoliticization of Marxist theory when he assumed that the homogenization of society is the way to overcome the need for any protocols for reaching social decisions. Lenin is led into an irreconcilable paradox: one could only be communist by passing beyond democracy. He reaffirms the idea that democracy and communism are two different systems.

Just as the need for democracy is overcome through the application of the social egalitarian model, so the communist society is introduced by the application of the economic egalitarian model. The Marxism of the Second International defined communism as a form of economic egalitarianism, and *State and Revolution* is a reflection of this tradition.

Chapter Five of *State and Revolution* is entitled "The Economic Basis of the Withering Away of the State,"[39] and in this chapter Lenin sets forth the economic presuppositions for the "higher phase of communist society."[40] Lenin adopts the productivist model of a communist society. For him, as well as the Marxism of the Second International in general, communism is impossible without economic abundance, and economic abundance is only possible if the potentials of modern manufacture are unleashed and communism outproduces capitalism. Lenin shows his dedication to the productivist model in the following statement. "This expropriation will make it possible for the productive forces to develop to a tremendous extent. And when we see how incredibly capitalism is already retarding this development, when we see how much progress could be achieved on the basis of the level of technique already attained, we are entitled to say with the fullest confidence that the expropriation of the capitalists will inevitably result in an enormous development of the proproductive forces of human society."[41]

Lenin capitulates to economism, because he assumes that technological development is the primary causal factor in a social structure. The first effect of the unleashing of industrial productivity under communism is social homogenization. Lenin describes the ending of social stratification in the following manner: "But how rapidly this development will proceed, how soon it will reach the point of breaking away from the division of labor, of doing away with the antithesis between mental and physical labor, of transforming labor into 'life's prime want' . . . we do not and cannot know."[42] Lenin says that although it is impossible to predict exactly advanced technology would eventually do away with social classes because social classes initially derived from the "division of labor." Technology would lead to social egalitarianism, erasing all social distinctions based upon unequal ability, or different forms of labor. Social egalitarianism means the leveling down of society to common norms attainable by everyone.

Social egalitarianism forms the basis of economic egalitarianism. Lenin remains in the mainstream of the Second International when he defines communism as an expression of economic egalitarianism. He writes: "The state will be able to wither away completely when society adopts the rule: 'From each according to his ability, to each according to his needs,' i.e. when people have become so accustomed to observing the fundamental rules of social intercourse and when their labor has become so productive that they will voluntarily work according to their ability. There will then be no need for society, in distributing the products, to regulate the quantity to be received by each; each will take freely 'according to his needs'."[43]

Lenin also applies the model of administrative egalitarianism to his vision of a communist society. *State and Revolution* contains the following passage:

> Accounting and control . . . that is mainly what is needed for the "smooth working," for the proper functioning, of the first phase of communist society. All citizens are transformed into hired employees of the state, which consists of the armed workers. All citizens become employees and workers of a single country-wide state "syndicate." All that is required is that they should work equally, do their proper share of work, and get equal pay. The accounting and control necessary for this has been simplified by capitalism to the utmost and reduced to the extraordinarily simple operations . . . which any literate person can perform . . . of supervising and recording, knowledge of the four rules of arithmetic, and issuing appropriate receipts.[44]

In the above passage, Lenin offers his "post-office" interpretation of social administration. Administrative egalitarianism is an attempt to overcome differences between people based upon talent stratification and the difference between mental and physical labor. He wants to prevent bureaucratic domination by ensuring that talent does not monopolize positions of bureaucratic power. The way to prevent bureaucratic or party domination, recognizing that talent stratification could not be erased, is to reduce all jobs to "extraordinarily simple operations" so everyone could perform them. Administrative egalitarianism is, in part, Lenin's response to the danger of party authoritarianism or Stalinism. Lenin understood that the way to prevent an administrative apparatus, i.e. a political party, from acquiring hegemonic power is to open that administrative apparatus to popular control.

Lenin looked upon communist society from the perspective of B.F. Skinner and *Walden Two,* as a behavioralist paradise. Lenin believed that people could learn to administer society without the constraints of politics. He writes: "For when all have learned to administer and actually to independently administer social production, independently keep accounts and exercise control over the parasites, the swindlers and other 'guardians of the capitalist traditions' the escape from this popular accounting and control will inevitably become so incredibly difficult, such a rare exception and will probably be accompanied by such swift and severe punishment . . . that the necessity of observing the simple, fundamental rules of the community will very soon become a habit."[45]

By "habituation," Lenin means customary behavior. Work in the post office, in large state syndicates, would teach uniform behavior. Lenin transfers the Taylor model of the assembly line from the factory floor to the administrative hierarchy, for he believed that the mechanical repetition of both factory and administrative jobs would train people into uniform behavior. By the word "habituation," Lenin describes the egalitarianism of intent and voli-

tion. Habituation through repetition teaches people to perform their social functions without the need for politics, because habituation brings about performance by consent rather than by compulsion.

The failure of bolshevism to develop a theory of politics for a communist society is not the fault of Lenin alone, but a problem for the entire Second International. A Marxist theory of politics was the black hole of the Second International, and Lenin's work is a reflection of this vacancy. This theoretical emptiness within the Second International stemmed from three primary terminological confusions: 1) the Second International assumed that conflict was the only ground for politics; 2) the Second International believed that the medium for overcoming conflict, i.e. politics, was egalitarianism; 3) the Second International was guilty of the linguistic collapse, of drawing the following syntactical equation: politics = state = class power. When the Second International accepted the linguistic reduction of state to politics, it entered upon a syntactical formula which only permits one escape from the state and that exit is only through anarchy, or "politicslessness." To be assessed correctly, Lenin's failure must be placed within the failure of the Second International generally. The disintegration of a Marxist theory of the state was endemic to an entire generation of the European left, and Lenin was an instance of this disintegration and not its cause.

The ultimate failure of Lenin does not detract from the sincerity and creativity of his quest. His project was to discover an alternative form and theory of politics in contradistinction to the bourgeoisie. Although Lenin did not succeed in this project, he did open new insights into the concept of democracy. He perpetuated the Marxist tradition of extending the applicability of democracy into the economic arena, and went a step beyond Marx by extending the applicability of democracy into administrative, bureaucratic, and vocational domains.

Lukács's *The Process of Democratization* is the transcendence of *State and Revolution* and the overthrow of bolshevik political ideology. It is the establishment of the fundamental principles of a Marxist theory of politics.

The Process of Democratization is dedicated to the repoliticization of Marxist thought. *State and Revolution* concludes with the supersession of democracy and politics in an economic and administrative egalitarianism. *The Process of Democratization* begins from the position that the need to adjudicate social disputes and to have a protocol for social decision making is axiomatic and that democracy is the way to insure that these adjudicatory and rule-making functions of governance remain accessible to the masses. Society always has need for governance and politics, and democracy is a means of ensuring that these arbitration and protocol functions are controlled by the majority.

State and Revolution applies the idea of democracy to Marx's theory of

labor, while *The Process of Democratization* applies the democratic principle to the anthropological idea of human activity. According to the Second International and Lenin, Marx defines all labor as equal, and the only differentiation of labor arises over the amount of time spent on laboring. This attempt to mathematize the qualitative distinctions of labor means that the democracy of labor is envisioned in terms of an egalitarianism of time. Democracy is seen as the guarantee that equal quantums of labor exerted are returned as equal quantums to the laborer. Lukács overthrows the association between democracy and the theory of value, beginning his speculations from the need to maximize human activity. Lukács's project is to think of the process by which democracy can lead to the enhancement of human potential. He does not begin from a mathematization of labor, but his axial concept is species activity. Based upon this anthropological core, Lukács looks upon democracy as the decision-making procedure most conducive to the valorization of human productive potential. Lukács remains bound to the Marxist intellectual tradition by beginning his political theorizing, not on the ground of labor theory, but on the basis of individual *praxis,* conceived as the full range of human potential. For Lenin the issue is an equal return of the commodity labor, while for Lukács the issue is the expansion of human talent.

Lukács is a major contributor to the reformulation of a Marxist theory of the state. The revolutionary changes in Marxist state theory are evidenced in the differences between Lukács's 1924 book on *Lenin: A Study on the Unity of His Thought* and his 1968 book, *The Process of Democratization.* The 1924 book is devoted to the revolutionary subject, that social class which has the power can make the social revolution.[46] The text applauds Lenin as a great tactician, but it is the proletariat which is presented as that class which is alone capable of making the socialist insurrection. When Lukács wrote his *Lenin* book in 1924 the revolutionary wave unleashed by the Bolshevik 1917 had spent its force, but the utopian hopes of a communist breakout into central Europe, Germany, Hungary, Austria, Italy, still resonate in its pages. In terms of Marxian political theory, Lukács's 1924 book is in full agreement with Lenin's *State and Revolution.* Three years after the beginning of Lenin's New Economic Policy, Lukács's book justifies the dictatorship of the proletariat. Proletarian hegemony can be carried out through the Soviets, and in 1924 Lukács still clings to the council movement as the best form through which to exercise proletarian democracy. In 1924, confronted with the death of Lenin, the need for Russia to undergo rapid industrialization and the political struggle over the successor to Lenin, Lukács ceases to speak of the "withering away of the state." Too many problems faced Russia, and Lukács thought it useless to speculate about an anarchist society so he terminated his political thoughts with the justification of the proletarian dictatorship.

Lukács's 1968 book, *The Process of Democratization,* moves from tac-

tics to social ontology. The philosophical presupposition of the *Lenin* book is the Hegelian idea of identity: the revolutionary proletariat shapes history in its own image. In 1968, Lukács ceased to look upon the industrial working class as the revolutionary subject, but focused instead upon the idea of social labor. In *Lenin,* Lukács's object is the tactics of political upheaval, while in *The Process of Democratization* his object is social labor. Not only have the object and subject of the 1924 and 1968 books changed, but also the source of the philosophy of identity. In *Lenin,* the philosophy of identity rests upon the activity of class, but in *The Process of Democratization* the ground of this unity is no longer class subjectivity but rather social labor.[47]

Lukács's movement away from the strategic aspects of Leninism toward a search for the principles of democratic socialist governance is not a rejection of Leninism. *The Process of Democratization* is anti-Stalinist, but not anti-Leninist. Lukács draws a sharp line of demarcation between Lenin and Stalin. Lukács condemns Stalinism, relating to it as a form of bureaucratic totalitarianism. He feels that the Leninist heritage is opposed to bureaucratic hegemony. In 1924 Lukács related to the Lenin who is a political tactician of the seizure of power, while in 1968 Lukács related to those parts of *State and Revolution* in which Lenin talks of "habituation" or "custom," seeing in these phrases a Leninist commitment to socialist democracy. For Lukács, adherence to Leninism is the best defense against Stalinism.

The views contained in this introduction seek to refute that school of Lukács interpretation which find him a spokesman for Stalinism. The major proponent of the Lukács-as-Stalinist school of interpretation is Leszek Kolakowski, particularly in the chapter "Lukács or Reason in the Service of Dogma" contained in the third volume of Kolakowski's impressive work *Main Currents of Marxism.*[48] The Lukács-as-Stalinist argument is also set forth in two earlier assessments, George Lichtheim's *Lukács,*[49] and Victor Zitta's *Georg Lukács's Marxism.*[50] The question of Lukács's relation to Stalinism is too complex to be discussed in detail here, and I recognize that he does embrace some aspects of Stalinism, such as the Russo-German Pact of 1939. But Lukács's anti-Stalinism after 1956 is irrefutable. (See his "Letter to Alberto Carocci."[51]) I argue that his anti-Stalinism, at least in the area of cultural studies, becomes evident in his work of the 1930s. In his struggle against Hitlerism, as he ponders how irrationalist racism threatened the German humanist tradition of the Enlightenment, Lukács associates himself with the democratic and rationalist aspects of eighteenth century German culture. Although he is aware that proletarian humanism had subsumed eighteenth century humanism, Lukács does identify Goethe as the classical expression of the bourgeois Enlightenment. Like Engels, Lukács maintains that proletarian culture both grows out of and surpasses bourgeois humanism.

Lukács's move toward democracy is also extended to his studies of Rus-

sian culture in the 1930s, and in his essay "The International Significance of Russian Democratic Literary Criticism,"[52] Lukács interprets Tolstoy and Chernyshevsky as expressions of the plebeian democratic Jacobin stream of the nineteenth century, which eventually erupted in the Russian Revolution of 1917. Between 1945–1947, Lukács is an advocate of "new democracy" in Hungary, an economic-political alliance between peasantry and proletariat patterned on the *Blum Theses* of 1928 and Lenin's New Economic Policy, and pivoted on the retention of private property by the farmers. Lukács's adherence to Lenin's concept of the "democratic dictatorship of workers and peasants" (based on the Soviet model of 1905), his adherence to the rationalist humanist and democratic principles of the German Enlightenment, his rejection of the Stalinist aesthetics of proletarian art in favor of his own form of "critical realism," clearly place him in opposition to major aspects of Stalinism. Far from a defender of Stalinism, he was a critic of it from its beginnings.

According to Lukács, Stalinism represents a deformation of Marxism. Stalinism is the bureaucratic disfigurement of socialism. Just as Lukács draws a distinction between Lenin and Stalin, so he rejects all attempts to associate Stalin with socialism and then to criticize socialism through Stalin. Lukács takes a different path than Rudolf Bahro in *The Alternative in Eastern Europe*,[53] in which Bahro fuses Stalinism and socialism and he ends up rejecting socialism. Bahro allows his anti-Stalinist opposition to become antisocialism, while Lukács remains a socialist partisan. In order to save socialism, Lukács finds it necessary to rid socialism of Stalin.

In *The Process of Democratization,* Lukács offers a new definition of socialism. He breaks with the productivist and economist models which characterized the Second International interpretation of socialism, an interpretation which flowed into Lenin and Stalin both. The problem of economic scarcity was paramount in the nineteenth century, and within this context socialism was defined as the overcoming of scarcity through abundance. Lukács breaks with this form of the privileging of the economic, and moves the definition of socialism from a question of economic distribution to a political one. Socialism for the Hungarian Marxist does not place the priority on commodity abundance but on democracy.

Lukács defines socialism as the only way to ensure the greater democratization of society. The nationalization of property is the only way in which democracy could be extended. One is a socialist because one advocates deeper democracy, for socialism is the only form democracy can take in its advance beyond bourgeois parliamentarianism.

The late works of Lukács, *Die Eigenart des Asthetischen, Zur Ontologie des gesellschaftliches Seins,* and *The Process of Democratization* form an interdependent trilogy, with the common purpose of contributing to the "renais-

sance" of Marxist thought. His project was to disassociate Marxism from Stalinism, to show that Marxism has creative potentials outside of official Kremlin ideology. He reaffirms living Marxism not only against Stalinism, but also the anti-Marxism of Western critics. Lukács was not Lezcek Kolakowski, an emigree from the Eastern world who fled to the West and became a leading voice in the denunciation of Marxism. Lukács remained a Marxist partisan. Just as Lukács wished to disassociate Marxism from Stalinism so he wished to defend a reformulated Marxism against its Western critics.

The most important theoretic element in the founding of a Marxist theory of politics is Lukács's recapturing of the distinction between civil society or species being and the state. The political question for Marx and Lukács is the site of political empowerment. The issue is whether power should be located in the state, which has grown insulated from the everyday life of man, or should it be vested in civil society, which is the more immediate expression of the species life of man? Both Marx and Lukács favor the political investment of civil society.

Politics, for Lukács, is the protocol of social decision making and the adjudication of disputes. Politics is an ever-present need in society. Lukács abandons the idea of Lenin in *State and Revolution* that a conflictless society is possible. He surrenders the Leninist idea that social homogenization can remove the universal cause of social disputes. Since politics is an ever-present need in society, the question arises as to which realm, the state or civil society, can become the site of the political, the exercise of power or decision making. Both Lukács and Marx believe in the politicization of civil society because they feel that civil society is the more direct and immediate expression of the everyday life of humankind. The Soviets are the proper institutions for this politicization of civil society. Rather than a political process being the result of irreconcilable class conflict, as Lenin in *State and Revolution* puts forth, a political process is the ground out of which democracy arises.

Lukács provides the program for a Marxist theory of politics. The agenda of a Marxist theory of politics calls for the invention of political processes and institutions which extend the reach of democracy. Democracy is not a status which is ever final, but a status which must be constantly redefined dependent upon the underlying social structure. A Marxist state theory has as its charge the discovery of political protocols which will move toward the universalization of democracy.

The difference between *State and Revolution* and *The Process of Democratization* is that Lenin defines the political in the class reductive mode, while Lukács defines the political as social procedure. Beginning from a class-reductive point of view, Lenin believes that the end of class spells the end of politics. Beginning from the procedural point of view, Lukács recognizes that society could never exist without procedural consensus. Lukács changes from a class to a procedural definition of politics.

Lukács replaces class with civil society. The substitution of civil society for class is crucial, because it focuses attention on the fact that without rules there is no civil society, and that politics is a necessary function in all civil life. The substitution of civil society for class is the sociological basis for the founding of a Marxist theory of politics. The substitution of civil society for class as the basic constituent of a Marxist theory of the state is the crucial paradigm shift in Lukács's political thought.

The remarks that I offer above provide the general principles of Lukács's attempt to revive Marxist political theory. *The Process of Democratization* is also a concrete book, and it is necessary to spell out some of its specifics in order to make the complex meanings of the work clear. Only as the details of *The Process of Democratization* are made visible, do the full dimensions of Lukács's renaissance of Marxist political theory also become visible. For the sake of clarity, I divide my discussion of the specifics into two parts: 1) the transcendence of bolshevik historiography, economism and vulgar sociology; 2) the principles of a founding of a Marxist theory of the state. Most of the following remarks will be directed at Lenin's *State and Revolution,* since one of the points I wish to prove is Lukács's supersession of this work and of the bolshevik theory of politics in general.

The Transcendence of Bolshevik Historiography, Economism and "Vulgar Sociology"

The Process of Democratization must be placed in its historical period, and there are four conditions which help define this work: 1) it was written after the Bolshevik 1917 Revolution; 2) it was written after the experience of the Second World War; 3) it was written after the death of Stalin and the twentieth Party Congress of the Soviet Union; 4) it was written after the Czechoslovakian Reform movement of Alexander Dubcek.

State and Revolution was composed in July 1917, about four months before the bolshevik seizure of power, and its emphasis rests upon the taking of power. It is a manual of revolutionary strategy.[54] *State and Revolution* is one of the primary reasons for the bolshevik destruction of a theory of politics: it substitutes tactics of insurrection for the art of governing a socialist society.

Lukács's *Blum Thesis* of 1928 is a search for an alliance policy by which to block the advent of fascism in Europe. Like Lenin's *Two Tactics of Social Democracy in the Democratic Revolution,* Lukács's *Blum Thesis* calls for the formation of a worker-peasant alliance but Lukács sees this alliance policy as a way to stop the march of totalitarianism. Later in the 1930s, Lukács is an advocate of a "Popular Front" strategy.

The age of fascism presented Lukács with only two choices, either authoritarianism or democracy, and Lukács chose the democratic option. Democracy has many forms, and the form of democracy which Lukács espoused in 1968 is different than the form he espoused during the anti-fascist crusade, but the theme which remains constant is the need of the proletarian forces to remain in contact with some form of the bourgeois democratic tradition.

Within broader sociological dimensions, Lukács exemplifies a central European intellectual of the generation of the First World War who is not averse to the mixture of culture and politics. Within a narrower political framework, Lukács is always the communist partisan. After he joined the Hungarian Communist party in December 1918, he never understood his role as anything but a tribune of the cause of communism. His political writings, then, must be understood as responses to immediate tactical situations. One function of the communist intellectual is to provide intellectual warrants to justify communist tactics. This does not mean that Lukács is either insincere or devious, it means that he is attempting to preserve the communist heritage by making it relevant to different historical environments.

It is widely assumed that Lukács surrendered political life after the furor brought on by the *Blum Theses*.[55] According to this wisdom, Lukács's expulsion from the Hungarian Communist party ended his active political involvement, and he thereafter devoted his energies to literary and philosophical studies. Such an interpretation violates Lukács's self-definition as a politically conscious intellectual, for Lukács never gave up a political engagement and the only question concerns the form of political engagement.[56] The ten years from 1918 until 1928 marks Lukács's entry into and expulsion from the Hungarian Communist party, and this is a decade of political activism in which he took part in the communist government of Bela Kun. After his expulsion from the Hungarian party and the rise of fascism, Lukács's political engagement underwent a change of form but not of intellectual commitment. Lukács's political activism stopped until his entry into the Hungarian revolutionary government of Imre Nagy in October 1956, but his political engagement continued in his writing which is rarely free of political import. In his struggle against European fascism Lukács's writings are intensely political. In his studies of the novel, either Russian or Western, he sees European cultural life polarized between fascism and democracy, and his advocacy of democracy at this time becomes the source of his demands for the democratic reform of communist society after the death of Stalin in 1953. Far from political disengagement or irrelevance, Lukács's involvement in the theoretic question of democracy acts as the speculative basis from which practical reforms are to be formulated and demanded. Lukács is a major source of East European dissent and revolution.

The historical context of *The Process of Democratization* is socialism as

it existed in Eastern Europe in 1968. His problem is not the question of the nationalization of productive property, the overthrow of capitalism or the uprooting of the bourgeoisie, for all this was already accomplished. *The Process of Democratization* redirects Marxist political theory to a concentration upon the protocols necessary for the democratic governance of a socialist society.

The Process of Democratization is written in response to the crushing of the Dubcek reforms by the Soviet Union in 1968. It is a statement of support for the anti-Stalinist reformist movement in Eastern Europe. Just as Lukács was a participant in the Hungarian Revolution of 1956, so *The Process of Democratization* is a philosophic justification on the basis of his social ontology of the Prague Spring in 1968.

Within these historical parameters, Lukács transcends bolshevik historiography by ceasing to think in terms of the three stage process from capitalism to socialism to communism. Lukács abandons this classical bolshevik historiography in two ways: he no longer speaks of the transition from socialism to communism and he substitutes the idea of a democratization of socialism for the idea of communism.

Lukács refers to the idea of communism in *The Process of Democratization,* but in order to understand its meaning a distinction has to be drawn between "communism-as-immanent" and "communism-as-heuristic." By the term "communism-as-immanent" I mean the repesentation of communism as a necessary historical stage which lay within foreseeable reach. "Communism-as-immanent" appears in the pages of *State and Revolution,* for Lenin thinks it must inevitably follow socialism. It is the goal of all historical development, and since it lay in the proximate future he attempts to define some of its characteristics. By the term "communism-as-heuristic" I mean the presentation of communism as future possibility. Communism-as-heuristic acts as a guide to the future, it refers to the continuous process of the perfection of democracy. Communism-as-heuristic is not a concrete final period of history, but a value toward which history ought to move.

When Lukács uses the term "communism" in *The Process of Democratization* it is employed as communism-as-heuristic. He means an "ought" which directs humankind into the future, he does not mean a necessary conclusive stage of history which is immanent. The word "communism" as used by Lenin, Stalin, and Khruschev was defined as communism-as-immanent, but Lukács changes the meaning of the word to communism-as-heuristic. The question of the immanent coming of communism ceases to be an issue for Lukács, and so "communism-as-immanent" drops out of his political vocabulary. This part of the ideological apparatus of classical bolshevism, the part which makes communism the justification of the historical process and of the proletarian revolution, is dead. Communism as millenialism ceases to exist for Lukács.

part of classical bolshevik ideology which Lukács jettisons is the ____ ___ _ ialism or communism is commensurate with classlessness. *The Process of Democratization* is a prolegomena, so there are features of a reborn Marxist political theory which Lukács cannot address in depth and the question of social stratification is one of those areas. The pages of Lukács's text, however, contain no mention that either socialism or communism-as-heuristic can be classless. On the issue of social stratification, it is clear that Lukács draws a distinction between class and other forms of social groups, or social strata. "Class" is a term which applies to the ownership of productive property, while "group" is a term which applies to social strata which are joined together by ties other than ownership. Within this definition, it is possible for a socialist society to have abolished class, but not other social groups, like professors, engineers, social workers and industrial laborers. Lukács abandons the idea of equating socialism or communism with social homogenization. In terms of the definition offered above, socialism is a society in which social stratification, groups, still exist, for the existence of groups, nonpropertied associations, is not destructive of democracy. In surrendering the idea of classlessness, Lukács overthrows the classical bolshevik idea of economic and administrative egalitarianism. The deepening of democracy does not lie in the homogenization of society, but rather in the political empowerment of all social strata, so that no social group is excluded from the exercise of political sovereignty.

Classical bolshevism presents communism as a final stage of history. A contradiction exists between historical materialism and bolshevik political theory. As a model, historical materialism is a form of social analysis which was based on the assumption that process is continuous in history, while in terms of political theory, bolshevism upholds the idea that communism is the final end of the historical process. Communism is clothed with millenial expectations, and from the point of view that it is considered a perfect society there is no progress beyond it.

Lukács does accept this separation between historical materialism and political theory. Communism is not considered an ahistorical state, rather political theory must be historicized. Lukács rejects the eschatological interpretation of communism, and realizes that political theory itself must be historicized. In his book, Lukács does not use the term "democracy" because this implies a static, fixed form of a certain type of government. Instead, Lukács uses the term "democratization," a term that implies democracy-in-process: that democracy is a never-ending search for ways to extend citizen participation in government.

Lukács stops using the word "communism" in its eschatological sense, as a New Jerusalem whose historical realization was imminent. Communism suggested ahistoricity, while Lukács attempts to found a Marxist theory of

politics on the basis of historicity. The aim of a Marxist political theory is not to describe a communist society, but rather to analyze how a socialist society can be democratized further. Lukács substitutes the idea of a deeper democratization of socialist society for the idea of communism. The socialist revolution is a victory for the democratization process, because it places productive property in the hands of the party. The movement of the socialist revolution calls for an extension of the process of democratization beyond the economic into the political spheres: party ownership of the means of production changes into the social ownership of this productive property.

Lukács is the death of classical bolshevist historiography, the attempt to periodize history as a necessary three-stage process. Not only does Lukács assign the paradigm capitalism-socialism-communism to the dustbin of historiography, but he also supersedes many other aspects of the classical bolshevik ideological apparatus. Concepts like "dictatorship of the proletariat," "proletarian state," "withering away of the state," "smashing" of the bourgeois state, "commune-state," all cease to appear in his late political writing. All these concepts were crucial to bolshevism as a tactics of insurrection, and the fact that they no longer have any relevance for a repotentialization of contemporary Marxist political theory means that an age in the history of socialist thought is at an end. Classical bolshevik ideology is outmoded, and the scrapping of all these theoretic concepts means that the ideational apparatus of bolshevism is dead. Just as the early political writings of Lukács, from 1918 until his *Lenin* book of 1924, provide some of the finest intellectual defenses of bolshevism, so his 1968 book *The Process of Democratization* officiates at the death of classical bolshevik political theory.

In order to see how it is possible for Lukács to supersede classical bolshevism while at the same time upholding Leninist bolshevism, it is necessary to draw a distinction between these two forms of bolshevism. By the term classical bolshevism I mean a common body of bolshevik thought that runs from Lenin to Stalin. Although there were differences between Lenin and Stalin there was also continuity, and the phrase classical bolshevism refers to those areas of thought in which there were continuities, such as the perpetuation of the political theory of the Second International. The separation between classical Stalinist bolshevism and Leninist bolshevism stemmed from the differences existing between Lenin and Stalin. It is possible for Lukács to attack classical Stalinist bolshevism while at the same time defending Leninist bolshevism. Stalinist bolshevism was synonymous with bureaucratic totalitarianism, while Leninist bolshevism looked upon the Soviets as the core of governance. The "Leninist opposition" is anti-Stalinist. The current reform movement in Eastern Europe and the Soviet Union, of which Lukács is a philosophic precursor, has succeeded in destroying Stalinist bolshevism and in affirming Leninist bolshevism.

A part of Leninist bolshevik ideology which Lukács retains and which characterizes the Leninist opposition, is the idea of the Soviets. He sees them as an institution which can help bring about the separation of party from the state, for the Soviets can take over functions of the state and lead to the disengagement of the party from the state. *The Process of Democratization* relies heavily upon the idea of the Soviets, since they are institutions of direct democracy. Lukács conveniently overlooks the fact that Lenin had inflicted a near mortal wound on them during the Kronstadt Rebellion.

Another aspect of the ideological apparatus of classical bolshevism which Lukács overthrows is the idea of statelessness and politicslessness. In *The Process of Democratization,* Lukács calls for the separation of party and state, making known his awareness that the state and politics are necessary features in all forms of governance. Additionally, when Lukács characterizes socialist society as governed by Soviets, or as a realm in which everyday life is politically empowered, it is clear that these kinds of activities cannot proceed without a state. Socialism is a stage in the odyssey of democratization, and democracy as procedure and protocol cannot exist without state. Lukács ensures that statelessness and politicslessness are erased from the lexicon of Marxist political theory and this is a further purification of the ideological integument of classical bolshevism.

In terms of philosophical foundations, Lukács frees a Marxist theory of politics of its utilitarian and behavioralist bias. Lenin's *State and Revolution* and the entire political theory of the Second International had, as their philosophical presuppositions, a utilitarian and behavioralist approach to man. The era of the Second International substituted psychology for political speculation. The underlying assumption of the Second International was that man could be psychologically conditioned to cooperate, and so the art of conditioning replaced the skill of the politician. Lukács transcends this reduction of politics to psychology, and resituates a Marxist theory of politics in the Greek *polis* ideal. Lukács seeks to restore the unity of the public and private man, instead of eradicating self-interest through psychological conditioning.

Jeremy Bentham is the philosophical godfather of the political theory of the Second International. His view of humankind, a perspective originally founded in the seventeenth and eighteenth centuries, considered humankind to be a creature of want. Humans had needs, and unfulfilled needs led to self-interest and self-interest was the seed of social conflict. Conversely, if needs were fulfilled, humankind was pacified and there was no social conflict. Pacification was the end, and gratification the means by which social conflict would be brought to an end. The underlying assumption of utilitarian psychology was behavioralism: through the proper adjustment of pleasure and pain and the gratification of wants humans could be conditioned into cooperative harmonization.

Adopting a utilitarian and behavioralist approach to human psychology, the Marxism of the Second International thought it possible to condition humankind into a nonconflictual society. If the gratification of wants was the surest way to overcome conflict, then politics could be superseded. If there were no conflicts and no self-interest to adjudicate, there was no need for any political order.

Lukács overcomes the philosophic foundations of Second International political theory. He rejects the psychologist approach to human behavior and commits himself to the idea of integrating the public and private person. He accepts a world of individuals and self-interest, and recognizes that social protocols and politics are needed to reconcile conflicting claims. Resurrecting the idea of *polis* integration, Lukács is not primarily concerned with the creation of nonconflictual situations, but more with the fulfillment of human potentials. Lukács commits himself to the Greek ideal of harmonized life, and once again joins ethics and politics. The Greek ideal of a harmonized life assumes the existence of separate self-actualizing individuals who can disagree, and the Greek ideal disposes Lukács to accept the need for a continuation of politics in the form of social procedure. Politics is not domination for Lukács, but a protocol which allows the integrated personality to appear.

Lukács also transcends the productivist definition of socialism. The economism of the Second International and bolshevism tended to focus attention on productive forces. If economic abundance was the aim, then the means to this abundance was an increase in technology. Attention was shifted away from relations of production to the technology of production. Socialism became the propaganda of the technological bureaucrat. The linguistic equation which captured the fascination for industrial modernization took the following form: technology is the basis for productivity; productivity is the condition for economic abundance; economic abundance is necessary before pacification could take place; pacification is the key to a nonconflictual society. In the economist model, communism is equated with advanced technology.

Along with the supersession of the productivist-economist interpretation of socialism, Lukács also jettisons "vulgar sociology," or the attempt to explain all social events in terms of class or economic income. Even though vast differences separated Lenin and Stalin, Lenin is a "vulgar sociologist," a position driven to the extreme under Stalin. Allied to vulgar sociology is the base-superstructure model. According to this model, the superstructure of a society—its culture, politics, laws—are merely reflections of its infrastructure, its class structure and means of production. The base-superstructure model can also be described as sociological epiphenomenology, a method of social analysis which claims that law, politics and culture are merely epiphenomena of class interest.

From the point of view of sociological epiphenomenology, the culture

and institutions of politics have no independent existence. The entire apparatus of politics, from political theory to political parties to state, is reducible to class interest. Sociological epiphenomenology lends itself to the conclusion that the elimination of class was simultaneously the elimination of politics *sui generis*.

Lukács transcends all forms of vulgar sociology. He believes this to be a slavish capitulation to objective forces. A Hegelian, Lukács accentuates the role of human activity in historical evolution. Objective forces, nature or economic tendencies, are never sufficient in themselves to account for social development, for the action of conscious subjects is that agency which provides the ends toward which social evolution moves. Because he wishes to defend the causal agency of human activity, the Marxian idea that men make their own history, Lukács rejects all forms of vulgar sociology, or sociological epiphenomenology.

The Principles of a Founding of a Marxist Theory of the State

Lukács hoped that his reformulation of a Marxist theory of politics would contribute to the renaissance of Marxism. The reconstruction of a Marxist theory of politics is one way to lead to the regeneration of Marxist theory in general, toward making Marxism relevant to a post-Stalinist world. The Marxism which Lukács wants to recreate is bolshevism as it exists 1921–1925. Lukács was always the tribune of bolshevism, but the form of bolshevism he seeks to resurrect is the Leninist bolshevism of the period of the New Economic Policy, or a counterfactual Leninist bolshevism, one in which Lenin had not completely destroyed the Soviet movement.

In order to understand Lukács's politics, however, it is necessary to place it within the context of his social ontology. He continues the Marxist idea that philosophy must form the speculative ground of every sociology. A liberatory social science or political theory is only reached when social science or politics is joined to philosophy, either as method or as axiology. It is impossible to discuss the full dimensions of Lukács's social ontology in the context of this essay. However, I begin my discussion of Lukács's theory of the state by relating that political theory to his social ontology in three areas: 1) social ontology: historicist; 2) social ontology: *praxis;* 3) German humanism and the *polis*-ideal.

Social Ontology: Historicist

Part 1 of *The Process of Democratization* is called "Bourgeois Democracy as a False Alternative for the Reform of Socialism" and offers a his-

toricist interpretation of democracy. Lukács attacks the "vulgar" idea of democracy, that democracy exists in one eternal form. Lukács suggests that democracy, like any other social institution, is constantly changing its form, that democracy must be interpreted from a historicist viewpoint.

Process is the crucial idea in Lukács's philosophy of social ontology. Human activity is a constant in the socioeconomic universe. Although Lukács uses the term "ontology," he uses ontology as synonymous with process. Assuming the essentiality of process, Lukács affirms that all historicity derives from social changes. Lukács begins from a Hegelian view of constant movement and adds Marx to the equation; social change is the basis of all change. Lukács does not want to make process a transcendental category in the style of Heidegger. Movement cannot become an existential atemporal category of existence. Lukács's social ontology is meant as a refutation of Heidegger, as a Marxist response to phenomenology and existentialism. It is an attempt to show that process is not a transcendental category but a socially produced category.

Social process is always a product of objective and subjective forces. Subjective agency, conscious human action, is goal oriented, while objective agency, natural or economic developments, move by a mechanical process of their own. This combination of subjective and objective forces is the dynamic for social evolution. Every society is a unique totality of separate social structures. Although Lukács does not reduce politics totally to economics, he understands that social structures influence political belief. As the social structures of societies change, so the politics of that society change. Just as social process is the inherent quality of historical existence, so democracy must be approached as a form of government which undergoes change. In Part 1 of "Bourgeois Democracy as a False Alternative for the Reform of Socialism," Lukács discusses two prior forms of democracy, Greek and bourgeois, before going on to analyze the socialist form of democracy. The historicist approach to democracy indicates that rather than speak of one form of democracy, it is more accurate to speak in the plural of the forms which democracy assumes throughout history.

Within this historicist vision of man, socialism is a stage in the human process of becoming. Lukács read Marx's *Economic-Philosophic Manuscripts of 1844* in Moscow in 1930 and was greatly influenced by them, particularly the social phenomenology of Marx in which Marx comments that history is the autogenesis of man. The theme of becoming remained a major motif in the thought of Lukács, and he looked upon socialism as a stage in the becoming of man to freedom. In the style of Hegel, Lukács views history as the self-educative process of mankind, and socialism is that part of this self-educative process in which democracy can be extended into areas of human *praxis* where it has never been extended before.

The socialist revolution is a necessary precondition for this extension of

human freedom. In order for freedom to enlarge into the realm of human activity, it is necessary to nationalize productive property. These forces must be placed under the control of society in general, so that society in general can learn how best to use them. There is a difference between nationalization and socialization. Nationalization refers to the transferance of title from private ownership to public ownership, while socialization refers to the process of governance. Nationalization is the initial step to socialization, for ownership must first be won before democratic governance of the means of production is instituted. Man can only be educated into his freedom if he first has the experience of controlling both his social labor and the social productive instruments of society. Self-consciousness is a part of self-determination; being aware of human capability in the abstract helps one decide how one should act in the concrete.

Social Ontology: Praxis

Influenced by the theme of human activity as stated in Marx's *Economic-Philosophic Manuscripts of 1844* and the *Theses on Feuerbach*, Lukács advances a philosophy of socially productive action. Human *praxis* is one of the forces which brings about social process, for it is a self-generative force which constantly modifies the world around it. Lukács considers social evolution to be the product of two developmental lines: human work, which is the subject, and the natural or social environment, which is the object. Human work is goal oriented, for conscious human beings establish ends. Social process comes from the interconnection of human *praxis* and the socionatural, comes when human consciousness attempts to use the socionatural for its own purposes. On this basis, Lukács opposes every social philosophy which looks upon change in history as stemming automatically from economics or technology. Objectivism is simply another form of mechanical materialism, for it maintains that change is solely explicable in terms of material forces. Soviet philosophy after Stalin became objectivist, and Lukács fought against the Kremlin's version of dialectical materialism because it canceled out any role for subjective intervention.

Lukács philosophy of practico-critical activity is built on the idea of the unity of subject and object. Human work is the connective link between the subject and the object. Human intervention is teleological, it sets forth purpose, and this purpose is the goal which uses the socionatural as instrument.

Lukács's idea of the dialectic of intervention preserves the Marxian thematic that history is the autogenesis of man. Human practico-critical work modifies the socionatural environment, the newly produced socionatural environment then modifies the subject, and the newly modified subject then re-modifies the objective conditions. History is the autogenesis of man because

the conditions which change the subject are conditions which are produced by the subject. The change of man is thus self-change. The dialectic of activity means that man is a constitutive agency which humanizes his objective social and physical surroundings in accordance with his own powers of objectification.

The thematic unity of the subject and the object is the logical basis for Lukács's belief in the unity between humankind and society. Work is again the connective link between humankind and society, for society is the objective which provides the conditions of labor upon which the subject can work. The bond between humankind and society arises because each is nonproductive without the other. Society provides the conditions which facilitate human constitution, and the individual is that generative force which modifies society. Lukács's philosophy of practico-critical activity substitutes productive capacity for citizenship as the ground for the revival of the Greek ideal of *polis* unity. The Greeks assumed that citizenship provided the basis for the integration of humankind within the *polis,* while Lukács assumed that the dialectic of work provided the connective links which bring about the reciprocity between humankind and society.

German Humanism and the Polis-*Ideal*

The Process of Democratization is an attempt to relocate the *polis* ideal of democracy in a socialist society. It places a Marxist theory of politics on a classical footing, since it makes the *polis* ideal the theoretical core of a socialist society. Some of the precursors of Lukács were Robespierre and Rousseau, who attempted to recreate the *polis* ideal for eighteenth century France.

The democracy which Lukács wants to bring to socialism is an antibourgeois form. Bourgeois democracy divides the political person from the private person. Based upon the doctrine of natural rights, which separates the economic from the political person, bourgeois democracy leaves the individual in capitalist society as a schizoid creature, his private economic life is totally divorced from his political life. Rather than unite the various parts of the human personality, bourgeois democracy sunders them.

Lukács feels that socialism provides the proper conditions for a revival of *polis* democracy. Lukács does not begin his political speculation from a natural rights tradition. His initial concern is not with personal rights, but with the unity between the citizen and the economic person. His primary intent is to restore the integration between the private and public person, not to build constitutional guarantees of individual liberty. He is antibourgeois because he does not think in terms of natural law or individual liberty, but rather in terms of social integration through the reciprocity of the work process.

In returning to the tradition of *polis* democracy, Lukács remains true to

classical German humanism. Standing at the beginning of the capitalist world in the eighteenth century, Schiller, Goethe and Hegel were all aware of the divisions opened between the private and public life by bourgeois society. The plays and novels of Schiller and Goethe frequently told of the destruction of gifted individuals by the philistine values of the society which surrounded them. Recognizing the tragic conflict between social conformity and personal giftedness, the German humanist philosophers looked upon the integrated life of the Greek *polis* as a means to escape this typical bourgeois dilemma.

In his book *The Destruction of Reason,* Lukács sees two polarities in German culture, irrationalism which led to fascism, and humanism which acted as the foundation of democracy. In this regard, Lukács is at variance with Stalinism, for as fascism arose in the 1930s Stalin condemned both Western socialism and bourgeois democracy as simply alternate forms of right totalitarianism. Lukács pursues a different course, seeing in democracy a defense against fascism. Stalinism led to the isolation of Russia from Western socialism and democracy, while Lukács's attachment to the bourgeois humanist Enlightenment leads him to espouse the tactics of a "popular front," an alliance of all democratic forces against Hitlerism. Lukács sees the need to elevate this bourgeois mode of democracy into a socialist mode, and he takes from the classical German humanist tradition its idolization of the *polis*. *The Process of Democratization* must be read as a continuation of the *polis* tradition which lived on in German classical philosophy.

Lukács seeks to show that this humanist tradition is represented best in Marxian socialism. Lukács's attempt parallels the cultural struggle of Friedrich Engels, who, *in Ludwig Feuerbach and the End of Classical German Philosophy,* tried to show that the proletariat was the legitimate heir of the German humanist tradition. Lukács's *The Process of Democratization* is an attempt at cultural legitimation, an attempt to show that the classical tradition had found its heir, in the words of Friedrich Engels, in socialism. As confirmation of this point, Lukács shows how *polis* democracy corresponds perfectly with socialism. In ranking the features of democracy which he values most highly, Lukács gives privilege to the idea of the unity between the public and private person, or the integration of the self and society, an ideal the German classical philosophers and, Lukács thinks unattainable in capitalist society.

The above discussion of the relationship between Lukács's theory of politics and his social ontology points out the rootedness of his theory of the state in his social philosophy. It is now possible to discuss his principles of a founding of a Marxist theory of the state more concretely. I discuss his contribution in six sections: 1) on the commensurability between species being and the state; 2) anthropology and emancipation; 3) the unity of the private and the

public; 4) towards the redefinition of democracy; 5) towards the redefinition of socialism; 6) the program.

On the Commensurability Between Species Being and the State

Lukács's theory of politics perpetuates the Marxian distinction between civil society and state. Lukács, however, anthropologizes this distinction and in *The Process of Democratization* rather than speak of the civil society-state dichotomy he speaks of the distinction between species being and the state. The idea of species being was a Feuerbachian conception, which Marx takes over in his *Economic-Philosophic Manuscripts of 1844,* and refers to as the universal properties of the human being. Feuerbach chose the term ''being'' because it provided an ontological status to the kind of anthropological vision he had, and Marx rejects this ontological definition of ''being'' in his *Thesis on Feuerbach* where he substitutes the idea of social becoming. Continuing the ideas set forth by Marx in *Thesis on Feuerbach,* Lukács is willing to employ the phrase ''species being'' as long as ''being'' is not thought of as fixed, but something that is continually recreated by human activity.

Assuming that when the socialist revolution nationalized productive property it also puts an end to class warfare, Lukács no longer looks upon civil society as rent by class struggle. With the elimination of the conflict image, presupposing the collectivization of productive property, Lukács writes of the commensurability between species being and the state. He assumes the unity of subject and object, and maintains that the conditions of work required by the species be made available to the species by society or the state and that the species through its activity modifies these provided conditions consequently engendering changes in society and state. This metabolic relationship between species and society is based on the reciprocity between need and accessibility. The species needs to work in order to provide its sustenance, while society makes the conditions of activity accessible to the species. When Lukács writes of the compatibility between the species and the state, he is offering a basis on which to integrate the public and private person.

The metabolic argument also provides the logic for the repoliticization of a Marxist theory of politics. The aim of a Marxist politics is the empowerment of civil society. Marxism is not the end of politics or the state, but the situation of political power in the social institutions of humankind so it will accurately reflect the species interests of humankind. The concept of the empowerment of civil society means the popularization of political power, it means placing political power in social institutions which are closest to the species needs so political power can accurately reflect these needs.

A Marxist theory of politics presupposes the distinction between civil so-

ciety, species being and the state. The definition of politics for Marx concerns the investment of power: politics is the art of investing power in the institutions of civil society so it can be most expressive of species interests. Not only does a Marxist politics concern investment, but it also has to do with trusteeship. A Marxist politics is directed toward granting civil society trusteeship over political power.

Anthropology and Emancipation

The Process of Democratization is a prolegomena to a Marxist theory of politics, and Lukács begins his speculations on the basis of an anthropological subsumption of the political. The site of political speculation is human anthropology and when Lukács locates a theory of the state in these contexts he overthrows the boundaries of bourgeois political thought.

According to bourgeois political science, humankind was primarily a selfish creature and, as Thomas Hobbes put it, in a war of all against all. Reflecting inherent human selfishness, natural rights were protective boundaries. Rights were legal protections for individual estates, or as Locke stated "property." Lukácsian political theory begins from completely different ethnological assumptions. Lukács does not look upon humankind as inherently selfish, but rather cooperatively joined to the species. Where bourgeois anthropology thought in atomistic terms, Lukácsian anthropology thinks in universalistic terms, the commonality of needs which all members of the species share. Rather than legal prohibition, Lukács commences his speculation from the point of view of humankind, which is its activity, and the primary human activity is work. Rather than see the primary human need as rights or protection, Lukács understands the primary human need to be *praxis,* or teleological activity. Lukács begins his political theory from the anthropology of work.

In the *Economic-Philosophic Manuscripts of 1844,* Marx introduces his idea that human activity is the primary generative force of social processes. The Marxian universe evolves mono-causally out of human *praxis.* Lukács continues the Marxist *praxis* theory when he bases his political theory on human activity. A Marxist political theory must be a *praxis* theory of politics, meaning that politics must be thought of as institutions which enhance total human potential.

Marx's text, *Theses on Feuerbach,* has great impact on Lukács. In opposition to Feuerbach's anthropological essentialism, Marx proposes two principles of social phenomenology: humankind changes the world through its work; the "being" of the species is a historical product recreated by human work in every generation. Marx's eleventh *Theses on Feuerbach* is the axis for all of the work of Lukács after 1930, for it contains an idea central to Lukács's social ontology, the idea that humankind creates its own history. Lu-

kács also learns from the eleventh *Theses on Feuerbach* that historical circumstances can only be changed through human action: human action is the hydraulic force for historical evolution.

Just as bourgeois political thought joined the legal and the political, so Lukács's political thought joins the economic and the political. The enhancement of human *praxis* coupled with the development of technological capacity leads to the reduction of necessary labor. In the first volume of *Das Kapital,* Marx draws the distinction between necessary and surplus labor: necessary labor is the labor needed to produce the sustenance of the worker and of society, while surplus labor is labor beyond the necessary which under capitalism is expropriated by the capitalist. With the increase in the powers and conditions of human labor, Lukács, like Marx, thinks it possible to reduce necessary labor, to cut the number of hours needed to sustain the life of the worker and society. Under socialism, surplus labor presumably disappears because property has been nationalized. Although surplus labor ceases to exist under socialism, necessary labor continues to exist, but the hours devoted to necessary labor are reduced. The curtailment of necessary labor means that every individual has more time to devote to his own development.

Lukács refers to the reduction of necessary labor and the corresponding increase of time that individuals can expend as they wish as the kingdom of freedom. In Volume 1 of *Das Kapital,* Marx is the first to use the phrase the kingdom of freedom and he means a society in which the maximum amount of daily time remains under the control of the individual. The kingdom of freedom is wealth, only this is the "property" of the individual, he is free to determine its use as he wishes. Freedom means the overcoming of necessity. Liberation involves a displacement of time: time once needed to be expended on necessary labor can now be expended on the self. The kingdoms of freedom and liberation are both expressions of self-determination: the possibility of using time, life time which was emancipated from necessary labor in terms of one's own conscious purpose.

This stress on individuality also marks a break with previous socialist thought, which was highly collectivist. Classical bolshevism, both in its Leninist and Stalinist forms, accentuated man's sociability to the practical exclusion of individuality. The stress on human sociability was intended as a means to overcome bourgeoise egocentricism. Lukács breaks with the tradition of socialist conformity and offers instead an ideal of self-development. Lukács's idea is that true individuality can only be developed in socialism. Where Lenin and Stalin both saw individuality as a hindrance to socialism, Lukács sees individuality as the highest instance of socialism. In breaking with the tradition of bolshevik sociability, Lukács adds two new themes to contemporary Marxist political theory: 1) the fusion of the Greek ideal with socialism; 2) making individuality part of socialist ethics.

A Marxist theory of politics must draw its inspiration from the anthropological vision of humankind which valorizes its social environment. For Lukács, politics is social governance which leads to the improvement of human productive potential. Politics must be subsumed under the image of humankind that humanizes its world. If politics then becomes a branch of anthropological *praxis,* the following definition of politics is appropriate: politics is the practice of *praxis,* it is the expression of *praxis* which leads to the facilitation of *praxis.*

In two extremely challenging works, Ferenc Fehér locates the origins of communist totalitarianism at the historical moment when politics was seen as a means of answering the problem of social inequality. In his book, *The Frozen Revolution: An Essay on Jacobinism*[57] and in his chapter "Why Is Dictatorship over Needs Not Socialism?" contained in the book *Dictatorship over Needs,*[58] Fehér maintains that left totalitarianism was born in 1793 when the Jacobins capitulated to the demands of the *sans-culottes* to standardize prices through political means: economic questions were subsumed into the realm of politics.

My view disagrees with that of Fehér, for I see no reason why the empowerment of the social should lead to autocracy. I offer two rejoinders to the theses of Fehér. 1) The origins of left totalitarianism did not stem from the subsumption of economics by politics, but rather because economics was defined solely in Babouvist egalitarian terms. Economics need not be defined as social homogenization, as the age of the Second International did, but as distributed control over productive property, or the "socialization" in the broad sense as opposed to mere "nationalization." 2) The origins of left totalitarianism did not stem from the politicization of the economic, but rather from the economization of the political, the fact that politics was reduced to social egalitarianism. If politics was not reduced to social homogenization, but rather seen as an autonomous form of social decision making concerning economic questions, it would not be considered inevitable that the politicizing of the economic produced left totalitarianism. It is possible for the decision-making process to obey democratic protocols, thus thwarting any totalitarian intervention, while at the same time investing the political with the power to make decisions concerning the socioeconomic condition of man. If the political was seen as decision making and representation in this political process awarded on the basis of the empowerment of civil society, it would only mean that society was represented and sovereign in the political process, but need not mean that the political process could not function according to procedures which were lawful, thereby immune from arbitrary control by an hegemonic party. Fehér's presentation is faulty because he does not make a distinction between representation in a process and the protocols of the process itself.

The Unity of the Public and the Private

The idea of the unity between the public and private person is captured in Lukács's phrase "everyday life." Lukács looks upon the *polis* ideal as the way to overcome the "citizen ideal" of the bourgeois West.

In a suggestive study, *Everyday Life in Bourgeois Society and Pietist Thought in the Work of Hölderlin,* Meinhard Prill shows how the fragmentation of daily life under capitalism was as much a concern for Enlightenment German humanism as for Lukács.[59] To the eighteenth century German poet, Hölderlin, everyday life was daily experience which was unmediated. Everyday life was the immediate unreflective experience of our social surroundings. To the eighteenth century poet, everyday life under an emergent capitalism divides the public from the private person, creates the citizen as distinct from the private self, and imposes conformity which aesthetic personalities could not tolerate, and Hölderlin turned to the ideal of the *polis* as a form of political organization in which the person was a harmonious unity. Whereas the eighteenth century German humanist tradition looked upon aesthetic experience as the medium through which the unification of man was to be achieved, Lukács replaces art with social labor. Hölderlin dreams of a harmonious man resurrected through beauty and contemplation, while Lukács sees a harmonious man produced by means of cooperative social activity. Like Hölderlin, Lukács returns to the image of the Greek *polis* and a sociopolitical environment in which harmony would replace estrangement and reification.

In later paragraphs of the Introduction I will show how Lukács redefines the nature of democracy: he defines democracy from a *polis* point of view and not from the perspective of Thomas Jefferson and the American Constitution. Western democracy was constructed upon the ideal of a "citizen," man as a politico-legal entity. Lukács wants to supercede the citizen ideal because it is based on the bifurcation of the person. It divides the person between "citizen" and "homo oeconomicus." Lukács sees two democratic traditions evolve in Western civilization: one is the "rights" tradition which leads to the "citizen" ideal and bourgeois democracy; the other is the *polis* ideal, which Lukács wishes to resurrect in a democratized form of socialism in which the Soviets play a crucial role.

Lukács's understanding of everyday life is predicated on the commensurability between individual *praxis* and society. Lukács's idea of work acts as the means of correspondence, bringing about the unity between the person and society: work binds humankind and society together in a reciprocity of need. Active persons need to make the conditions of work accessible, and society needs productive persons to use these conditions to carry through the process of social reproduction.

veryday life "immediate daily concerns"[60] are connected with "universal" questions.[61] The process of democratization, which requires a socialist society, produces a situation in which economic problems are immediately connected to political issues. Lukács thinks of the Athenian market place in which issues of state were discussed as people conducted their private lives. Everyday life becomes a convention, a place where people congress to debate the larger general questions of society.

The institutions in socialist society which act as the facilitators between the public and the private realms are the Soviets. They are the congresses which facilitate the debate of universal problems in the context of the everyday. The Soviets are forms of direct democracy, an everyday assembly in which political issues are debated. Lukács is captivated by the image of the Soviets during the revolutionary periods of Soviet history in 1905 and 1917, for in the course of these revolutions the Soviets combine everyday life with political practice: they were councils at everyday work places which not only activated the demands of the workers but also acted as strategic centers when the workers crossed the line to practico-critical revolutionary activity.

Lukács's political theory conjoins the Soviets and the *polis*. Such a fusion is perfectly consonant with Lukács's assessment of the role of the European proletariat, for he believes that the proletarian movement can be the heir of the classical humanist tradition. The fusion of Leninist bolshevism with *polis* integration is perfectly consistent with the role which Lukács assigns to the proletariat: perpetuate the Greek and the eighteenth century German form of humanism.

Politics, for Lukács, entails turning the workplace, in the style of the revolutionary Soviets, into conventions of public debate. Politics means the creating of popular and everyday assemblages at the work place where issues affecting the state are debated. In this way, everyday life is joined to the universal.

Toward the Redefinition of Democracy

The Process of Democratization presumes that the continued development of democracy only takes place within socialism. Democracy only survives as a historic enterprise with the elimination of private property. A society is democratic if it increases the unity between humankind and society, the person's private and public existence. Although Lukács does reopen the issue of individuality in socialism, he remains a collectivist in terms of the productive property of society. For him, a society is most democratic when it increases the sense of oneness between an individual and his species.

Democracy also concerns economics. A society is democratic if it leads to the reduction of necessary labor time. Only a person who lives above want

can be self-determining, for economic enslavement is the chief barrier to self-determination.

Toward the Redefinition of Socialism

Lukács breaks with the economist model of socialism and offers a German humanist definition of this form of society. Socialism is a stage in the self-educative process of mankind. Lukács thinks in terms of Hegel's *Phenomenology of Mind,* which described consciousness becoming self-consciousness and therefore self-determination. The development Hegel described was a movement toward greater degrees of self-reflection: consciousness learning its abilities by reflecting on its own previous activity, and upon learning its own capacities it then becomes self-determining. For Lukács, socialism is a stage in the educative process of society: by placing the means of production in the hands of society it allows society to determine the end to which these productive means are to be placed.

One indication of Lukács's redefinition of socialism is his restatement of value. Stalinist Marxism defines value as labor time, claiming that the value of an object was the quantity of labor time it took to make the object. Like his historicist definition of democracy, Lukács also offers a historicist definition of value. The understanding of value changes in terms of the society in which the category finds itself. A society is a totality which influences particular parts of the whole. Two definitions of value reflect the different societal contexts of which it is part: 1) value under capitalism; 2) value under socialism.

Value Under Capitalism. The labor theory of value was a capitalist invention, found in the writing of Adam Smith and David Ricardo. Marx was influenced by these economists, although Marx himself worked through to a historicist definition of value. Marx's focus on the labor theory of value reflects the capitalist environment in which he lived. The interest in the labor theory of value expresses the interests of capitalist society, for in the age of factories labor did seem to be the sole source of value. Stalinist Marxism continues the capitalist definition of value. The definition of value found in Soviet Marxism is merely a vulgar form of the definition of value which the bourgeois economists invented. Vulgar economy began with Smith and Ricardo, but was perfected under Stalin.

Value Under Socialism. Stalinist Marxism assumes that exploitation does not take place under socialism. The Stalinist argument is based upon the idea that labor is the major means of exploitation: if labor exploitation does not exist then no exploitation exists. Labor exploitation exists, according to Stalinist Marxism, because of the capitalist class. If the capitalist class is destroyed, la-

bor exploitation ceases because no class exists to carry out this exploitation. Socialism is a society in which labor exploitation does not take place because socialism uprooted the capitalist class.

Lukács points out that exploitation does take place under socialism. He is aware that a bureaucracy is as exploitative as a capitalist class. Indeed, bureaucracies are classes and are as exploitative as capitalists, an argument first put forth by Djilas in *The New Class*.

Lukács can penetrate to the exploitative nature of Stalinist socialism because he defines value in a different way. Value is not restricted to human labor, but Lukács defines value as total human creative capacity. Even though socialism in Eastern Europe does not eradicate all forms of exploitation, bureaucratic exploitation still exists, it provides a new perspective from which to redefine value. With the means of production now in the hands of the state, with the uprooting of the capitalist class, it is now possible to define value not simply as labor but in more universalist terms.

As a stage in its historical evolution, value in a socialist society means the societal commitment to enable individuals to develop the full range of their abilities. Value means human creativity. From this point of view, education and an educational system are value, science and scientific knowledge are value, technology is value, because they all enhance the ability of an individual to produce. Just as under socialism the definition of value is universalized beyond labor, so also under socialism the definition of exploitation is universalized. Under capitalism exploitation means the expropriation of labor, but under socialism exploitation means the expropriation of any aspect of full human capacity.

The definition of socialism also experienced a historical evolution. From the framework of nineteenth century capitalism, socialism was given a productivist-economist definition. From the framework of economic scarcity, in which nineteenth century capitalism could not produce enough goods to be distributed to the proletariat, socialism was defined as economic abundance. In the Lukácsian definition, socialism overcomes its economist deformation and is defined as that society which increases total societal value. Lukács offers a humanist definition of socialism, for it perpetuates the classical humanist ideal that humankind is an end in itself. Humanist socialism is aimed at the increase of social productivity, so that humankind can be liberated from its dependency on nature, and through that emancipation reconquer labor time which can then be accumulated as free time.

The concept of freedom also underwent historical evolution. Freedom under bourgeois society means freedom from the noninterference by external factors into private decisions, or the curtailment of external compulsion. Under socialism, the idea of freedom changes to freedom to perform all human functions. Freedom-to accentuates facilitation, the allowance to fulfill internal

capacities. Bourgeois freedom is negative, directed against external forces; socialist freedom is positive, concerned with permitting internal expression.

The Program

Although *The Process of Democratization* is not programmatic, it does contain suggestions of concrete political reforms Lukács wants. The reforms Lukács advocates are expressions of the "Leninist opposition," and they also serve as barometers of the current reform movement in the Soviet Union and Eastern Europe. I discuss the program Lukács sketches under the following categories: the separation of party and state; the restoration of the Soviets; the restoration of the trade unions; NEP and the reprivatization of property; the retention of the Leninist party; the transcendence of statelessness; the replacement of habituation by democracy; socialist democracy and the repoliticization of Marxist political theory.

Separation of Party and State. Lukács calls for the separation of party and state because he wants to liberate society from the control of the party. He does not want to overthrow the single party system, as I shall show later in a section on the retention of the Leninist party, but he does want to emancipate other social institutions from direct party domination. This emancipation of social institutions is simultaneously the political empowerment of these recovered institutions, because it allows them to participate in the decision-making process of society. The separation of party and state is intended to allow suffocated social institutions to regenerate themselves and exercise some authority in the social decision-making process.

The Restoration of the Soviets. With the retraction of the party from its authoritarian control over the institutions of civil society, the Soviets can emerge as a major form of the political organization. Lukács advocates the re-Sovietization of communist society, as one political form through which society can be repoliticized.

Lukács takes the period of the New Economic Policy (NEP) in the Soviet Union as the model upon which to reform East European society. Lukács overlooks the fact that Lenin had destroyed the Soviet movement, and assumes that the Soviets remain viable political institutions during the NEP period. The justification or denunciation of Leninist bolshevism rests upon one's assessment of the NEP period.

The Restoration of the Trade Unions. Lukács draws reference to the debate over trade unions which divided the bolshevik party during the 1920–1922 period. In his essays, "Once Again on the Trade Unions, the Current Situation and the Mistakes of Trotsky and Bukharin" (1921), and "The Role and Func-

tion of the Trade Unions Under the New Economic Policy'' (1922), Lenin spells out his attitude on the position of trade unions in a socialist society.[62] In this debate, Lenin did battle against the syndicalist opposition led by Shlyapnikov, as well as those who wished to enslave the unions to the party, like Stalin. Lenin was not a syndicalist, he did not want the bolshevik party to renounce its leadership role to the labor unions, but he recognized that the labor unions play an important intermediary role between the party and society. Lenin is not a Stalinist, he does not believe in authoritarian party hegemony over the labor unions, but rather sees them as important points of transition between party and populace. Lukács wishes to return to the Leninist position regarding labor unions.

NEP and the Reprivatization of Property. During the NEP period, Lenin allowed small businesses to remain in private hands and for the small peasant to own his land. Understanding property as productive property—waterfalls, oil wells, hydroelectric plants—Lenin nationalized productive property but was willing to allow property that did not contribute to total social value, like shoe stores or bakeries, to remain in private hands. The NEP was Lenin's political compromise with the peasants, and it produced social peace in Russia after the Civil War. It was a *quid pro quo:* Lenin allowed the peasants to keep their own land in return for the political support of the peasants.

The Process of Democratization does not contain a direct statement supporting the reprivatization of small businesses or land. But Lukács's frequent praise of NEP, his belief that it represents Leninist bolshevism in its best form, leads one to surmise that he favors the privatization of nonproductive property, that kind which does not contribute to total social value.

Three years after Lukács wrote *The Process of Democratization,* he published *Record of a Life,* where he affirms his favor for privatization and the use of the market where it is effective. He writes: "The principle of Marxism: the democratic reorganization of production (the internal connection between democratization and the quality of production). Capitalism is effective in certain tendencies of the market where it is impossible to manipulate total production centrally. But it would be an illusion to believe that such elements of the market could lead socialist production along the right democratic path."[63]

The *Record of a Life* also documents Lukács's commitment to peasant ownership of land, which Lukács affirms in his *Lenin* and in the *Blum Theses.* Lukács's dedication to peasant ownership continues into the 1945–1948 period in Hungary, the period of "new democracy," during which he advocates the privatization of small peasant holdings. For Lukács, the alliance of the proletariat and the peasantry offers the economic basis for a new democracy, for he sees in this coalition an electoral majority of the poor, a majority which can provide the democratic enfranchisement of socialism. Lukács writes: "In

fact, the course of later history vindicated the *Blum Theses* completely. For the period 1945–1948 in Hungary was the concrete realization of the democratic dictatorship of the workers and peasants for which I argued in 1929. After 1948, of course, Stalinism created something quite different . . . but that is another story."[64]

The phrase the "Leninist opposition" must be expanded to include all those who favor Lenin's policy of an alliance of workers and peasants on the basis of small farm ownership as the economic foundation of a democracy of the poor. In underdeveloped countries a coalition of workers and peasants would be a majority and democracy on this class basis would be simultaneously anticapitalist and prosocialist. The phrase the "Leninist opposition" must be understood as those seeking to create a coalition of the poor on the assumption that a majority of the underprivileged would be socialist. It was a way to provide a mass sanction for socialism. In upholding the Leninist idea of a "democratic dictatorship of the workers and peasants," Lukács again revealed his anti-Stalinism, for at the same time that Stalin began his First Five Year Plan which called for the nationalization of the land and the expropriation of the peasants, Lukács issued a plea for the peasant proprietorship of the land.

The Retention of the Leninist Party. Lukács does want a multiparty system for Hungary. He does not want to bring the bourgeois parliamentarian system to Eastern Europe. He wants to retain a single party system and looks upon the Communist party as exercising an educational platocracy. Like Lenin, Lukács continues to think that a higher level of consciousness must be brought to the working class from a source outside of the proletariat. The source which brings advanced consciousness to the general population is the Communist party.

Lukács favors the internal democratization of the single party system. He does not want a plurality of parties outside the Communist party, but rather a plurality of viewpoints inside the Communist party. On this issue as well, Lukács returns to the Leninist model of "democratic centralism." In 1905, at the Tammerfors Unity Conference of the Russian Social Democratic Workers party, Lenin proposed a democratic reorganization of the party. His essay, "The Reorganization of the Party," shows that Lenin recognizes that after the victory of the bourgeois democratic revolution in 1905 in the Tzarist Empire, the Russian Marxist party must also cease being an underground party and embark upon internal democratization. Lenin believes that the former conspiratorial organization of the party distorted it, and that it must undergo a democratic restructuring in order to meet the challenge of the new political realities of Russia.[65] Lukács is an adherent of the Leninist version of democratic centralism, but rejects the Stalinist debasement of the principle. The bolshevism

of Lenin retains single party rule, but accepts an innerparty plurality of viewpoint or debate, of contested votes, and of freedom of conscience.

The Transcendence of Statelessness. In one of the few areas in which he dissents from Lenin, Lukács criticizes him on the issue of statelessness. When Lukács abandons the theme of statelessness, he not only transcends *State and Revolution,* but also classical Marxist and bolshevik thinking on the nature of communism, the central concept of classical Marxist and bolshevik political theory which was made synonymous with anarchism.

According to Lukács, Lenin's approach to the issue of democracy is divided into two parts: democracy-as-plebeianism and democracy-as-bourgeois.

Lenin accepts democracy-as-plebeianism, as rule of the majority of the population through the institutions of the Soviets and the Communist party. Lenin uses the phrase "democracy of the poor," but since the vast majority of the population in Russia were poor the democracy of the poor automatically means rule by the vast majority. Lukács recognizes the democracy-as-plebeian spirit of *State and Revolution* and so identifies this book as a great democratic statement. For both Lenin and Lukács, democracy-as-plebeianism is the content of democracy.

Lenin rejects democracy-as-bourgeois for this is a corrupt form of democracy. Democracy-as-bourgeois was synonymous with the class rule of the bourgeoisie, and the institutional expressions of that class rule, multiparty system, parliamentarianism and the state. Lenin's attacks on democracy were specifically attacks on the bourgeois form of democracy which violates the content of democracy and Lukács joins him in this condemnation. As an attack on the bourgeois form of democracy, Lukács recognizes that *State and Revolution* is an important historic document.

Lenin's problem arises when he confuses his condemnation of democracy-as-bourgeois with statelessness or anarchism. Democracy-as-bourgeois is tantamount to government by class, and when Lenin rejects the form of bourgeois democracy he also commits the mistake of rejecting the ideas of class and state. Lenin falls victim to the "linguistic collapse," of confusing democracy with class rule and in assuming that a rejection of class rule necessitates the overcoming of democracy.

State and Revolution takes a wrong turn when Lenin confuses democracy-as-plebeianism with statelessness. Lenin commits the linguistic collapse when he does not assign a political form to democracy-as-plebeianism, or the content of democracy, but he never addresses the question of the proper form for the content democracy-as-plebeianism.

State and Revolution descends into anarchism because Lenin does not perform a form-content analysis of the state. In *State and Revolution,* Lenin does perform a form-content analysis of democracy, in which democracy-as-plebeianism is content and democracy-as-bourgeois is form. He halts this his-

toricist analysis at the question of the state, and does not attempt to separate the content of state from the form of state. Lenin becomes enmeshed in fetishistic thinking, because he assumes that the form of state, which presumably existed throughout history, is the eternal form of state. Lenin descends into vulgar political theory, because he takes state-as-class-rule as unchanging. By becoming entrapped in fetishistic political thinking, Lenin could only escape from the vulgar definition of the state by calling for the abolition of the state, which is the institutionalization of class rule. Lenin's embrace of statelessness and anarchism rests upon his joining of democracy-as-bourgeois with a vulgar or formal definition of the state.

Lenin does not perform a complete historicist analysis of the state; he never asks about its content. Carrying through a complete form-content analysis of the state and politics could have shown a definition of politics as the social protocol of decision making. When Lenin does not carry through his form-content analysis, he is left without a content of state and politics. He is left with a form of state-politics, which equates it with class rule.

Realizing the mistake of Lenin, Lukács defines politics as the protocols of decision making, as the substitute for statelessness. For Lukács, democracy, understood as procedure through which to reach decisions, replaces anarchy. In *State and Revolution,* democracy requires statelessness, while in *The Process of Democratization* democracy is only possible inside a political order.

Replacement of Habituation by Democracy. Lukács also adopts a two-track analysis of Lenin's concept of habit. In *State and Revolution,* Lenin uses the idea of habituation as a substitute for political procedures, and as a synonym for the most extreme form of democracy. Lenin had already committed himself to statelessness and politicslessness. He then had to answer the following question: if neither a state nor a politics exists, by what rule are the functions of society to be carried out? Lenin's answer is habituation, for without a state and without a politics he could only maintain that people become accustomed through training to the performance of social duties. Habit is customary social behavior, which makes any rule making unnecessary.

When Lukács evaluates the idea of habituation as an extreme form of democracy, he praises it highly. One aspect of *State and Revolution* is its democratic plebeianism, and the actual processes of society would be vested in the people in general. When Lukács evaluates the idea of habituation as a substitute for political procedures, he only has negative comments. Lenin wants to show that learned responses, behavioralism, could perform the same tasks that social protocols do: behavioralism would ensure that people perform social functions without political compulsion. Lukács replaces behavioralism with democracy: he replaces psychology with politics. He recognizes the need of protocols to enable society to reach its collective decisions.

Socialist Democracy and the Repoliticization of Marxist Political Theory. The Process of Democratization is a form-content analysis of the ideas of democracy and state. It is a demonstration that, while the forms of democracy and state alter, the content of democracy and state stay the same. The content of democracy and state rests on the need for every society to have both procedures and institutions which facilitate social decision making. At their most basic level, democracy is universally agreed upon procedure, while state and politics are institutions which facilitate that procedure. By penetrating to the content of democracy and the political, Lukács shows that this content must be a part of a socialist society. Socialist society is another form for democracy, but a form which enables democracy to be extended. Socialist society is not the last form of historical evolution, so it too needs the content of political organization. *The Process of Democratization* points to the political institutions, Soviets, which facilitate the radicalization of democracy under socialism.

The Process of Democratization transcends *State and Revolution* because it remains rooted in the historicist method.[66] *State and Revolution* violates the historicist principles of Marxism because it presents communism as the final stage of history. Whereas Marx never sees any end to the historical process, *State and Revolution* suggests, at least in the questions of politics and the state, that communist society is millenial. *State and Revolution* presents a messianic vision, that the history of class and state is solved forever.[67]

The Process of Democratization returns to the historicist method of Marx. It is not sufficient to think of statelessness or classlessness as the eschatology of social evolution. Statelessness and classlessness must be decentered, the "end of politics"[68] superseded and history seen as the continuous process of democratization.

A Marxian political theory, preserving its historicist underpinning, can be defined in the following way: invent new political institutions which are commensurate with the changing historical-social environment and which radicalize the possibilities of democracy. But this recreation of political institutions must always find its center of gravity in an expressivist anthropological vision of humankind: humankind is productive activity and any political institution must valorize human capacity.

Notes

1. Lukács wrote this book in German and the actual title of the text held in the Lukács Archiv in Budapest is *Demokratizierung Heute und Morgen,* which translated literally means *Democratization Today and Tomorrow.* A West German edition of this work produced by Frank Benseler carries the title

Sozialismus und Demokratizierung or *Socialism and Democratization*. I use the title *The Process of Democratization* because it gets closer to the historicist nature of democracy which is one of the major themes of the text. Lukács is not concerned with either democracy or socialism as a prefigured form, but rather with both democracy and socialism as a process.

 2. The Introduction, *On the Transcendence of* State and Revolution, was initially written in 1988, about eighteen months before the revolutionary upheavals that swept Eastern Europe and the Soviet Union in 1989–1990. The main theme of the Introduction deals with Lukács's reformulation of classical Leninist political theory as exemplified in *State and Revolution*. Clearly, the entire landscape of Eastern European and Soviet political life was restructured by the earthquake of 1989–1990, but in order to understand Lukács's relevance to all these events it is first necessary to answer the problems of his relation to Leninism in terms of a theory of the state. The major goal of Lukács's *The Process of Democratization* is to set forth the principles of a new Marxist theory of politics and he achieves this by applying a form-content analysis to the concepts of democracy and state and by reasserting the historicist basis of all Marxist political theory. Although he is an admirer of Lenin, Lukács brings an end to the Leninist domination of Marxist political theory. Since these are the questions that *On the Transcendence of* State and Revolution primarily addresses, I publish it as written because these are the questions that must be resolved before any further advance can be made in a Marxist theory of the state. Additional questions speculating on Lukács's attitude toward Gorbachev, his probable position toward the Eastern European revolutions of 1989–1990, properly belong to separate studies.

 3. Lukács, Georg, *Die Eigenart des Asthetischen* (Berlin: Luchterhand, 1963).

 4. For an excellent discussion of Lukács's relationship to Nicolai Hartmann and Martin Heidegger, see the essay by Nicolaus Tertulian, "Lukács's Ontology," in *Lukács Today,* ed. Tom Rockmore (Boston: D. Riedel, 1988), pp. 243–274. The presentation of Tertulian is at odds with the Lukács interpretation of Agnes Heller and Ferenc Fehér. For another work that explores the similarities and differences of Heidegger and Lukács see Lucien Goldmann, *Lukács and Heidegger,* trans. William O. Boelhower (London: Routledge & Kegan Paul, 1982).

 5. Lukács, *Zur Ontologie des gesellschaftlichen Seins* (Berlin: Luchterhand, 1972).

 6. See my book *Dialogue Within the Dialectic* (London: Allen and Unwin, 1984). In particular see Chapter 5, "Hegelianized Leninism" and Chap-

ter 6, "The Dialectic and the Yenan Way." In these chapters I use the phrases "Leninist bolshevism" and "Stalinist bolshevism" to distinguish between the forms of bolshevism represented by Lenin and Stalin. Looked at chronologically, "Leninist bolshevism"refers to the type of Marxism that emerged in the Soviet Union through 1924 and "Stalinist bolshevism" alludes to the type of Marxism that characterized the Soviet Union from the rise of Stalin until Gorbachev exclusive of the Khruschev interlude.

7. Lukács, *Sozialismus und Demokratizierung,* ed. Frank Benseler (Frankfurt: Sendler Verlag, 1985), pp. 131–136. I mentioned this book in footnote 1, and in the German edition Benseler has written an editorial comment in which he describes his correspondence with Lukács during the period in which *Demokratizierung Heute und Morgen* was written. Other interesting comments on the evolution of this text will be found in Lukács, *A Record of a Life,* ed. Istvan Eorsi (London: Verso, 1983), and in the essay by Agnes Heller, Ferenc Fehér, Gyorgy Markús and Milady Vajda, "Notes on Lukács' Ontology," in *Lukács Reappraised,* ed. Agnes Heller (New York: Columbia University Press, 1983), pp. 125–153.

8. Ibid.

9. Fehér and Heller, *Hungary 1956 Revisited* (London: Allen and Unwin, 1983).

10. Fehér and Heller, *Dictatorship over Needs* (Oxford: Basil Blackwell, 1983), p. 290.

11. Fehér and Heller, *Hungary 1956 Revisited,* p. 118.

12. Ibid.

13. Remark made to me in a private conversation with Agnes Heller.

14. Lukács, *Record of a Life.*

15. Ibid, p. 168.

16. Ibid, p. 129.

17. Ibid, p. 168.

18. I offer a fuller discussion of the various meanings of the word "politics" in my article "On the Repotentialization of a Marxist Theory of Politics" in *Praxis International* (July 1988). The word "politics" has several meanings, and it is only possible to understand Marx's political thought by coming to an understanding of the different meanings of the term "politics" for Marx. Only one of these meanings has to do with the state, and to assume that the end of state meant the end of all politics for Marx is to fail to grasp the

other meanings of the concept politics. Most political functions continue after the end of the state for Marx, and it is only by grasping the various meanings of politics for Marx that one is then able to clearly surmise the exact political functions which continue after the eradication of the state.

19. Marx, Karl, *Economic-Philosophic Manuscripts of 1844* ed. Tom Bottomore (New York: McGraw-Hill, 1964), pp. 63–65.

20. I have written on the utopian elements of *State and Revolution,* in particular pointing to the anarchist assumptions of the text. See my article, "Lenin's Utopianism" in *Studies in Soviet Thought* (June 1985). In this article I attempt to point out that Lenin did not have an adequate definition of the concept of politics, a problem which I refer to as the "linguistic collapse," and this was one of the reasons why he assumed communism was synonymous with the absence of all governance.

21. This neologism is my creation.

22. Lenin, Nicolai, "State and Revolution," in *Lenin: Selected Works* (New York: International Publishers, 1967), Vol. II.

23. Colletti, Lucio, "Bernstein and the Marxism of the Second International" in *From Rousseau to Lenin,* trans. John Merrington and Judith White (London: New Left Books, 1972), pp. 45–108.

24. Charles Bettelheim has written an insightful analysis of the hold of the economist model of socialism over the entire Second International. See his book *Class Struggles in the USSR: 1917–1923,* trans. Brian Pearce (New York: Monthly Review Press, 1976).

25. Lenin, "The Proletarian Revolution and the Renegade Kautsky," in *Lenin: Selected Works,* Vol. III.

26. Kautsky, Karl, *Die Diktatur des Proletariat* (Berlin: Dietz Verlag, 1919).

27. Lenin was familiar in his early years with a great number of the texts of Marx and Engels. The exact dimensions of Lenin's Marx-Engels bibliography has never been explored, but it should be because it would reveal much about Lenin's knowledge of Marxism in his formative period. I made a modest attempt to uncover the extent of Lenin's knowledge of the texts of Marx and Engels as well as German social democracy in my article, "The Germanization of Lenin" in *Studies in Soviet Thought* (July, 1988), pp. 88–101. The major thrust of this article is to see the depth of influence which German social democracy in total had on Lenin. It is the thesis of that article that Lenin was far more influenced by German theory than has previously been recognized,

and that former interpretations of Lenin's intellectual development stress the Russian side too heavily to the disadvantage of the German stream of thought.

28. Lenin, *State and Revolution,* pp. 424–427.

29. Ibid, p. 424.

30. The early Lenin was extremely critical of bureaucracy because he saw this as an instrument of Tzarist control. Bureaucracy as it was used by the Romanovs was simply a tool to further the repressive policies of the Romanovs. On Lenin's early condemnation of bureaucracy, see the following essays: "What the Friends of the People Are and How They Fight the Social-Democrats," in *Lenin: Collected Works* (Moscow: Foreign Languages Publishing House, 1972), Vol. I, pp. 129–332; "The Heritage We Renounce," in *Lenin: Collected Works,* Vol. II, pp. 491–534.

31. Lenin, *State and Revolution,* p. 428.

32. Ibid, 475.

33. Hal Draper is one of the most perceptive students of Marxist thought writing today. On the issue of the meaning of the "dictatorship of the proletariat" for Lenin see his *The "Dictatorship of the Proletariat" from Marx to Lenin* (New York: Monthly Review Press, 1987). Draper is one of those scholars, like Neil Harding, who stresses the democratic currents in Lenin's thought. His work is a refutation of the work of Richard Pipes and Adam Ulam who interpret Lenin as an autocrat.

34. Draper has another book on the dictatorship which traces the evolution of the concept from the Jacobins to Blanqui. See his *Karl Marx's Theory of Revolution: The "Dictatorship of the Proletariat"* (New York: Monthly Review Press, 1986). Draper's grasp of the bibliographic material is always impressive, and he has an eye for catching a phrase or sentence that has eluded other scholars. I find myself in complete agreement with his views on Marx and Lenin and consider his work a welcome and long overdue corrective to the Tkachevian interpretation of Lenin propounded by Pipes and Ulam.

35. Lenin, *State and Revolution,* p. 461.

36. Ibid, p. 473.

37. Polan, A.J. *Lenin and the End of Politics* (London: Methuen, 1985).

38. Ibid, pp. 473–474.

39. Ibid, p. 474.

40. Ibid, p. 478.

41. Ibid, p. 479.

42. Ibid, p. 480.

43. Ibid, p. 482.

44. Ibid, p. 490.

45. Ibid, p. 492.

46. Lukács, *Lenin: A Study of the Unity of His Thought* (London: New Left Books, 1970). Norberto Bobbio has written some penetrating insights into the failures of the political theory of the Second International. Although I reached my conclusions independently of Bobbio, much of what he says corresponds to my own beliefs and it is always pleasant to find support for one's conclusions. Bobbio's work deserves to be studied because he also explores the relationship between socialism and democracy which is at the heart of contemporary socialist theory. See his book *Which Socialism*? (Minneapolis: University of Minnesota Press, 1987).

47. Heller, "Lukács' Later Philosophy," in *Lukács Reappraised*, pp. 177–190.

48. Kolakowski, Leszek, "Lukács or Reason in the Service of Dogma" in *Main Currents of Marxism* (Oxford: Oxford University Press, 1982), Vol. III.

49. Lichtheim, George, *Lukács* (London: Viking Press, 1970).

50. Zitta, Victor, *Georg Lukács's Marxism* (The Hague: Martinus Nijhoff, 1964).

51. Lukács, Georg, "Brief an Alberto Carocci," in *Marxismus und Stalinismus* (München: R. Piper, 1970.)

52. Lukács, Georg, "The International Significance of Russian Democratic Literary Criticism," in *Studies in European Realism* (New York: Grosset and Dunlop, 1964).

53. Bahro, Rudolf, *The Alternative in Eastern Europe* (London: New left Books, 1977).

54. The contemporary discussion of the relationship between socialism and democracy was the fruit of the Euro-Communist movement of the 1970s. Norberto Bobbio's work on this issue must be seen as an expression of the Euro-Communist movement that was successful in riding socialist thought of much of outmoded bolshevik political ideology. Bobbio was particularly penetrating in seeing that Leninist revolutionary strategy of 1917 eventually be-

came the basis of a bolshevik theory of the state. See his essays "A Socialist Democracy?" and "Is There a Marxist Doctrine of the State?" in *Which Socialism*?

55. See the essay by Ferenc Fehér, "Lukács in Weimar," and the one by Agnes Heller, "Lukács' Later Philosophy," both of which appear in *Lukács Reappraised*. Both Heller and Fehér interpret the later Lukács as retreating from politics to both ethics and aesthetics. While correctly identifying the 1930 period as a turning point in the career of Lukács, they both see his late work, *The Specificity of the Aesthetic,* as forming the axis of his thought after 1945. The views expressed in this Introduction contradict the evaluation of Heller and Fehér. Heller sees Lukács as writing a "philosophy of history," Fehér paints him as embracing a Weimarian "classicism," and both portray him as distancing himself from political engagement, as abandoning the role of the active "partisan" in search of an ethics and a contemplative aesthetics. Fehér's essay, "Lukács in Weimar," maintains that *The Specificity of the Aesthetic* argued that the unity of subject and object could only be realized in the aesthetic experience, and I reject this view because it seems to neglect Lukács's persistent involvement in politics, his writing of 1968. The attempt to portray the later Lukács as retreating to a Weimarian "classicism" seems to me to violate Lukács's consistent search for a philosophy of action, as well as his awareness that the ontology of human existence is always grounded in society. Contrary to the Heller-Fehér interpretation, I uphold the view that Lukács remained an intellectual partisan, a politically engaged member of the intelligentsia, and that his writing cannot be understood unless taken as responses to the political situations confronting Lukács. Even after the *Blum Theses,* even after his eviction from the Hungarian Communist party, Lukács's work after 1930 intentionally reflected the political events of his time. To see Lukács as escaping to a Weimarian "classicism" is to distort the tenacity of his political commitment. Heller and Fehér present an idealist interpretation of Lukács, because they seek to detach him from his own "ontology of social existence" and present him as a Kantian, as someone in search of an "ethical democracy," or as someone escaping the harshness of twentieth century politics in a realm of contemplative aesthetics.

56. Sziklai, László, *Georg Lukács und seine Zeit* (Wien: Europaische Verlag, 1986). Sziklai is the Director of the Lukács Archiv in Budapest, and in this book he adopts a position antithetical to that of Heller and Fehér, arguing that Lukács was always the partisan and it is the Sziklai position which I espouse in this introduction. Concentrating on the period after 1930, Sziklai shows how Lukács's intellectual endeavors after that time were shaped by the struggle against fascism and Stalinism. In his struggle against Hitler, Lukács associated himself with the democratic traditions of the German Enlighten-

ment. In his struggle against Stalinism, Lukács also associated with the humanist traditions of the German Enlightenment. According to Sziklai, Lukács's writing can never be detached from immediate political exigencies, but this should be seen as a strength, the force of political engagement.

57. Fehér, *The Frozen Revolution* (Oxford: Oxford University Press, 1988).

58. Fehér and Heller, *The Dictatorship Over Needs*.

59. Prill, Meinhard, *Burgerliche Alltagswelt und pietistische Denken im Werk Hölderlin's* (Tübingen: Niemeyer, 1983).

60. Lukács, *Demokratizierung Heute und Morgen*, p. 92.

61. Ibid.

62. Lenin, "Once Again on the Trade Unions, the Current Situation and the Mistakes of Trotsky and Bukharin" and "The Role and Function of the Trade Unions Under the New Economic Policy," *Lenin: Selected Works*, Vol. III.

63. Lukács, *Record of a Life*, p.168.

64. Ibid, p. 178.

65. Lenin, "The Reorganization of the Party" in *Collected Works*, Vol. 10.

66. On this point see A.J. Polan's *Lenin and the End of Politics*. Polan is correct in assuming that *State and Revolution* contains no political theory, but he was wrong in assuming that Lenin's totalitarianism was the cause of the absence of a political theory. Polan's major thesis is that *State and Revolution* offered scriptural legitimation for bureaucratic authoritarianism, and that the seeds of Stalinism are to be found in Lenin's text. Although Polan sees that Marxist political theory was brought to an end in *State and Revolution,* he remains unyielding in his refusal to see any democratic elements in the text. Polan is committed to seeing Lenin as a totalitarian, and refuses to allow him to ever escape that imprisonment. *Lenin and the End of Politics* follows the argument that a direct line of development connects Lenin and Stalin, while I reject this interpretation. Not only do I draw a profound distinction between Lenin and Stalin, but I also subscribe to the thesis that a democratic spirit flows through Lenin's political writings.

67. Harding, Neil, *Lenin's Political Thought* (London: St. Martin's Press, 1977), 2 Vols. Harding's work stands in direct contradiction to that of A.J. Polan, particularly the chapter which Harding devotes to *State and Revo-*

lution. It is a daring chapter, bold in its assertion of the democratic presuppositions of the work. Harding reads *State and Revolution* as a radical democratic document and he is correct. There is a naïvete to Lenin's radical democracy, but Harding was also aware of that. Lenin was a part of the plebeian democratic tradition which stretched back to Robespierre, not the Robespierre of the Committee of Public Safety, but the Robespierre who was responsive to the demands of the Paris Commune. Polan's totalitarian interpretation of Lenin totally overlooks the plebeian democratic elements of his thought.

68. The phrase "the end of politics" is taken from A.J. Polan's book. I have written a detailed review of Polan's book in which my criticism is more fully developed: see my review in *Internationalwissenschaftliche Korrespondenz* (Sept. 1987). In this review I point out the ideological blind alleys which led Lenin to renounce a Marxist theory of politics. Lenin is both a victim and perpetuator of the ideological dead ends which the Marxism of the Second International had entered. Polan does not appreciate this ideological decay, and so wrongly resorts to condemning Lenin's dictatorial proclivities for the death of a Marxist theory of politics.

*The Process
of Democratization*

Notes on the Translation

Lukács wrote The Process of Democratization *in a race against time. Written between September and December, 1968, it was composed with extreme haste and bears all the marks and imperfections of a hurried first draft. During the composition of this incomplete monograph, Lukács's creativity and mortality were pressed from three sides.*

The composition of this manuscript started a month after the Soviet extinction of the Dubcek reform movement in August, 1968. Lukács was aware that he suffered from incurable cancer and he was to die in 1971. Recognizing that he only had a few more years of life, he was under great pressure to get something of his response to Soviet imperialism down on paper.

Since he wished to respond to the crushing of the Czech reformation of Marxism, Lukács was compelled to cease the writing of his Ontology of Social Existence. *He had completed his revision of Marxist aesthetics in 1963, and in his* Ontology *hoped to also revise Marxist philosophy. In order to embark upon* The Process of Democratization, *Lukács would have to suspend his work on the* Ontology, *a project he ardently wished to finish. In addition, Lukács desperately hoped to complete an Ethics. As I noted in my Introduction, he initially thought that* The Process of Democratization *might be incorporated as part of his proposed Ethics. In order to get* The Process of Democratization *down in words, Lukács had to interrupt the writing of the* Ontology *and postpone the beginning of his Ethics, which he never did start. Under these conditions it was no wonder that he sped through the labor of writing* The Process of Democratization.

Lukács's age was also a factor. Born in 1885, he was eighty three when he commenced the writing of his treatise on a Marxist theory of politics. Lukács had devoted his last years to the reformulation of Marxist theory. He rushed because he did not want either age or death to rob his powers before he was well into the renaissance of Marxism.

The original text of The Process of Democratization *is awkward and sometimes almost impenetrable. The translators were left with a hard choice: to smooth out the flaws of the text in order to make it more readable or to present the text basically as Lukács left it, even though it is flawed.*

The approach of the translators was to present the text as Lukács left it, where such a presentation did not interfere with the readers ability to understand it. Lukács was the greatest Marxist theoretician of the twentieth century. He had earned the right to speak for himself and it would be presumptuous to alter his phrases even if many of them, taking into account

the constraints under which he worked, fell below his normal level of excellence. He can stand on his own.

The translators felt that the presentation of a text that closely mirrored what Lukács actually wrote would provide a sense of immediacy to the reader. Including some maimed portions of the text was the best way to have the reader experience what Lukács himself was experiencing, the enormous pressure to get his thought on a Marxist theory of the state down in print before time or death stole his faculties.

For these reasons, the reader will find two places in the text in which Lukács actually repeats himself. One of these occasions deals with a quote he took from Marx's On the Jewish Question *and the second are comments on the Marquis de Sade. Lukács employed the Marx quote twice and the de Sade comments twice. The translators have left these repetitions stand so the reader will have a sense of the stress under which Lukács labored.*

In The Process of Democratization *Lukács used the traditional, although sexist, words "man" and "mankind" when referring to humankind. He was deeply influenced by both the philosophy and language of Classical German Humanism which was itself sexist. But Lukács was an East European intellectual writing in 1968. The Feminist movement was then still in its incipient stages and Lukács could hardly be expected to be aware of the gender-prejudices of languages before this issue was exposed by a later and more mature Feminist movement. The translators made the decision to leave Lukács's gender-prejudice language in the text.*

Lukács sometimes referenced his sources and sometimes did not. The reader gets the impression that when the quote was easily accessible to Lukács he cites the source in a note. But if the quote was not easily accessible, if it required time to ferret out, he would frequently not add a reference assuming, perhaps, that he would add it at a later time. The translation reflects this and so many quotations in the text do not carry a note.

At the end of the manuscript, all the footnotes are supplied in German. Lukács himself mined German sources and so they are provided in the original. For consistency, German footnoting conventions are also used. The German word Ebenda *is equivalent to the English word Ibid and in German the letter S equals the English letter P for page.*

Preliminary Methodological Remarks

The most significant moment of Marxism is its monumental reduction of historical development to a succession of class struggles and this has fascinated but more often repelled broad sections of the nonsocialist intelligentsia: "Freeman and serf, patrician and plebeian, lord and serf, master and journeyman, in short, oppressor and oppressed stand in continuous opposition to each other, lead an uninterrupted, sometimes hidden and sometimes open struggle, a warfare which everywhere ends with a revolutionary reorganization of the entire society, or with the mutual destruction of the contending classes."[1] With the exception of the concluding statement, this view of history serves as a guideline for the supporters of Marxism whose approach to sociology, consciously or not, is rather abstract, while enemies of Marxism find it difficult to accept such a historical interpretation. The attempts to conceive of every historical phenomena as absolutely unique, to exclude historical regularities from historical theory, have been rejected. With good reason. Such a glaring opposition between historical particularity and universality must lead on the level of theory to irrationalism, and on the level of *praxis* to complete unimaginative and vacuous "realpolitik," which not only hinders socialist attempts to master historical reality but also blocks the practical application of the social manipulative tendencies inherent in neo-positivism. Political theory, which at least in its external appearances has been influenced by the natural sciences, from the perspective of universal epistemotogical categories has become accustomed to consider state forms, social forces, and tendencies as social realities.

Such methodological approaches can easily become habitual, if one repeatedly assumes he finds support for them in the honored classics of western thought. Aristotle and Rousseau, for example, appear to illustrate this aspect of our problem for they claim that democracy is most adequately defined as a universal category. In fact, the methodological ground of the discussion over dictatorship and democracy during and after the events of 1917 until the present day debate over "totalitarianism versus democracy" is to be sought in the overwhelming number of cases in these categorical alternatives, in the opposition between the particular and the universal.

We believe that any attempt to set the particular and the deterministic in opposition to each other to be unfounded, and in any case not a true Marxist approach. In the classical theory of Marxism, particular sociohistorical phenomena and their generalization into deterministic laws are never perceived as contradictory, but on the contrary as an indivisible unity. Particular social existence is, above all, a sociohistorical category, the necessary manifestation of the contradictory interplay of active socioeconomic forces within a social conflict at a certain stage of development. From the point of view of theory and

praxis, the understanding of the characteristics of a social particularity is as important as the perception of general regularities and sociohistorical determinism. For *praxis*, whose affirmation only takes place in the concrete "hic and nunc" of a real sociohistorical situation, the adequate comprehension of a particular historical situation is an inescapable priority. The manipulators and fetishists of abstract-universality necessarily err if they believe they can call Marx to their support. There is sufficient evidence in Marx's *Eighteenth Brumaire of Louis Bonaparte*,[2] for it is immediately clear that in all classes and class developments, changes of state and government are presented in the light of those concrete social situations which the revolutions of 1848 called into life in France. Generalizing on these concrete examples, Marx concludes that since every economic formation is simultaneously a unity of deterministic necessity and historic particularity, superstructures, in our case democracy, must be similar in their origin and being. For that reason, the attempt will be made here to consider democracy historically (better said: "democratization," since the analysis itself primarily concerns a process and not a condition), as a concrete political force for the organization of a contemporary economic formation from whose soil it arises, an economic formation which acts, becomes unstable, and perishes. Here, as everywhere else, dehistorization creates negative fetishes which instead of throwing light on concrete historical movements (and the social laws they call forth), mystifies and camouflages them. In these questions, one speaks frequently of democracy as a fixed condition and thereby forgets to consider the active process of development in the structure of contemporary conditions, although an accurate picture can only arise through the use of the notion of process. In order to emphasize this crucial point, we prefer the term democratization to that of democracy.

Part I
*Bourgeois Democracy
as a False Alternative
for the Reform of Socialism*

1

Democracy and Its Various Economic Formations

It would be a misleading simplification to assume that the leading theoreticians of political theory, beginning with Aristotle, failed to address the problem of the variety of forms of democracy. But their observations, their clarifications and most of all their value judgments do not proceed from an analysis of the relationship between economic base and democracy as a political superstructure, but only from naturalistic determinations (such as the size of the state) or from legal considerations (such as the status of a citizen). In this way, only very general categories or evaluations can arise, but there can be no adequate perception of how the concrete existence of the various forms of democracy emerge from primary socioeconomic developments. For these leading theoreticians of political theory, more difficult to grasp than the problem of the genesis of democracy was a knowledge of the growth and decline of a particular type of democracy founded within a particular economic formation. Any speculations by these past political theoreticians regarding a particular type of democracy remained abstract generalizations, which cannot possibly be understood as reflecting the "thing-in-itself," the self-movement of a specific societal totality.

Marx was the first to proceed from the elementary facts of social life. Even though he comes to speak of *polis* democracy, the original, and through many centuries, the most ideologically influential model as the paradigmatic form of democracy, the economic is still his primary presupposition. The commune "as state . . . is from one perspective an interrelationship of free and equal private property owners, their association against external enemies, and is at the same time their protector. The community consists of working land owners and allotment farmers. The independence of the allotment farmers originates through association as members of the commune, the guarantee of the *ager publicus* for the needs and renown of the community. Only members of the community can acquire landed property, but as a member of the community he is a private property owner. Thus, the individual's position as

a private property owner is closely linked to the social existence of the community: individual self-preservation means community self-preservation at the same time."[3] The type of democracy which develops from this economic constellation is not merely based on general forms of human existence and human *praxis*—that are valid for every society—but is associated with a concrete form of social existence in which individuals actively participate. To be a citizen of the *polis*, an active participant in *polis* democracy, is not merely a determinate-specific category of the political superstructure, but every private citizen of the *polis* is inseparably connected with the economic foundation of societal being.

That conclusion had important consequences for the whole life of man in this type of social formation. Above all, social existence took precedence over individual private life. The real being of all citizens, their cooperation in democratic life, is intimately tied to a specific economic formation. As this economic foundation disintegrates—a consequence of the necessary development of productive forces—the existence and functional capacity of *polis* democracy is destroyed. Forces of political decay compelled this most highly esteemed and luminous model of democracy, above all in the classical models of Athens and Rome, into their own dissolution. Marx clearly recognizes these economic forces of decay: slavery as the basis of such a society. The struggle over democracy played itself out inside a privileged minority while the great active productive masses were in principle excluded from the democratic struggle as from all active participation in societal life.

If the original economic foundation of the *polis* is transcended, the relative equality of private allotments destroyed, a proletariat emerges which according to Sismondi's analysis lives at the expense of society, whereas under capitalism, society lives at the expense of the working classes. The relationships between labor, property, and membership in a political community, the principle of *polis* democracy, is in its origin a primitive form of social organization. According to Marx, early man lives in clans and membership in a tribe is the condition for the ownership of property. With the beginning of what Marx calls "the receding of natural barriers" the interconnection between clan membership and property vanishes. This Greek form of democracy loses, precisely as a result of its economic advancement, the civilizing effect of its exemplary humane qualities. The individual at this stage of historical development has not yet acquired a modern "unique" identity. A citizen of the *polis* holding an allotment, belonging to the tribe—those are the socioeconomic conditions of his existence and consequently the essential features of his identity. The secondary importance of the private life of the *polis* citizen is due to the fact that human existence and personal development is synonymous with the fulfilling of one's political duties, is coincidental with his functioning as a political subject in this form of democracy.

As far as political consciousness is concerned the great French Revolution, which represents the classical form of modern bourgeois democracy, was influenced to a large degree by the Greek ideal. Socioeconomically, however, it is the exact opposite. By stressing this contradiction, Marx simultaneously emphasizes that freedom and equality, the central ideological modes of expression of modern democracy, can receive extremely various formulations. Freedom and equality are molded by socioeconomic conditions, they are not idealized constructs, "not only esteemed in exchange which rests on exchange-value, but the exchange of exchange-values is the productive real basis of all equality and freedom."[4]

Despite all inherent contradictions, the factual realization of freedom and democracy during the French Revolution signifies enormous progress in the history of human society. Real human sociability, the objective real foundation of the species being of the human has entered into existence with the realization of freedom and democracy. Political categories which were assumed to be the natural barriers of social existence are negated. The social struggle through which this annulment takes place is directed in its modern form against the division of French society into estates which come into existence in and from feudalism. The feudality which young Marx calls a "democracy of unfreedom" imparts to the contradictions of society "an immediate political character" in which "the elements . . . of bourgeois life, as for example private property or the family or the shape and mode of work . . . in the form of lordship, of Estates, and the corporations were raised to the elements of political life. . . . These elements determined . . . in the form of the relation of particular individuals to the State, i.e. its political relation."[5]

The French Revolution radically destroys this entire feudal structure and in so doing reveals for the first time in history in purely sociological terms the actual relation between the state and civil society. Marx correctly points out that the historical mission of the French Revolution is to construct a unitary state on the ruins of feudal decentralization. Political life, irrespective of any bourgeois categories, becomes a subject of general public interest. For the first time in history, human reason is taken to be the most reliable architect in the planning of social existence, ending a century long dispute over the proper purpose of the "Kingdom of Reason."

However, as Engels later correctly states, this Kingdom of Reason proves itself to be the idealized Kingdom of the Bourgeoisie. Idealized is not to be understood as a politico-ideological critique, but as an objective scientific assessment of a real developing social structure. Marx himself says in the theoretical discussion of the above quoted passage concerning the transformation of an entire social formation that the state arose as an ideality through its overturning of feudalism and so establishes a fundamental contradiction between political life and the "complete materialization of bourgeois society."[6] He

shows that this contradictory unity of state and bourgeois society, of ideality and materiality in the life of society and the life of every individual man, is the key to understanding the documents of this transformation which are the texts of the constitutions of the French Revolution.

These texts proceed from the correlative opposites of *homme* (bourgeois) and *citoyen*. *Citoyen* stands for the idealization of the citizen, who is detached from all material ties with socioeconomic existence while *homme* (man) is a member of bourgeois society. Marx also emphasizes that within this indivisible unity (insofar as every citizen is also a *homme*) the revolutionary constitutions degrade the status of citizenship by making it dependent upon so called human rights. In so doing, these constitutions implicitly recognize the real social supremacy of material, productive (private) men over the idealized citizen.

At the same time, these texts clearly depict the position of this bourgeois form of democracy in the great developmental process of humanity, the rise of the human species, the anthropogenesis of man. With a view to the social situation of the concrete individual created by bourgeois society, Marx says that his "personal freedom is not facilitated but rather that other individuals form a barrier to his own freedom."[7] That is the fundamental social reality of capitalism: the egoistic and for that reason the merely partial/fragmentary man appears as the subject of the real *praxis* of society. Simultaneously, as a necessary component of this developmental stage, expressing the socialization of labor which takes place under capitalism, the species nature of man also reaches an objectively higher social level as compared to earlier less socialized formations. Consequently, this species nature, the real cooperative life of man, which evolves in Marx's lifetime in the cooperative labor factories, appears "as a contrast to his material life."[8]

Naturally, in the stormy upheavals of the great French Revolution all this is expressed with more exuberant pathos than later on in the prosaic moments of literary composition. Ever since the Renaissance, this recurrent reference to the ancient ideal of *polis* democracy is typical of this revolutionary enthusiasm. This is not literary or intellectual eccentricity. Marx states that it is necessary for the French Revolution to make heroism a part of everyday life. The great actors of the revolution needed ideals, even self-deceit "in order to hide the limited bourgeois content of their struggle from themselves and raise their passion to the heights of great historical tragedy."[9] This historical enthusiasm often leads to a historically false identification of both Greek and bourgeois forms of democratization, with a careless ignorance of their societal contradictions. However, the revolution gains the victory and starts a real process in which the existing categories of bourgeois democracy become the ruling forms of both the capitalist state and civilization. The luminous symbol of the *polis* was overcome by social reality. Even after the victory of the revolution,

when these dreams of antiquity are used as a legitimating device, they appear as intentional deception. The socioeconomic reality of the living and acting allotment owner of Greek *polis* democracy can never be resurrected. His social being has nothing in common with that of commodity exchange or with bourgeois freedom and equality. The social being of bourgeois life, the world of commodity trade, finds its political expression in the superstructure of the modern capitalist state.

2

The Necessary Developmental Tendencies of Bourgeois Democratization

So far we have only shown the contradictory economic foundations of Greek and bourgeois forms of democracy. In contrast to fashionable contemporary theories, social structure is not a static and therefore anti-historical principle, but development is the inherent quality and primary dynamic basis of every social formation. We have seen how the equality of allotment owners in *polis* democracy was destroyed by the necessary economic development of the forces of production. Let us now look at the dynamic developmental tendencies of bourgeois society that unfold out of the contradiction of the materiality of middle class society with the ideality of the state.

Above all, it is the general dynamic character of bourgeois society to subject every part of this social formation to its own tendencies. In agreement with all the impartial and accurate observers of this period, Marx describes the influence of *homme* on capitalist society, its institutions, and its real superstructure as follows: "The bourgeoisie acts towards the institutions of this system as the Jew towards the laws; he avoids them as often as it is possible in every individual case but he wants all others to abide by them."[10]

From a historical perspective, there is nothing strange about this general mode of behavior. The state in every social formation, functions as an ideological weapon in the fighting out of class conflicts. When a class of *polis* citizens helps break up the allotment community by buying up the property of the impoverished they initiate the destruction of *polis* democracy regardless of their original intentions. Even though such activity undermines *polis* democracy, as Marx and others recognize, it paradoxically promotes the economic development of capitalism and at the same time brings a later political superstructure in correspondence with the unfolding economic base. On the basis of social ontology the democratic state must retain its ideal character, but the democratic state is an effective instrument and increasingly adapts to the economic needs of the *homme*. The fact that this state is manipulated by influential groups, that the ideology of these influential groups is looked upon as a

general social norm, does not alter the overall principle of the adaptability of the capitalist state. Our studies will only consider those social movements which possess sufficient strength to call forth a transformation of the economic base, and because the economic base stands in such a dynamic determinate relation to the political superstructure it can shape the form of state. Those who wish to follow such transforming social movements and not fetishize them may never forget that such mass movements are only a particular kind of synthesis between personal and public acts. There is deep socio-ontological justification in Marx's description of mass movements in terms of individual acts and his view that the fetishing of mass movements is founded on the attempt to distort the species being of man (immediate individual: his relation to his fellow men).

Although this may appear contradictory in terms of formal logic or epistemology, the ideality of the superstructure proves to be the most effective means and therefore a historic success in facilitating the complete triumph of the materialistic-egoistic tendencies in capitalist social life. It is no coincidence that under these circumstances the abstract formalism of law flourishes and enjoys the greatest esteem. It is also no coincidence—to return to our basic problem—that the present and most advanced ideality of political forms of government is the most appropriate instrument for the complete conquest of egoistic-capitalist individual interests. This process is disguised under idealized slogans of public interest. Bourgeois representative systems are themselves separated from the real life of society. The more parliamentarianism, the crucial and typical realization of this political Ideality, is established as the perfect organ of popular sovereignty the more it becomes the most appropriate instrument for the justification of the egoistic interests of capitalist organizations. Parliamentarianism is able to do this by disguising the terms "unlimited freedom" and "equality." Perhaps, the term "disguise" is not entirely correct. It is not simply the "disguise" of freedom and equality which is established, but more accurately its economic essence, the real idea of capitalist commodity-exchange.

Political life since the great revolutions of the seventeenth and eighteenth centuries has been driven by the quest for the pure form of parliamentarianism, (i.e. universal and equal suffrage) with its omnipotent legislature and bureaucratic control. Some of these struggles do not require lengthy discussion, like those against the remnants of feudal estates: they belong to the past, at least as far as the capitalist countries are concerned. It seems more important to concentrate on the fact that the decisive steps in the attempt to call into being a democracy in the sense of the Great Revolution are results of the mass movements which must be conceived as democratic correctives to "pure" parliamentarianism. Plebeian-radical democracy, whose masses served in Cromwell's army at the time of the English Revolution, and the plebeian revo-

lutionaries of the Paris sections, put Parliament under pressure. They necessarily dissolved and decimated them, in order to create organs which were capable of giving expression to the real interests of the working population. First, the "Glorious Revolution" in England, then the government of Louis Phillipe and later the Third Republic were capable of excluding such "unauthorized" interventions to ensure that Parliament defined freedom and equality in accordance with the interests of the leading capitalist groups. One may, however, never forget that in times of crises—it is sufficient to mention the Dreyfus Affair—there emerges on the political horizon, although in a weakened form, the possibility of plebeian-democratic intervention. This contrast between democratic populism and parliamentarian liberalism evidenced itself in the political theory of the nineteenth century. It is not necessary to emphasize the almost unchallenged triumph of parliamentarian liberalism.

3
Bourgeois Democracy Today

It cannot be our task to comment specifically on the contrast between parliamentarianism and plebeian-democratic intervention. Only the basic tendencies are relevant here, and Marx already finds illustrations for them in the Great French Revolution. These tendencies later attain unlimited domination in developed capitalist societies. What one is nowadays accustomed to call freedom is the result of the undisputed victory of the inner forces of capitalism. It is only too obvious that capitalism underwent many qualitative changes in its evolution from its very beginnings to the present day, modifications that brought about changes in its political superstructure, and the freedom of bourgeois democracy. Yet, in a Marxist sense, the fundamental structure of capitalism has not essentially changed. On the contrary, it is necessary to say that in the course of its evolution its inner quality of life, the fundamental characteristics of its essence, functions in a more sharply focused way than would have been thought possible in its illusion-filled revolutionary beginnings.

Thus, our discussion of bourgeois democracy and its manipulation of the concept of freedom has to be based on the contents and forms that specifically characterize contemporary capitalism. A politician or political theorist with abstract ideological views might indeed be under the delusion that he can conjure up a previous or utopian form of freedom. If his efforts are to have any real practical meaning they must deal with the reality of the contemporary capitalist economy which is the foundation of its corresponding form of government. This is especially true for those ideologists who perceive bourgeois democracy as a real alternative to contemporary socialism. They want to show a continuity stretching from Cincinnatus to Rousseau from Cromwell to Robespierre. Reality, however proves that only a bourgeois democracy as defined by Nixon or Strauss is possible under the present sociopolitical conditions. Later on we will return to the necessary consequences of such widespread pseudo-alternatives to socialist democracy. Yet, we find it necessary to briefly point out the absolutely existential priority of the present as distinct from a desired and attractive past.

The apex of a centuries-long development, contemporary capitalism, abetted by techniques of social manipulation that establish a dominating imperialism, is a contrived and regulated social formation. We are quite aware of the fact that by the standards of respectable modern researchers it is a major breach of integrity not to put terms like imperialism or colonialism in quotation marks. Sharing the general rejection of the nineteenth century because it was an age of ideological conflict, all the present-day social sciences, nevertheless, are intensely ideological and have the common purpose of showing the present as superior to and as qualitatively different from that prior age. This is how the term "pluralistic" society is counterpoised to "totalitarianism," how the attempt is made to construct and widely propagate throughout the world the thesis that both fascism and communism stem from a common spiritual heritage. The increasing capitalization of the consumption and service industries, and the embourgeoisement of the proletariat as buyers of commodities, are used to prove that the proletariat can be derevolutionized and that the theory of surplus value is wrong. In fact, Marx's surplus value theory has not proven incorrect, but rather the relative surplus value form has only replaced the absolute surplus value form. Marx not only predicts the growth of relative surplus value over absolute surplus value under technologically advanced capitalism, but this process is itself determined by the merely formal subsumption of production under capitalist categories. Consequently, all traces of the class struggles of prior epochs disappear in modern industrial society partly due to the fact that the social democrats often completely turn their backs on Marxism in order to become participating members of the establishment. The role played by Stalinist and post-Stalinist communist theory and *praxis* in these developments will be discussed subsequently. In any case, the trade unions nowadays stand almost universally to the left of the social democratic parties. In addition, occasional large strikes disclose that economic class struggle has never been totally renounced. Although the liberation of hitherto existing colonies is interpreted as proof of the disappearance of every trace of the old colonial exploitation and repression, in fact every new policy in the United States, despite its public refutation of colonialism, is essentially nothing but a continuation of the old policies masquerading in new technological means. Following the basic traditions of Warren Hastings, German imperialism etc., not only is the domination of the most reactionary classes over the Third World sustained by economic and military means, but every attempt for reform on the part of the liberal-bourgeoisie in the underdeveloped areas is suppressed by brute force. The fact that these forms of domination created through foreign intervention are labeled "Freedom" by the capitalist propaganda machines does not hide the continuity of western imperialism as shown in the cases of Santo Domingo, Indonesia, and Vietnam.

We are attempting to point out the inherent socioeconomic tendencies of

capitalism and their human, domestic, and international consequences. In this regard, we use as evidence the problem of species being and how this principle of human-social development receives a new form in the more complex class struggle engendered under capitalism in comparison to earlier societies. Marx emphasizes that the species life of man stands in contradiction to his natural life. In order to understand the central theoretic-practical importance of this statement we must refer to those problems which play a decisive role in the conceptual founding of Marx's materialism. In his VI *Theses on Feuerbach,* Marx criticizes Feuerbach's perception of the essence of man arguing "that the essence of man is not an abstraction inherent in each particular individual. The real nature of man is this ensemble of social relations." Since Feuerbach does not understand the connection between human essence and the real totality of social relations, the fact that human existence originates in the development of social relations, he is therefore obliged to "abstract from the historical process" and postulate an idealized isolated human individual. Hence he conceives of the nature of man "only as a species: as an inner, silent bond composed of the natural similarities between men which is their universality."

Feuerbach's idea of the species lacks any real social-human content, and as every purely logico-epistemological category it has to remain abstract and "silent." Marx expresses this by only recognizing Feuerbach's "species" as relevant to the domain of the organic nature, where it can be conceived "as an inner, silent bond composed of the natural similarities between men which is their universality."[11] The becoming of man to his social essence, his real species being, takes place in the historical process, is precisely overcoming this silence.

Marx can content himself with this aphoristic contrast, for from the very beginning he makes every effort to interpret species being as molded by sociological conditions, as no longer abstract and therefore no longer silent. Even the statement we took as our starting point that in bourgeois society the species life of man contradicts his material existence presupposes a fundamental and therefore sociohistorical interrelation between individual and species. In the *Economic-Philosophic Manuscripts* this thesis receives another highly important concretization: "It is above all necessary to avoid postulating 'society' once more as an abstract confronting the individual. The individual is social essence. His manifestation of life, even if it does not appear in the immediate form of a community which is consummated in association with other men is, nevertheless, both an objectification and an affirmation of social life."[12] Obviously, the resultant unity of individuality and species is not a gift of nature, but the product of a sociohistorical process that needs to overcome and surpass many barriers before the naturalistic categories of life cease to exist. These naturalistic barriers deter the rise and concrete development of such a unity

between man and species. Society must radically socialize itself; the material barriers preventing a socialized life must be pushed back. In order to make this species being of man a reality, man must emerge out of the animal life from which he stems. Capitalism carries out this process in the economic sphere and through the economic to the totality of society.

Without assuming any kind of teleology in the total process, the historical movement leading up to the appearance of socialized man is causally necessary. Although in capitalism a genuinely socialized man unfolds (also in itself a development of human species being) it is simultaneously a society which can only be kept going by internal indissolvable contradictions. It is a society in which man himself, due to economic necessities, is not capable of elevating himself to genuine species being, to essential human existence. We emphasized above the contradiction which separates species life from the material life of each individual as well as from the whole society. The species being of man advances to the degree in which these contradictions are destroyed in the particular and total economic process of society and are replaced by species universality. "Society" means the interdependence of man that is created by humanity and never before did it reach such a peak of practical and technical realization as in present day capitalism. At the same time, capitalism is contradictory because those socioeconomic forces that objectively produce and reproduce this material dependence do not create a complete connection between man and man but rather the contrary, the separation of man from man. Individual freedom as both a presupposition and product of society "lets every man find in another man not the enlargement but much more the limit of his freedom. . . . The human right of freedom is not based on the association of men with men but much more on the separation of man from man. It is the right of this separation, the right of limiting by individuals who are limited themselves."[13]

It is a mild and reserved description to use the word "limit" to characterize this activity of men hindering each other. Hobbes rather brutally describes the condition as "homo homini lupus," and it is certainly no coincidence that the Marquis de Sade has recently been quoted as a major ideologue of this transition to "individual rights." For de Sade, the sexual in the mere physiological sense is the crucial point. It is important to the theory of de Sade that the sexual act is not a matter of cooperative action of two human beings, of their common life. In his writing men do not look upon the women as human beings, but rather as mere objects. Despite all exaggerations, the inherent truth of this statement is again made obvious in Kant's definition of marriage. He translates de Sade's cynical egoism into the language of capitalist economics, into that of commodity exchange. Kant says: Marriage is "a contract between two people of the opposite sexes for the exclusive prossession of their sexual organs for a lifetime."[14]

The category which is simultaneously subjective and objective, which determines the individual and society, which comprises both social presuppositions and consequences, is that of possession. On this point, Marx says: "Private property has made us stupid and one-sided, biased enough to believe that an object cannot be ours unless we possess it, i.e. it exists for us as capital, or unless we can immediately eat, drink, wear it or live in it, in short, use it. Therefore, the physical and mental senses have simply been replaced by the sense of possession which is the alienation of these senses."[15] It would be ridiculous to assume that these capitalist social categories which were universal in economic and human terms, would disappear at the end of the nineteenth century. Quite the contrary. These categories have reached their peak in the industrial society of the twentieth century. Marx provided the first theory of this form of alienation almost 150 years ago, and it is no accident that the contemporary economic, social and human relationships of alienation, which in the nineteenth century remain hidden behind the question of economic productivity, become in our day a universal, social-human problem. Marx already points out that this universality of estrangement ensnared both the exploiter and the exploited. But it is only today that these social consequences of capitalism are perceived as questions of general human concern. This shows that Marx's discovery that capitalism determines the various modes of human existence is the essence that extensively and intensively still controls the totality of human life. Present day capitalism is not a transcendence, but a culmination, a dissemination and a deepening of its hitherto existing nature.

How is contemporary capitalism to be interpreted from the standpoint of our problem concerning democratization? Outwardly, it is its perfection, its universal dissemination. What, however, are the new social contents of its continuing consolidation and spread? On the surface, the immediate force is the subtle manipulation of the market which has become completely capitalist. Advertising has become the model of political "enlightenment" with the aid of an outrageously persuasive mass media. (Hitler already clearly understood this when he looked upon a good soap advertisement as a shining example for all political propaganda.) A direct connection between Hitler and capitalist advertising is out of the question, in fact, a strict contrast exists. Hitler's political propaganda was overtly ideological (it is hardly necessary to mention the quality of its contents and arguments). Political life after the victory over Hitler in the time of the Cold War, of the politics of the "rollback," has invented a new ideology of de-ideologization as a weapon against totalitarianism (which above all means socialism). We do not need to discuss the inner instability and self-contradiction of these Hitlerian and capitalist political weapons. We have already answered this question by calling this attempt at de-ideologization an ideology. In the sense of Marx, every ideology serves as the means for fighting out socioeconomic conflicts and as every class society necessarily

produces such conflicts it cannot function without these socioeconomic conflicts expressing themselves in permanent ideological struggle. Yet, the term de-ideologize has a concrete meaning even in the context of its fundamental self-negation: the market needs to be confirmed as the universal model. Every person can act in political life, vote in elections etc. In the same way he is forced to act with the help of advertising propaganda to "freely" buy the commodities allegedly most adequate for his needs of consumption. We put the term "free" in quotation marks when referring to the market. The societal relations of manipulated capitalism and the prestige that consumption necessarily develops in it makes the idea of "freedom" highly problematic. Subtle manipulation consists precisely in the fact that the acquisition of a certain commodity is suggested to the buyers in such a way that they are deluded into believing their purchase was a free choice or even an expression of their personality.

This principle of manipulation can easily be adapted to the participation of citizens in the ideal of public life. The dynamics of capitalism, a jagged contradiction to its beginnings, must transform the relation of men to their own social institutions. As a result of this transformation, bourgeois materialism has become the dominant ethos. In accordance with the above discussion, Marx represents the effects of this capitalist relationship on the *praxis* of individual men as follows: "The bourgeoisie acts towards the institutions of this system as the Jew towards the laws; he avoids them as often as it is possible in every individual case but he wants all others to abide by them." This selfish mode of acting, its necessary universalization in society leads to the ideal world of the *citoyen* increasingly becoming in *praxis* a mere instrument of bourgeois egoism. Obviously, not every egoistic act receives public sanction under capitalism. The class struggle in bourgeois society brings about a whole scale of differentiation ranging from the simple prohibition of certain bourgeois modes of behavior to tacit acceptance, to outspoken toleration or to the sanctioning of specific forms of individual violations of the laws. This scale of differentiation reflects a complex set of forces which strive for universalization. It is of secondary importance to the fundamental facts themselves whether we deal here with legislation as such or just with the administrative tendencies, i.e. the interpretation of the law. What matters is the clear perception of the universality of this penetration by the egoistic materialism of bourgeois society into this ideal sphere of freedom and equality.

It is not our purpose at this point to offer a detailed analysis of this concrete and extremely refined process of penetration. It is only important to point out that the ideal forms of freedom and equality are never called into question. Rather, these forms become mere vehicles for the class-oriented egoistic interests of the bourgeoisie (defense of the legality of the segregation of the "colored" people in the name of the constitutional autonomy of the

separate states in the United States etc.) In no way do freedom and equality disappear in the process, but rather their increasingly hollow forms are filled with increasingly bourgeois interests and contents. The less freedom is linked with the original ideals (and illusions) of its substance, the greater the glorification of the empty fetish of freedom. The more the interests of the great lobbies control everyday life, the greater the tribute paid to this fetish as introduction and as crowning moment of any propagandistic statement. De-ideologization as a practical substitute for ideology as well as the ideological glorification of the concept of freedom that has become vacuous, forms a real and therefore intellectual contradiction. Nevertheless, de-ideologization and the ideological glorification of freedom are complementary principles of *praxis* under capitalism although not merely in this abstract-intellectual formulation.

The fetish of freedom requires socially powerful organs of leadership and enforcement in order not to sink from an ideologically effective and socially credible position to empty phrase mongering. The CIA is the organ of enforcement that helps the most important groups of monopolists achieve their goals and vital interests. It is the CIA that ultimately conducts the "defense of freedom" on the part of the United States—from South America to Vietnam. It is this organization which also guarantees the domestic triumph of monopolist propaganda. Prime examples are the assassinations of the two Kennedys, or of Martin Luther King. The clarification of both these cases is still unresolved. In the first case, even the judicial inquiries have not led to any definitive conclusions. The factual chronology of the events of Kennedy's murder is still unclarified, yet everyone whose reasoning is not totally manipulated knows that things could not have possibly happened in the way the Warren Report depicts them. In addition, it is not possible to keep secret the fact that the death rate of potential witnesses in these cases far exceeds the average in America. Such secrets seem to stand in glaring contrast to the unlimited power of public opinion in the "free world." To some extent, the division between free public opinion and uninvestigated secrets is established by means of brute force, by acute mortal danger that threatens everyone who attempts to bring the naked facts to public attention. The ideological apparatus of the mass media persuades the broad population to accept secretiveness as legitimate, the same secretiveness that surrounds the life and work of the "great men" of underground organizations as they appear in the best-selling books and in the successful movies. Whoever pursues the historical development of capitalist society knows that the power of elected public bodies continuously declines in comparison to its military and civilian bureaucrats working under "official secrecy."

If one compares the relationship of democratic bodies at the time of the French Revolution to the events in the French Army at the time of the Third

Republic one receives an informative picture of this social transition, the outcome of which at the moment is the CIA. This is really not a radically new phenomena, it is nothing more than the radical actualization of a long, necessary process.

The fact that the past few years have produced signs of the beginnings of a systematic crisis in the United States need only be mentioned marginally here. At the moment, oppositonal movements are still highly undeveloped both in the material and ideological sense. No wonder. When inner contradictions begin to come to light in a society, an opposition starts with a theoretical critique. At these early stages, a countermovement is unable to make itself conscious, to outline an alternative perspective. It is unhistorical, therefore, to contemptuously reproach the dissidents in the United States for their lack of ideological sophistication. Even the Luddites did not produce more than the negativity of violent protest but they were still a forerunner of the revolutionary proletarian movement. Whoever contemptuously dismisses the antiestablishment movement in the United States should remember the Luddites and other frequently recurring examples in history. The contemporary era is an age of manipulation, and it has already been assessed as the climax and perfection of history. Yet it is powerless to provide appropriate answers for its failure to solve the questions of Vietnam or the status of blacks and the reasons for this lack of self-awareness must be revealed.

Even if only with a cursory glance, we must look at the systemic crisis of capitalism because the whole present discussion of democracy is directed toward one theoretical question: is bourgeois democracy a real alternative for the socialist world as many inside that world believe? This question is raised when the systemic crisis of socialism also comes to light. Our answer is a clear decisive: No. Never! A small section of the deeper reason for this answer can barely be illustrated in the following chapters in which the problems of the Stalinist era and its consequences will be discussed. The following simple and direct political statement may be made: if a state, which has been led into a social crisis by Stalinist epigones, converts to the alternative of bourgeois democracy one could predict the future with a high degree of probability without being a prophet. Before long the CIA would make this state into another Greece. Sincere intentions are not good enough, and one must not only rely upon honest convictions of the many ideologically committed people within the socialist world who seek a way out of the impasse of Stalinism. The purity of their intentions is not to be doubted. These Eastern European reformers, their supporters and sympathizers, in spite of the sincerity of their convictions, share a failure of imagination and can only suggest a corrupt bourgeois democracy as an alternative to the crisis of socialism. It is of no objective consequence here to speculate upon what they think in the depths of their heart. It is only necessary to return to historical facts. Who doubted fifty years ago that

Lloyd George in England and Clemenceau in France had been ardent, even left Democrats with good intentions? Nevertheless, in 1919 they organized interventionist armies against the Hungarian Soviet Republic. They also dismissed the social democratic government which they themselves had proposed (the leaders of which were also ardent bourgeois democrats) and thereby laid the foundation of the Horthy regime. It is not enough to have good intentions, but one must be a realist. There was no army of intervention in the Greek Civil War of 1947–1948, but in the background there stood the CIA and those officials in the Greek government who were directly or indirectly manipulated by it. History does not repeat itself exactly and cannot be predicted, but there is a general line of social necessity. And in this sense we can definitely say: to look upon bourgeois democracy as a possible alternative during times of crisis in a socialist state implies a Greek outcome.

Part II
The Pure Alternative:
Stalinism or Socialist Democracy

4

Theoretic and Historic Presuppositions of a Concrete Problem

If we have rejected a bourgeois democracy as an alternative to a socialist one we have done so primarily on the basis of practical political considerations. An analysis of contemporary experience clearly indicates that every attempt to substitute a bourgeois variant for socialist democracy inevitably leads to the liquidation of socialism (and most probably to democracy itself). If we now attempt to discover the true political alternatives, we must approach this problem with the methodological procedure of polar opposition. From this perspective, it is impossible to present socialism (or the contemporary prevailing views of its essence) in the dogmatic declarative sense as the polar opposite of democracy. On the contrary, we must first of all strive to understand the present and existing mode of socialism, to understand its present concrete being from a sociohistorical perspective. After we have reached this understanding we will try to formulate more accurately the problem of democratization.

The actual social being of existing socialism is that complex of institutions, tendencies, theories, tactics which emerged from the crisis of the Stalin period. This crisis was given its first theoretic-practical expression at the twentieth Congress (1956) and the consequences stemming from that congress. It is not possible to understand the theoretic-practical work of reformation begun at the twentieth Party Congress, its value and direction, unless we proceed from the actual intent and structure that underlay this reconstruction.

It is also indispensable to discuss briefly the characteristics of the Stalin era itself. The twentieth Congress portrayed this period of socialist evolution as a "personality cult." Some perceptive critics immediately raised objections to this descriptive phrase and the societal content which it suggested was the substance of the crisis of socialism. It was above all Palmiro Togliatti who refused to look upon the personal characteristics of Stalin as the final cause of such a profound crisis in the development of socialism. He demanded a penetrating and exhaustive economic and sociohistorical analysis of the entire Stalinist period. He argued that without this kind of thorough investigation it was

impossible to clearly formulate in a Marxist-Leninist sense the positive and negative contributions of Stalin to this stage of socialism. We must unfortunately admit that an analysis which would have satisfied these demands has not yet been carried through.

The short, hurried and highly schematic sketch the reader has before him cannot fulfill these more exacting requirements, cannot satisfy the legitimate needs for a definitive scientific analysis of the Stalin period. But Togliatti's call was not intended as a summons for a detailed academic appraisal. His expectation was much more for an explication of the governing principles of this pivotal and fateful era of socialist history so that a correct program of reconstruction could return the sick to a healthy life, could mend the crippled.

If we want to fulfill Togliatti's legitimate demand, one must begin at the beginning. In terms of Marx's understanding, the proletarian revolution in Russia was not a "classical embodiment" of such a world historical transition. According to the prognosis of Marx, such a revolution must first break out in a developed capitalist country. In addition, Marx assumes that a proletarian revolution by its very nature would act as a model for the rest of the civilized world. The question which above all concerns us, even if we overlook this second feature of the classical paradigm of revolution, is the development of socialism in an economically and therefore socially underdeveloped country. Lenin never doubted that the Russian Revolution was exceptional, that it did not completely conform to the prognosis of Marxism. When Lenin came to speak on the international significance of the Russian Revolution in his work *The Infantile Disorders of Communism,* he correctly emphasized its significance. But he did not forget to immediately add: "Naturally, it would be a very great error to exaggerate this truth and apply it to more than a few basic features of our revolution. Likewise, it would be wrong to leave out of account the possibility that after the initial victory of the proletarian revolution in Russia another Proletarian Revolution could also break out in a developed country in all probability after a sudden socioeconomic collapse. In this situation Russia would no longer be a prototype, but exist again as an underdeveloped country, (in the sense of socialism and the Soviet system)."[16]

It is not difficult to see what Lenin meant by this statement. The transformation of a capitalist society into a socialist one is above all an economic issue. In a country in which a victorious revolution takes place, the higher the development of capitalism the more immediately and adequately can the specific foundations of socialism be cemented. On the contrary, in an underdeveloped country a number of questions must necessarily be placed on the agenda which from a purely economic perspective would have already been solved during the course of the evolution of capitalism. At issue here—and in economic reality both questions form an interdependent totality—is the relationship between heavy industry and agriculture. On the one side there is a

problem of the quantitative as well as qualitative degree of development of great industry in the decisive branches of mass production. On the other side lies the problem of the proper distribution of the working population in either industry or agriculture. It is a problem of the proper allocation of resource in order to achieve a balanced economic growth, the interrelation and further advancement of agriculture and industry which is capable of sustaining development in the various fields of economic life. No one doubted in 1917 that capitalist production in the Russian Empire had solved the problem of the relationship between industry and agriculture. Capitalism in the Russian Empire was still underdeveloped and left many economic problems unsolved.

If we accept these conclusions does this not prove that the violent overthrow of the capitalist regime in the great October Days was a mistake, as social democratic theory has wanted to show from the very beginning? We believe: No. Great historical decisions, revolutionary turning points, are never unleased in a purely theoretical manner as if in a scholars study. They are answers to alternatives which an agitated people, concered about everyday life as well as the great political issues, urge upon the parties and their leaders. In 1917, the conditions in which decisions were taken were above all, determined by the First World War. The war called into being a crisis of socialism and the various Marxist parties attempted to overcome this crisis in their own ways. Every resolution of the Second International expressed an opposition to the war, but with few exceptions the actions of the majority of the European socialist parties tacitly supported the imperialist war. The February Revolution, the overthrow of Czarism, did not change this basic situation. On the contrary, the continuation of the war became a primary goal of most Russian parties, especially the Mensheviks and the Social Revolutionaries. The struggle of the Bolsheviks for state power was consonant with the burning desire of millions of people for an immediate ending to the war. This urgent question which consumed the population became a decisive issue in the concrete alternatives of October; due to the conditions of the time, it was first necessary to ovethrow the bourgeois-democratic regime in order to bring an immediate end to the war. (The entire history of the Weimar Republic until Hitler's seizure of power illustrates the social consequences produced by postponing a decision for revolution until after a irreversible military collapse.)

Likewise, the internal political alternatives in Russia in October were also clearly demarcated. In 1917, the fundamental problems of Russian social development throughout the nineteenth century reached their explosive apex. This crisis concerned the liquidation of the prevailing feudal remnants, the emergence of a peasantry exploited in the late nineteenth century by capitalism rather than feudalism. In the course of 1917, in spite of the fierce resistance of the "democratic regime" of Alexander Kerensky, a continuous increase in peasant revolts and the spontaneous redistribution of land pro-

ceeded in an uninterrupted fashion. Here, too, the question was simply put: without the fall of the bourgeois-democratic system a real solution of the peasant problem was impossible. Hence, in October two questions coalesced, one concerning the imperialist war and the other concerning the question of the peasantry. Both these questions were associated with the preservation of Russian society and both provided opportunities for social insurrection. Neither of these questions possessed an immediate socialist character, but under the circumstances of the time it was only by revolutionary overthrow of bourgeois domination that a solution could be found satisfactory to the overwhelming majority of the working masses. For this reason, October 1917 amounts to a revolutionary situation in the broadest sense of the term: the ruling classes could no longer govern in the old manner and the oppressed and exploited masses refused to continue to live in the old way (Lenin's definition of a revolutionary situation). For these reasons, the decision of 1917 may not be placed into question unless one takes this social context into account.

There is no doubt that the decision for a nonclassical solution to the transition to socialism was politically justifiable. However, even the most substantial validification of this political revolution did not overcome the real economic problems. A few years later this disparity between the political and economic proved itself to be the central problem for the continued economic advances of Russia. First of all, the young Soviet Republic had to fight for its existence against German imperialism and later against various armies of intervention. In so doing, the Soviet proletariat demonstrated a force, a mass determination and an ability for superior politico-military leadership. This heroic period of the Soviet proletariat heightened and deepened the attractiveness that this young socialist state held for the peoples of the farthest reaches of the world. It was not until the successful completion of the Civil War that the economic problems inherent in the nonclassical form of transition to socialism became the focus of Soviet life.

When Lenin approached this complex of issues theoretically he did not forget to emphasize that they dealt with problems that were radically new. "Marx did not even consider writing a single word about this," he says in 1922.[17] The problems appeared to be purely economic and Lenin repeatedly refers to the practical consequences which result from this. Yet he focuses on the fact that the alliance between the proletariat and the masses of peasants was shattered by the economic situation left behind by the Civil War. He says: "the fundamental, decisive task to which all others are subordinate is the establishment of an alliance between the new economy which we have started to build (very badly, very unskillfully, but for all that we have still started a new system of production, a new system of distribution on the basis of a radically new socialist economy) and the peasant economy which is the economy of millions and millions of peasants."[18]

Even this goal shows that Lenin grasps in a practico-intuitive manner the character of socialism as a specific social formation, even though he never addresses this problem in a universal-theoretical fashion. In earlier social formations the change of an economic structure occurred on the basis of an inherent determinism. But this does not rule out that the first great instance of socialist transition enters into existence as the teleological directed *praxis* of conscious (indeed often with false consciousness) individual men. The socialization of the means of production, their concentration in the hands of the working class, is a necessary consequence of a social consciousness which looks upon society as a totality of economically interrelated parts. For that reason, the working class was called upon to change from the dominated to the planners of the social development of man. The transformation of specific social structures should be a result of the consciousness and social being of the proletariat. Consciousness must become the directive telos of society, from planning its economic functions to looking upon socialism as a preparatory stage to communism. Lenin correctly perceives that 1917, and with it the destroyed interrelationship between town and country, introduces a new period in the social activity of man that begins with the seizure of power by the proletariat, with the destruction of capitalist or traditional semi-feudal private possession of the means of production. This new age requires a new definition of human progress. It is no longer possible to allow history to be governed by blind determinist forces, but it is now necessary for objective-economic forces to be guided by human consciousness. Marx's third theses on Feuerbach asserts that "the Educator must himself be educated," an actuality that can no longer be avoided.

Socialism in part means the control of human evolution by human consciousness, or societal self-determination. One property of consciousness is that it is educable. The agent for this self-education of man—in world historical terms self-education for genuine human being in the Marxist sense—is socialist democracy. The socioeconomic development of the human species had thereby posed a question which only Lenin out of all the successors of Marx depicted as the central problem of socialist transition and made the basis of his teleological action. The fact that the educators, the leading societal strata of the socialist revolution, must themselves be educated is a critique, on the one hand, of every utopianism which suggests that rational persuasion is the motor that propels human development to a future state of absolutely harmonious existence. On the other hand, it is also a repudiation of mechanical materialism that simply presents every outcome as the spontaneous and necessary product of the development of production. For Marx the economic world, ("the realm of necessity") is never the sole basis for the self-creation of the human species. Marx refers to the conscious self-creation of man as "the realm of freedom." He further defines the essential contents of "the realm of freedom" as

"the development of human powers, which is valued for itself as an end in itself." At the same time, he clearly states that such *praxis* must be qualitatively different than the merely economic, and that this human teleological consciousness is a vital, new generative contradiction of the economic. Human evolution, for Marx, is a dialectical interconnection between determinism and teleology, and this dialectic life *praxis*"can only bloom when the 'kingdom of necessity' is its basis.''[19]

The nonclassical character of the Revolution of 1917 rests above all on the fact that socialism starts its evolution from a developmental stage in which the existing levels of production and distribution were still insufficient to serve as the basis for a concrete preparation of the "Kingdom of Freedom." Thus, an intermediary period had to be introduced in which this economic underdevelopment was overtaken, an intermediate period in which the accelerated advancement of the economic to higher levels must become the central preoccupation in the guidance of social life by consciousness. Lenin, evidently understood that a high level of industrial development was an economic precondition for the growth of socialism. As we have shown, he recognized the importance of the industrial base when he suggested that if a socialist revolution were victorious in an economically developed country this nation would appear as the vanguard in the construction of socialism, taking over that role from the Soviet Union.

Up to this point in history, no one, not even Lenin, was capable of formulating the crucial problems of such a nonclassical construction of socialism, of such a preparation for communism, in theoretical terms. From our present perspective, a theoretic generalization of these problems may be stated in the following manner: in this type of transitional period what is the relation between a pure economic *praxis,* which is called upon to surmount industrial underdevelopment, and the desired socialist content that intends to create democratic proletarian actions, institutions etc.? It was clear to Lenin—and he never lost sight of the fact—that previous socialist thought, to be found in Marx and Engels, did not and could not supply a theoretic solution to the problem of correlating the development of the economy with the development of democratic institutions. The problem of the relationship between the economic and the political is of great societal-ontological importance for it demonstrates that the Kingdom of Freedom is qualitatively different than the economic Kingdom of Necessity. It also shows that the Kingdom of Freedom can only be reached on the basis of the Kingdom of Necessity. This definition expresses both the societal dependence of the "superstructure" on the "base" as well as the qualitative difference between these two social categories. The term "Kingdom of Freedom" already implies much more than the mere superstructure and its functions in a class society. The ontological leap announces itself in the fact that in socialism the foundation of economic *praxis*

must be directed by conscious teleology toward producing a society of universal human interdependence.

Socialism (and communism in a greater degree) are economic formations in which the entirety of society is placed under the guidance of conscious teleology, and as a result they increasingly abandon the qualities of capitalism. Even though socialism is directed by the consciousness of man to final humanistic purposes, it is still a social totality that functions in terms of causal laws. There is no doubt that the domain of social causality complicates the problems of the transition to socialism. It is not always necessary to abolish capitalist structures, for some actually prepare the way for socialism. Engels had already detected this in relation to joint-stock companies and Lenin knew that the capitalist monopolies were transitional structures to socialist property. These problems of socialist transformation, in spite of all their legitimacy, may not blur the ontological leap inherent in any movement from a capitalist to a socialist social formation. In the growth of socialist humanity, the essentially new is that the evolution of the economy will be henceforth governed by a universal teleology. This teleology, not to be defined as causal-objective law, must be understood as a human subjective-conscious design for the species self-determination of social development. In this context, the fact that Marx himself portrays such causal-objective laws as the Kingdom of Necessity is socio-ontologically correct. For the economic is always the process of the material reproduction of society in which the individual human being ultimately remains the object of the reproductive process, in which human intelligence is always directed to the maximal utilization of the objective possibilities. In the Kingdom of Necessity there is no place for those activities that serve the human species as an end in themselves. The continued existence of the Kingdom of Necessity is socialism does not weaken in the slightest the fact that the socialization of the means of production possesses the quality of an ontological leap. First of all, it is no longer possible for individuals or groups to exploit the economy in the service of their own private interests. Second, and as a direct consequence of this, the possibility arises of placing the objective choices of economic development at the disposal of the conscious designs and humanistic goals of the species. In the case of the private ownership of the means of production, the subordination of these means of production to the higher goals of the species is at best a remote possibility.

Lenin had a deep insight into the relationship between subjective and objective forces, and he was an advocate of human self-determination. He wished to place a knowledge of the power and creativity of the subjective and objective in the service of the coming Kingdom of Freedom. He realized that the problem of Russian underdevelopment, which assumed catastrophic proportions as a consequence of World War I and the Civil War, could not be overcome on purely economic grounds. He subordinated the economic prob-

lem to the communitarian experimentation which a socialist society could support. We proceed from this exact principle when we mention that he perceived the shattering of the alliance between proletariat and peasant as the central danger of the crisis of the transition. From Lenin's viewpoint, the ontological leap into socialism consisted of a social and socially conscious union of the industrial and agricultural working population for the purpose of raising their material and spiritual existence through their own labor and experience to the level of meaningful cooperative species life.

Whether and to what degree Lenin's plans were practically realizable is today of secondary importance. One should not forget that his fatal illness soon made him increasingly unfit to carry out regular governmental activities during the period when the New Economic Policy was concretized. The greater part of his theoretical work during these years consisted of sketches for innovative socialist experiments. Lenin himself had no illusions regarding the visionary properties of his statements. In any case, he was increasingly incapable of pursuing their real practico-concrete execution, or of controlling them by means of self-criticism which *praxis* forces upon one. He considered these visions as only theoretical designs of the innermost tendencies of a new, emerging societal reality, and looked upon these conceptions as a heuristic plan for the future socialist existence of the productive classes. The provisional character of all his economic designs reveals itself in the fact that the centralized planning system which developed later in the Soviet Union still played a highly subordinate role in his thinking of the NEP era. His later, much quoted statement that the Soviets plus electrification would result in socialism should not be taken as indicative of his definition of this future society. The way he wanted his concrete plans to be realized manifests a particular methodology, however, and this methodology still retains its theoretical significance. Lenin approved conscious intervention into reality. Through this experimentation, through the reflexive character of human reason, men would become aware of their ability to control the theoretic-determinist properties of social conditions. Lenin often quoted the following phrase of Napoleon I: "One engages it and can direct it." We believe that Lenin's methodology still forms a healthy counterbalance to many fantasies regarding economic planning, which in consequence of their abstract-apodictic nature are very often based on ill-founded inference. Because they can be easily manipulated, these illusions regarding centralized planning are divorced from the real meaning of a socialist society.

To a certain extent, Lenin saw the danger of confusing centralized planning with socialism. The growing bureaucratization of Soviet life, in the state as in the party, was his main concern during the entire period of his illness. Anyone who carefully studies his writings during the pre-1917 period, will easily learn that for him the self-activity of the proletariat, ranging from ev-

eryday life to the great political decisions, represented a major barometer for the preparedness of the working population to carry out a socialist revolution. Nevertheless, Lenin not only tolerated but even sometimes assisted in the development of an even stronger bureaucracy. This was the case during the Civil War, when it was necessary to overcome many immediate problems. This was true above all for the military, but due to its practical success this kind of bureaucratic organization also flowed into the civilian sector. One of his major goals after the victorious end of the Civil War was the deconstruction of this bureaucracy and the return to the normal life of a society. This tendency was most clearly expressed in the debate over the trade unions. Trotsky put forth a plan for the nationalization of the trade unions so that their organizational potentials could be utilized in the interests of improved production. For Trotsky, this appeared to be eminently feasible since he did not believe that the proletariat required any protection against a worker state. Lenin, on the other hand, emphasized that the state was in fact "a worker state with bureaucratic aberrations." For that reason, he summarized his viewpoint as follows: "Our present state is constituted in such a manner that the proletariat in its totality must protect itself and we must use these workers' organizations to protect the workers against their state and to protect the state through the workers."[20] Anyone familiar with Lenin's work and letters in the last years of his life knows that he fought a tenacious and stubborn struggle against bureaucratization in all areas of state and social life and that he even wanted to exclude otherwise respected colleagues (e.g. Ordzhonikidze) from the party because they damaged the principles of proletarian democratism by falling back upon certain procedural methods of the Civil War.

On the question of mass participation, Lenin had much earlier taken a theoretically correct position. In *State and Revolution,* his major statement on the question of the political, he took up the issue of the "withering away of the state." The state will only become extinct when "the people, once they are liberated from capitalist slavery, from the innumerable atrocities, brutalities, inconsistencies and conspiracies of capitalist exploitation, will habituate themselves to the most rudimentary rules of social cooperation, rules that have been known since ancient times and utilized in every instance of social collaboration, without force, without compulsion, without submission and especially without the apparatus of domination called the State."[21] As always, Lenin concentrated upon the concrete task standing before him. This means that he did not enter upon the more complex problems of Marx's Kingdom of Freedom, but focused exclusively upon the "withering away of the state." But his position, if one grasps it in purely methodological terms, refers to the entire scope of the problem of the state. It is above all important that even here he takes into account the totality of everyday human existence. He is far from attempting to force something of a "citoyen character" upon the idea of de-

mocracy in socialism. In an earlier part of the *State and Revolution,* while relating to other aspects of the political problem, he took a negative position towards bourgeois democracy. Democracy in socialism is not a mere extension of democracy. Quite the contrary, socialist democracy is the direct opposite of bourgeois democracy. Above all, democracy should not be an idealistic superstructure of the inherent materialism of bourgeois society, but an active element for progress in the social world itself. Democracy should no longer be based on numerous material barriers, as, for example, democracy in the *polis,* but rather on social ontological being which is in the process of self-completion. It is therefore the purpose of socialist democracy to penetrate the totality of human existence and to present its social nature as the product of the activity and participation of all men, stretching from everyday life to the most important question of society. In acute revolutionary times, this activity and participation circulates from bottom to top and from top to bottom with an explosive spontaneity. We should recall that the great decisive questions in the life of the Russian Soviets concerning both domestic and foreign affairs did agitate the public opinion of the entire world. This changes in periods of "consolidation," in which necessarily, for example, secret diplomacy or the secrets of military preparations must be withheld from domestic public opinion.

We will again take up this question later on in a different context. The center of our interest here is how socialist democracy can penetrate into everyday human life and make it active and participatory. Lenin speaks of habituation as the most important cause for the "withering away of the state," for it enables the people to organize their cooperation with their fellow men without power, without force, without submission. Habituation is certainly a universal sociological category which must play a significant role in every functioning society. Habituation relates to behavior, but it is entirely indifferent to the object to which man himself becomes accustomed. But Lenin's meaning surpassed such abstract-sociological universality. By habituation he meant a social-teleological process in which all action, state and social institutions are employed to accustom the people to adapt cooperative modes of behavior. Certainly, elements of such a teleology exist in every society. The whole legal structure of class societies is necessary in order to habituate the population to voluntarily act in a prescribed manner. In accordance with Marx, however, we have described how the legal rights of a class society limit wherever possible the behavior of the other person and not the self, for these rights remain subject to the "economic egoism" of each individual. Habituation to this mode of behavior necessarily strengthens the egoism of the ordinary person and the view that his fellow men are merely barriers to his own existence and *praxis.* We also know that according to Marx, bourgeois law remains operative in the period of socialism, although not without certain modifications. In

order to encourage men, all men, to habituate themselves to a new and reformed society, it is necessary that a sudden transformation of actual circumstances take place. It cannot be a mere ideological transformation, but above all it must revolutionize everyday material existence and activity from the ground up. The *Communist Manifesto* distinguishes between bourgeois and communist society on the basis that in bourgeois society the past ruled over the present while in communist society the present ruled over the past. In bourgeois society the sufficient cause of human *praxis* is always reduced to an objective determinist self-movement of the material conditions of life. In communist society it is possible to set forth a conscious teleological design for a future life and to use this design for the qualitative transformation of actual existence.

From the first, one of the essential intentions of the inner dialectic of Lenin's doctrine of habituation was to assist in the capacity of species being to dominate the past. For this reason, he was interested in and supported every social impulse toward the evolution of the self-determination of the species. His vehement struggle against bourgeois tendencies was based on his highly critical observations of the ultimate ineffectiveness of bureaucratic manipulation. It was also based on the insight that every form of bureaucracy, through its own internal routinization, necessarily conceals within itself a drive to harden the domination of the past over the present. Reacting to this problem, Lenin looked upon the emergence of the so-called "Communist Saturday" as an expression of the desire to surpass the domination of the past by means of the spontaneous self-activity of social men. This species self-activity was capable of acting as the ground of socialist democracy, the preparation of the Kingdom of Freedom even though the journey was long and filled with contradictions and temporary setbacks. A socialist economy is the indispensable foundation for such species self-determination, its necessary point of origin and its corresponding content. The creation of the self-activity of the species is not, however, a determinist product growing out of the economic conditions of the past but a teleological consequence of the initial conquest of the domination of the present over the past. Lenin described the social essence of the Communist Saturday in the following terms: "Up to this point, there is nothing specifically communist in our economic system. The 'communist quality' only sets in when the Communist Saturdays appear i.e., when there is unpaid labor voluntarily given to the need and benefit of every aspect of society without the intervention of any public office or any state authority."[22] It is clear that Communist Saturdays and other similar social expressions must lose their communist quality as soon as they are co-opted by bureaucratic planning. When this occurs these social expressions become mechanical, mere cogs in the assembly line of bureaucratic hegemony.

It is no accident that Lenin's definition of communism called forth both

universal enthusiasm for and universal repudiation of the proletariat revolution. The desperate economic conditions in the young socialist country were, however, obvious. Lenin reacted with great passion and revealed the humanist foundation of his political being. Despite his uncompromising realism toward the deficiencies of the Soviet economy, its underdevelopment etc., he never surrendered his commitment to and belief in the coming of a socialist future and he viewed social democracy as the indispensable core for any constitution of a socialist society. It is in any case remarkable that Lenin's commitment to democratization, even if his democratic convictions were not always correctly understood, was highly influential outside of Russia due to its message of the social anthropogenesis of the human species. Permit me to call the readers attention to my essay "The Moral Mission of the Communist Party" which dealt with Lenin's exact views on the Communist Saturday, although my interpretation of Marxism at the time was tainted with an idealist bias.

As a Marxist, Lenin always emphasized his differences with the vulgarizing theories of social democracy. The social democrats believed that with the "withering away of the state" democracy would also wither away, that communism was a social formation in which the question of democracy was no longer relevant. Unfortunately, Lenin's deepest democratic-socialist convictions regarding the period of transition are forgotten today. (Of course, the need of bourgeois ideology to prove that the Stalinist distortion of democracy started with Lenin plays an important role in the evolution of this forgetting. The conservative bureaucratic principle of Stalinism and the bourgeois ideological Cold War against communism share a common goal: to trace as much as possible Stalin's theory and *praxis* back to Lenin.) Only a genuine Marxist critique of the principles of Stalinism can illustrate the real theoretic-practical discontinuity between Stalin and Lenin. In terms of the great strategic questions surrounding the Bolshevik Revolution and the period of transition, such a genuine Marxist critique would also show that Stalin distorted the tradition of Lenin. After his return to Russia in 1917, Lenin criticized both Kamenev and Stalin because of their misinterpretation of the revolution. Later on, in the question of labor unions, Stalin represented the line of thinking of Trotsky and not that of Lenin.

Since we have arrived at a discussion of the problem of continuity, it would be instructive to determine the socialist traditions which influenced Lenin and those he continued. It is surely clear to the readers of our quotes on "habituation" that Lenin did not consider as radically new the rules of human collaboration and cooperation which characterize socialist democracy, as the beginning stages of a new theoretic development. Rather he looks upon them as elementary principles which have been in existence for centuries but which can only achieve their social universality in socialism. This is shown by Lenin's methodology which connects him so deeply with Marx and separates

him as thoroughly from Stalin and his additional followers: the organic connection between the continuity of specific historical tendencies and their necessary radical structural change in the great revolutionary transitions and upheavals. The refutation of every form of utopianism, which Lenin shares, rests upon the methodological principle of the relationship between evolution and revolution in history. According to the utopians something radically new can be born in the world by means of reason, whereas in Marxism, the radically new is the result of a revolutionary change at specific social junctures in sociohistorical development. In the deepest human sense, nothing new exists in history. From the evolutionary point of view, historic leaps occur at specific moments, but these structural changes merely raise the previously existent human social being to an unprecedented level by means of social universalization. Lenin describes the organic connection between evolution and revolution in his comments on habituation and in his general methodology of Marxism. Lenin offers the following interpretation of this methodology: "Marxism gained its world historical significance as the ideology of the revolutionary proletariat owing to the fact that it did reject the achievements of the bourgeois era, but on the contrary, adopted it and comes to terms with all the values of more than two thousand years in the development of human thought and culture."[23]

It is not improper to emphasize at least in outline, this aspect of Lenin's Marxism. Lenin's ideas on continuity and discontinuity help us evaluate certain contemporary trends. On the one side, the opinion that history only presents us with the alternative between the old and new, between the stagnation and the revolutionary emergence of the radically new. (Lenin's observations are directed against theories of this kind; i.e. the "Proletcult" of the 1920s. This revolutionary interpretation was represented by the Andrei Zhdanov theory of Marxism. From the methodological perspective, this idea of radical discontinuity was not far from the futuristic conception of art.) On the other side, Stalin and his successors practiced a widespread fetishizing of continuity. These successors nowadays flatter themselves with the belief that they have broken with the "personality cult" of the past. They believe (or at least maintain) that the existent, concrete accomplishments of the Stalin period (we will discuss this later) exclude a radical break with its methods. This standpoint of total evolution and continuity is just as deeply unhistoric and non-Marxist as the standpoint of total revolution and discontinuity.

In order to conclude our unfortunately very cursory remarks, it is important to point out that Lenin did not bequeath an infallible formula for the systematic solution to the problems of the transition to socialism, nor did he inherit such a formula from Marx or Engels. It is useless to speculate on how Lenin, if he had remained active for a longer period of time, would have mastered the problems of this transition. It is also useless to debate whether there

existed any objective possibilities for the solution of the massive problems that arose out of the nonclassical nature of the Russian Revolution. Nevertheless, we believe that our attempt to illustrate the most important principles and methodological foundations that motivated Lenin's political *praxis* at the time is justified. We cannot be concerned at this point with giving a detailed history of the entire period. (Naturally, this would be highly desirable.) What is of burning importance today is a clear perception of how Lenin's successors radically broke with his methodological principles and how this inevitably led to multiple distortions of Marxism itself. Lenin continued the thought of Marx, but the inheritance of both Lenin and Marx was lost in the Soviet Union even though the overwhelming majority of the most important politicians during the 1920s and 1930s in Russia were deeply convinced that they were using the real method of Marx to analyze the historical situation. The politicians of the period created the illusion that they perpetuated the deepest intentions of Lenin, but this belief was also erroneous.

5
Stalin's Victory Over His Rivals

In the period immediately following Lenin's death the struggle among various leaders to become his successor was intensely politico-ideological. In the entire history of socialism this is the era that is the least investigated by the standards of exhaustive historical research. Much of the evidence has been destroyed. During the time of the Great Purges and in the following years the majority of the theoretic-political documents, above all those opposing Stalin, were withdrawn from public circulation. Since these documents were no longer accessible to the public, their authors were effectively rendered invisible, became non-people. Because of this lack of evidence, objective-historical descriptions and well-documented theoretic discussions concerning the transition from Lenin to Stalin became almost impossible. What has been published by the opponents of Stalin suffers from the same flaws as the official Stalinist version. Often supported by documents, the anti-Stalinist thesis for the most part proceeds from prejudicial political grounds. Even the noteworthy work of I. Deutscher is not free from a tendentious and biased distortion of the facts. The remarks we make below do not claim to fill this gap of exhaustive, objective research. However, the author of these lines followed those debates with great interest at the time, and so he may take the liberty of commenting in the most general terms on the fundamental methodological problems of this sea-change in the Soviet thought, while conceding their impressionistic character.

    The so-called Last Will of Lenin that comprises his assessment of his major Bolshevik colleagues is among the most pessimistic historic documents ever known. In his Last Will, Lenin evaluated six of the leading communists upon whose collective leadership, he—with great skepticism—thought the future development of the transition to socialism depended. Owing to the fact that Lenin did not think Kamenev's and Zinoviev's false assessment of the October Revolution to be a mere accidental mistake, but an inherent flaw in their analytical abilities, his doubts concerning their capacity for historical interpretation were reaffirmed. With the three other elected numbers, definitely

in the cases of Trotsky and Pyatakov, and somewhat indirectly in the case of Stalin, he saw them as representing a serious danger to the future evolution of Russia. All three tended to treat matters of principle in administrative terms (even willing to solve them by the use of force, an approach most strongly represented by Stalin). With Bukharin, the only one who demonstrated the abilities of a theoretician, Lenin expressed his reservations over the accuracy of Bukharin's interpretation of Marx. Since Lenin looked upon these six political personalities as forming the collective center of Bolshevik leadership, who could and should ensure the continuation of his life's work for the construction of socialism, the Last Will must be judged as an expression of an extremely far-reaching despair.

This pessimism soon proved itself as justified. In the years immediately following Lenin's death, the Bolshevik Party and the Soviet state were flooded with a multiplicity of views concerning the course of the future development of Russia. But all these views displayed a deep-rooted similarity between their fundamental theoretical and methodological principles. No one remained dedicated to Lenin's burning desire to construct a socialist democracy through the extension and strengthening of the foundations already in place. The centrality of socialist democracy in Lenin was superceded by the pure economic question, although each of the successors of Lenin had different views on the industrialization process in Russia. These differences between the epigone of Lenin also had important consequences in questions of foreign affairs. This shift of emphasis in terms of goals and the shift from the process of democratization to rapid economic industrialization had important consequences for the tactics used by those who desired to be Lenin's successor. Especially in the bourgeois world and among the social democrats, if he was recognized at all, Lenin was seen as a shrewd tactician. Although inspired by a sense of fairness, this was a continuous misinterpretation of the man. Tactical decisions were never primary for Lenin. He was indeed an extraordinarily insightful analyst of prevailing circumstances and of the resulting alternative possibilities. For good reasons he continually demanded a concrete analysis of a concrete situation and for equally good reasons spoke often and forcibly about the significance of Marx's law of uneven development. In his eyes, tactical decisions were only transient moments in the universal historic development of the human species. Lenin drew a distinction between the general march of human development and the tactical needs of the moment. Only by understanding the universal movement of human history was it possible to arrive at the appropriate tactical decision in relation to human *praxis*. Tactics could only be effective if they corresponded to the general historic strategy. Lenin referred to the general historical tendencies as strategy, and to the concrete moment as tactics. Only within a historical, scientific-theoretical, and strategic framework could one advance to the formulation of a realistic tactic, i.e. to a concrete analysis of a concrete situation leading to a concrete *praxis*.

Above all it was Lenin's successors who abandoned the priority of historic-strategic considerations. They all considered themselves as facing situations that required immediate decisions and in which theoretic-historical perspectives had no place. In so far as tactical decisions were connected with a long-term perspective, these also remained without a genuine Marxist theoretic-historical grounding in most cases. The movement of events ran in the direction of the absolute priority of existent concrete circumstances. A theory of total revolutionary development was later added to these tactics of immediacy because a supplementary and secondary theory could be easily amended. Because theory was not taken seriously as a guideline, new tactical decisions could be improvised or even turned into their opposite. Stalin and his generation had lost contact with the true message of Marx and Lenin. Such a shift of theoretic procedures after the death of Lenin amounted to an ideological-structural revision that took place earlier within European social democracy. Just as the debate over Bernstein marked off one era of socialist history, so the rigidification of Marxism after the death of Lenin was the historical divide for another era in the history of socialism. But in drawing comparisons between European socialism and Russian communism two crucial points must be alluded to: the moment when revolutionary Bolshevism separated itself from the pacification of European socialism and the moment when the priority of tactics calcified both post-Leninist Bolshevism and European socialism. The pactification of European social democracy was associated with Bernstein. In later party programs, this social democratic distortion of Marx led to an open break with the revolutionary theories of Marx, to a spiritual-practical adaptation of the techniques of social accommodation as employed by bourgeois parties. In contradistinction to social democracy, Leninism was oriented to a conception of revolutionary *praxis* and strategy in the sense of Marx even before the Congress of 1903. On the other hand, the retreat from Leninism by his successors did for that reason represent a non-Marxist and non-Leninist revision that resembled tendencies within European social democracy, the priority of tactics was raised to the level of real Marxist theory. In contrast to Marx and Lenin, theory was no longer the spiritual foundation of tactical decisions, but rather its belated, rationally contrived, frequently sophisticated "justification." But it was necessary for Stalin and those of his era to establish their legitimacy by demonstrating that they represented the heritage of Marx and Lenin. Even though in truth they were the deformation of Marxism and Leninism, these opinions were intended to show Stalin and his contenders for succession as the lineal continuation, application, and extension of Marxist theory.

This peculiar "further development" of Marx's method was not simply invention or contrivance. It sprang immediately out of the real situation in which the revolutionary workers movement found itself at that time and was always mired in the immediate. It was characteristic of the first phase of the

founding and organizational consolidation of the workers movement that Marx was considered its undisputed international head in whose personality theoretic and practico-tactical leadership were organically united. After Marx's death these functions were delegated to Engels, but no qualitative change of theory occurred. Problems began to surface in social democratic parties only after Engels death such as how can Marxist theory and daily organizational *praxis* be brought into unity? For a long time it appeared as if the combination of Kautsky-Bebel could solve this problem. However, at the time of the first great crisis (the Bernstein debate) the party leadership proved to be wedded to the supremacy of the tactical: theory seemed only as a supplementary justification of what had independently turned into *praxis*. (Theorists like Mehring and Luxemburg basically remained without influence.) Viktor Adler, a pure tactician, still controlled the leadership of Austrian social democracy in spite of the great number of theoretically more capable comrades in the party. Initially, Plekhanov's position in Russian social democracy appeared to be completely different, but the "european line" asserted itself even here, although with many variations. Gradually, Lenin won a position in the Bolshevik movement which was reminiscent of that obtained by Marx and Engels, and Lenin's fame rose to an international peak as a consequence of the Revolution of 1917.

The struggle over the leadership of Russian communism centered on finding a successor to Lenin who could combine the function of providing the communist movement with an encompassing theoretic as well as practical-tactical stewardship in the sense of Marx, Engels and Lenin. Trotsky, the powerful tribune of the period of revolutionary ascendancy, was totally unsuited for this role due to his complete ineptitude regarding correct tactical action which even his admirer and biographer I. Deutscher admits. Except for some concrete factors which we will come to speak about later on, Stalin's victory over Trotsky was that of a clever, calculating and superior tactician. It was also part of Stalin's tactics to paint his victory as representing the correct doctrine of Lenin over the distortors of Lenin. But it belonged to the essence of Stalin's personality that after his victory over his rivals as he did not merely intend to function as Lenin's loyal disciple. Gradually—often with ingenious tactical skills—he created situations in which he presented himself to public consciousness as the true epigone of his great predecessor but with superior leadership skills. In the struggle over the inheritance of Marx and Lenin, Stalin stepped forth as the victor for he managed to establish a Marx-Engels-Lenin-Stalin line of descent for the revolutionary workers movement. Even though Stalin actually deformed Marxism, during the historical age of Stalin he was accepted as the true perpetuator of this tradition equal to Lenin.

Yet Stalin himself was nothing more than an extremely adroit and subtle tactician. (We will see that his political career reveals both the positive and

negative features of this kind of one-sided talent.) Even in the immediate period after Lenin's death, he always understood how to maneuver ingeniously. Often without taking a decisive stand himself he knew how to disguise his tactical caution as an example of the highest political principle. Stalin allowed the contending tendencies and personalities that stepped into the foreground at that time to mutually annihilate each other. He also skillfully stole from his opponents any ideas of programs that could be useful to him. The most important practical accomplishment of his tactical adroitness was the gradual concentration into his hands of every instrument of political domination (party, state and the mass media of public opinion). It was the crowning moment of his entire mode of governance that he put himself in the position to declare any of his decisions as commensurate with Leninist democratism. At the same time as he destroyed Leninism, Stalin was able to exploit the Leninist heritage to consolidate his own power.

Earlier, we tried to point out that for Lenin the central strategic question was the preservation and continuation of the popular revolution (the alliance of proletariat and peasantry). The reconstruction of industrial production, the immediate crucial question of NEP-politics, above all was for him an indispensable instrument for the rebuilding of this alliance which, in the revolutions of 1905 and 1917, formed the axis of his politics. He always looked upon the expected lengthy and contradictory process of the building of an industrial base from this political perspective. It is generally known that he was even prepared to grant concessions to foreign capitalists to participate on a temporary basis in the economic restoration of Russian industry. It was not his fault that this plan remained an unfulfilled dream. After his death, the central question became: who should be the beneficiary of this process of economic restoration and who should pay the price for its practical realization? The left wing (Trotsky and Preobrashensky) demanded a policy of "original socialist accumulation," i.e. a single-minded and rapid construction of large-scale industry at the expense of the peasantry. The right wing (Bukharin) perceived the central economic question of the restoration and higher development of industry as the ability of industry to supply the countryside with the necessary commodities (Slogan: "Enrich yourself.") Essentially both wings reduced the problem to a purely economic category, which had extremely far-reaching political consequences. For both wings the perspective that Lenin viewed as crucial, the political alliance of proletariat and peasantry, was partially and theoretically excluded. For that reason also, the struggle over the course of the development of Russia was concentrated solely on tactical alternatives, which in most cases—again in contrast to Lenin—conformed to the contours of the party leader's personality. Stalin did not distinguish himself from his opponents by the theoretic level of his arguments but he was superior to them only in terms of tactics. Stalin approached the tactical question from the perspec-

tive of blocking Trotsky from becoming the leader of the party. He maneuvered ingeniously between both left and right, allowing each of them to wear down the other so that after the political destruction of both wings he could usurp the program of "original socialist accumulation" and develop it with greater energy and with extremely brutal means.

The struggle over the course of Russian development was complicated by a problem which stepped to the forefront only after Lenin's death. It was the problem of socialism in one country. After 1921, proceeding from the theory of uneven development, Lenin was firmly convinced that the socialist revolution would not spread beyond Russia and achieve global victory. However, before 1921, like many of his contemporaries, he was initially committed to the idea that the Russian Revolution only formed the beginning of that wave which, as a solution to the crisis of the war, would soon overwhelm the most important capitalist countries. Only in the last years of his life, and above all after his death, did events demonstrate that in spite of objectively revolutionary conditions and sporadic short-lived revolutionary successes in individual countries the worldwide victory of socialism was rendered impossible by the failure of subjective factors. In addition to overcoming the nonclassical nature of the Russian Revolution, there was now added an additional question: how could the revolution preserve itself in one country and work its way, unassisted by any external source, through to the construction of a socialist society? Within the objective social-historical reality, both of these problem complexes formed an inseparable unity. Due to the isolated position of Russia, the surmounting of its economic underdevelopment became the central focus of political considerations. As far as the solution of this problem of underdevelopment was concerned, the Russian Soviet Republic was now left exclusively to its own economic resources. However, the Soviet Republic did receive moral-psychological support on a global scale. The ideological influence of the working people in the capitalist lands, their sympathy for the Russian Revolution, indeed, were highly important attitudinal factors. These moral-psychological elements could not only be spiritually effective, but often, especially in moments of danger, could rise to actual physical support. While the Soviets received moral support, they did not receive economic aid. The ideological commitment of the international proletariat did not offer any practical solutions to the central, inner economic problem of Russia. The historic destiny that confronted Russia assumed the following form: thrown back completely upon itself, was it possible for Russia to both retain the victory of socialism in one country and to produce by itself the industrial base necessary for the construction of socialism?

The answers to these highly disputed questions illustrate the various forces that struggled for power in the Soviet Union. They also illustrate how these contentious forces abandoned the dynamic methodological principles of

Marx and Lenin. After the death of Lenin, these combative camps were solely directed by tactical moves and countermoves. Above all, the problem of the nonclassical origin of the Russian Revolution disappeared from party discussions. The general theoretical principle of debate increasingly reduced itself to the belief that the nationalization of the means of production—the state form of the dictatorship of the proletariat—provided all the essential answers to the complex questions facing Russia. For a long time, the overcoming of economic backwardness remained the central issue for the Soviet government. Since the question of backwardness was exclusively addressed from the standpoint of economics, precisely those questions that related to the problem of democracy, political questions were excluded from the debate. The Russian Communist Party became mired in economism and did not address the democratic aspects of the development of socialism in Russia. The issue of socialism in one country superseded the more important question of the nonclassical nature of the Russian Revolution, and so the Soviets debated the wrong issue. Even the question of socialism in one country was simplified to whether socialism could possibly develop with a single country. In answering this question priority was again given to purely tactical considerations. Everyone had to be aware that the development of socialism in one country necessarily entailed a lengthy historical process. If one, however, came to the conclusion that the development of socialism in one country could only be completed by means of a socialist revolution above all in the developed countries, then the tactical and ideological consequences that must follow took the following two forms: either the world revolution must be speeded by all means, or, since the world revolution was not developing the party must commit itself to build the industrial base of socialism with the greatest speed regardless of the human cost to the population and without certainty that even these draconian measures would produce the requisite industrial foundation. Trotsky, who believed in the international perspective, was certainly far from viewing the dilemma in such a brutally simplified alternative. In the absence of a genuine theory of revolutionary development, it was unavoidable that the false alternative played such an important role in public opinion.

A shrewed tactician, Stalin, by using abstract propagandistic expressions made these distorted alternatives into the central focus of the economic debate. He affirmed that the only possible Marxist answers to the issue of the Soviet course of growth was the complete construction of socialism in one country. Of course, years later he was misled by this exclusively tactical-propagandistic solution, which he seemingly mistook for a true theoretical one, to the blatant nonsense that not only socialism but also the transition to communism was possible in a single country. For that reason, and on account of the capitalist encirclement of Russia, he argued that the state and all its external and internal means of represssion must continue to exist. In Stalin's com-

munism, as one contemporary wit explained, everyone would be locked up in the concentration camps according to their needs. We will not at this time draw the intellectual similarities between the content of this ironic remark and the priority of tactics within Stalinism, for we shall return to the point later on. It may in any case be useful to point out that the priority of tactics remained unassailed even up to the time of the assault on the "personality cult" at the twentieth Party Congress. Although he criticized Stalin frequently and passionately, Khrushchev remained an economist. He proposed that the introduction of communism was dependent upon the achievement of a certain level of economic productivity. When Russia reached that level of productivity, which would surpass that of the United States, communism would become an actuality. Khrushchev only considered the economic presuppositions, and the idea that communism also entailed political and democratic presuppositions lay beyond his intellectual horizons. Regardless of the criticism of Stalin, Khrushchev remained imprisoned within Stalinism, because he made socialism and communism synonymous with economic productivity and did not allow the theory of socialist democratization to enter the debate.

But let us return to our present subject. After Stalin, with the help of the Bukharin group, rendered the Trotsky-Zinoviev-Kamenev faction powerless he appropriated the economic content of their program of "original socialist accumulation." He disguised his ideological theft by never using the same terminology of the Trotsky-Zinoviev-Kamenev faction. He then turned against his former Bukharinist allies and employed the ideas of the Trotsky-Zinoviev-Kamenev camp as tactical slogans in his destruction of the Bukharin group. We cannot enter here upon the details of Stalin's devious policies, although an exclusive Marxist analysis could be highly useful. We can only allude to those principles of action out of which the totalitarianism of Stalin emerged. As we have seen, Stalin's methodological principles were the absolute priority of the tactical perspective, the complete subordination, even disregard of any Marxist theory of the totality of the process of socialist development. Stalin's victory was objectively facilitated by the fact that his opponents were as far removed from establishing their tactics on Marxist-Leninist theory as Stalin himself. Even though his opponents committed the same methodological errors as Stalin, the difference was his superior political maneuverability as well as his more adept organization of the government apparatus of domination. Trotsky always proceeded from a universal revolutionary perspective which, given the waning of the worldwide proletarian revolution after 1921, remained rhetorical. Bukharin proceeded from dogmatically contrived semipositivistic considerations that were never thought through in a dialectical manner. Because of these methodological flaws, the tactical abilities of Trotsky and Bukharin, already inferior to Stalin's, were additionally weakened. Lacking any theoretic insight, they became rigid and

inflexible which again diminished their essentially limited tactical abilities. Under such conditions, the victory of Stalin was not accidental. His triumph did not express the inherent talents of the individuals involved in the struggle, for Trotsky and Bukharin were certainly more gifted than he. His triumph came from his tactical sagacity. Some people cling to the illusion that Trotsky and Bukharin were better equipped than Stalin to lead Russia on the path of socialist construction But this is an illusion that overlooks the fact that none of Stalin's rivals really had a fundamental Marxist-Leninist program which corresponded to the real circumstances. They also displayed massive theoretical differences. On the other hand, it is a supplementary reflection that Stalin was always able to represent himself as the only legitimate heir of Lenin. He presented himself as the true successor to Lenin, and this helped legalize his domination. For decades, this idea rooted itself in the communist movement and due to its continued survival after Stalin's death has prevented an accurate historical description of the concrete genesis of this struggle for power between Stalin, Trotsky and Bukharin.

6

Stalin's Method

We have already emphasized that the crux of Stalin's method rested on the principle of the priority of tactics over strategy, and even more the priority of tactics over the total evolutionary path of mankind which is the content of the ontology of social being. But we have also seen that this methodological problem cannot be attributed to Stalin alone. The priority of tactics was not an exclusively Russian or Stalinist problem. It was the dominant trend within late nineteenth and twentieth century European socialism and this hegemony was manifested in a variety of forms. It was the prevailing tendency in European social democracy which used this methodology with completely different class contents and therefore with completely different goals and political procedures. The hegemony of tactics within Russian communism was not a uniquely Soviet phenomenon, but rather the adoption of an existing and preferred contemporary tendency. It was—consciously or not—an example of an adaptation to the so-called "realpolitik" of the bourgeoisie, which became the dominant mode of action within the countries of western Europe on various ideological grounds. On the whole, it was not the case that the successors of Lenin were mere imitators of their western counterparts. We have already pointed out that Bukharin, for example, was disposed to a positivistic interpretation of Marxism and we must add that long before Lenin's death Zinoviev's *praxis* revealed tendencies which showed close affinity to the manipulative internal party practices of social democracy.

All this must be specifically illuminated through exact historical research. The decisive conceptual motif is easily detectable: it is the break with the Marxist conception of the role of the economic in the total process of the development of society. An erroneous view of the role of the economy was widely disseminated at that time throughout the entire worker's movement. Marxism degenerated into economic reductionism. This was directly connected with the fact that the specialization of knowledge led to the separation of the sciences from each other. With slight variations, the working class movement and its ideology adopted this division of labor, the independence of

scientific disciplines from each other. Marx had defined the economic as the material foundation of a more total historical process. In the twentieth century, the definition of the economic had been changed to that of a more or less "exact" individual science, so that, for example, Hilferding, from this positivist perspective, could explain Marxist economics as compatible with any world view. The economic as an individual science, as the sole causal determinant of social evolution, had lost its organic connection with the historical destiny of the human species. Marx had seen the economic as one factor of social evolution, and as organically interconnected with other social causal determinants. For this reason, sciences which are individualized, removed from their interdependence with other causal agents, easily slide into mere tactics. Lenin stood completely opposed, alone among his contemporaries—supporters and detractors—to this distortion of the Marxist conception of the economic as mere industrial productivity.

This process of converting the economic into an isolated science laid the methodological foundation for its capacity to be manipulated. This development did not conquer all political parties or movements. It was only in the communist movement that this ability to manipulate the economic was completely realized. Within social democracy, economic manipulation was aimed at an adjustment to bourgeois society, and this led to revisionism, or to a complete break with Marxism. Stalin first distorted the meaning of the economic on the theoretical level, and this distortion then became an instrument for his brutal manipulation of socialist development. When Stalin distorted the economic as a specialized positivist science, when he detached it from any political connectedness, he could claim to be building socialism by exclusively concentrating on industrial growth while totally ignoring the question of socialist democracy. One should not leave out of the account that Bukharin much earlier had defined, in a positivist-mechanistic reduction, the Marxist idea of the forces of production to mean simply technology. The theoretic falseness of this conception cannot be dealt with in detail.[24] We point out only one important theoretic-practical consequence of this interpretation. Bukharin assumed that slavery in the ancient world was one economic consequence of technological underdevelopment, while Marx himself traces this technological underdevelopment back to the slave foundation of the ancient world. It is clear that the theoretic dead end that Bukharin's technological determinism must lead to is based upon a limited notion of the economic. For Marx, the economic is more than just technology, more than a specialized individual science, but one causal factor within a larger total social formation. Marx places the priority on the concept of social totality. With regard to the level of development of the natural sciences in the ancient world, a higher advance of technology was entirely possible. Indeed, where the social totality did not place limits on further developments, technological achievement did advance

to higher levels, as, for example, in the armaments industry.[25] We only mention Bukharin's methodological conception because in its major outlines it became the dominant ideology under Stalin, although with many modifications, as we shall point out later. Under the appearance of Marxist orthodoxy, this methodology (the economic as an exact individual science separated from the total historical process of the social anthropogenesis of humanity) also proved to be an instrument for the construction of a system for the bureaucratic manipulation of society in socialism.

This is clearer in Stalin himself than with Bukharin and the other contenders for leadership. Relatively late (1952), at the time of his completely consolidated autocracy as theoretic and political leader of world communism, as the allegedly legitimate successor of Marx, Engels, and Lenin, Stalin published a small treatise on *The Economic Problems of Socialism in the U.S.S.R.* Its main tactical and propagandistic purpose was to cure the economic theory of socialism of its "subjectivist" aberrations and lead it back to its original Marxist-materialist foundations, to make the Marxist theory of value—under the conditions of socialism—the foundation of economic theory and *praxis* again. However, subjectivism in the era of Stalin could only be interpreted as the bureaucratic manipulation of production. The bureaucracy manipulated economic figures in order to present questionable developments (or even stagnation) as progress, specific procedures as the necessary price one had to pay for rapid progress, and outlawed every critical insight. One ought to remember that in the 1930s, the calculation of production figures on a per capita basis was, for a time, prohibited because it was called a bourgeois aberration. The purpose of this prohibition was not to let the population know that the rise of Soviet production lagged behind that of the capitalist world. Taking into account the vast size of the Soviet Union, the comparison of present production with previous years could occasion great differences in the interpretation of the statistics—and with the ban on critical examination and free access to the facts—the real tempo of economic development could be hidden from the population. The restoration of the Marxist laws of value had the—in itself correct—purpose to restrict the most extreme forms of bureaucratic manipulation (the subjectivism which falsified economic reality).

But what is the real meaning of Stalin's return to the Marxist law of value? Above all, he, perhaps less out of error than from tactical considerations, confused the law of value itself with the appearance it assumed in commodity exchange. Thus he referred to the significance of the law of value in production in the following way: "The matter in question is that the articles of consumption, which are necessary to guarantee the expenditure of labor power in the production process, are themselves produced and realized in the form of commodities which are subject to the effects of the law of value. The effect of the law of value on production becomes apparent here."[26] In this

context, we are interested in his method which manifests itself all the more clearly when he comes to speak on other crucial aspects of the law of value. As we have seen, in order to account for the fluctuating role the law of value played in the planned economy of the Soviet Union and to determine its actual value, he was forced to place himself in open contradiction to Marx. His political needs required him to violate Marxist methodology. He calculated that because of his hegemonic control of the party, no one in Russia at that time would point out his own contradiction of Marx. He posed the question of value openly and unambiguously:

> It is said that the law of value is a permanent law, indispensable for all periods of historical development, and even if the law of value ceased being an effective regulator of exchange relations in the period of the second phase of communist society, it would still stay in force as a regulator of the relations between the different branches of production and the distribution of labor between them.
>
> This is absolutely incorrect. Value, like the law of value, is a historical category and thus related to the existence of commodity production. If the production of commodities ceases to exist, value in its manifestations and the law of value likewise disappears.[27]

We have quoted this passage at great length in order to clearly describe Stalin's thoughts and to demonstrate their contrast to Marx's. Marx speaks about the various forms of the law of value, not in an extremely inaccessible passage, but in the beginning of the first volume of *Kapital*. Marx isolates at least three distinct forms of the law of value; for example, with Robinson Crusoe, or with a self-supporting peasant family in the Middle Ages, or, finally, in socialism itself. Labor time, i.e., the present socially necessary labor time, the immediate economic materialization of value, has a double function: "Its socially planned distribution regulates the correct relationship between the different function of labor and different needs." On the other hand, Marx adds, "labor time serves as a measure of the individual producer's share in common labor and therefore also of the individually consumable portion of common production."[28] Whereas Marx defines labor time as the substance of value, Stalin defined value as commodity exchange. In direct contradiction to Marx, Stalin affirmed that it was not just commodities serving individual consumption that remain subject to the law of value, but the producers' entire share of the total social yield of commodities, and this makes an enormous difference. For Marx, labor exploitation can exist under socialism if labor time is expropriated from the laborer, since "the share of every producer to the means of subsistence is determined by his labor time." For Stalin, however, the law of value cannot exist under socialism because socialism destroyed commodity exchange, and commodity exchange was the basis of

exploitation. Thus, Marx and Stalin disagreed in their analyses of the socialist stage of history, for Marx maintains that surplus labor can continue under socialism, while Stalin thought that since socialism destroyed commodities it must also destroy surplus labor.

For Marx, the law of value is not dependent upon commodity production. Yet Stalin insisted on this interconnection, and it was by no means a mere slip of the tongue. Stalin's distortion of the methodology of Marx had practical consequences, for it led him to distort the definition of socialism. A fallacious definition of the construction of socialism was presented in a propagandistic fashion, as if Stalin consciously wanted to substitute a false interpretation of Marx for the true one. For this purpose, Stalin used the trick of depicting classical economic categories as if they were merely historical manifestations of capitalism and thus no longer operative in socialism, although according to Marx these classical economic categories are applicable to any mode of production. Stalin's intent was to present his manipulative form of socialism as the theoretic and political fulfillment of Marxism-Leninism. The first step toward an understanding of the connection between the Stalinist formulation of Marxism and the prevention and even destruction of socialist democracy is an analysis of Stalin's misinterpretation of Marx's concept of surplus value in his *The Economic Problems of Socialism in the U.S.S.R.* The need to politically legitimate his rule made it mandatory for Stalin to portray his Soviet Union as on the correct path to socialism, and in order to prove this Stalin had to falsify Marx. Political need led to the necessity to distort methodology, and a false methodology led to flawed and misguided policies. "I have in mind," Stalin said, "such concepts as 'necessary' and 'surplus' labor time." According to Stalin, Marx had correctly employed these categories in the analysis of capitalist production, but showed how they would lose their meaning after the socialization of the means of production. "It is likewise bizarre," he continued, "to talk of 'necessary' and 'surplus' labor now, as if under the present conditions the labor performed by the worker for the benefit of society, for the expansion of production, for the development of education, for Public Health, for the organization of defense, was not as necessary for the presently ruling working class as the labor performed for the gratification of needs is for the individual laborer and his family."[29] In other words, under socialism, surplus labor no longer existed, but only necessary labor.

We are dealing here with Marx's distinction between "necessary" and "surplus" labor and we are concerned with the economic reproductive process. In opposition to Stalin's thesis, it must be said that the difference between the labor necessary for the reproduction of the worker and the labor he performs in addition to that, (surplus labor) is by no means a specific feature of capitalism. Surplus labor is an important and an indispensable economic feature in the development of the reproductive process generally from its pri-

meval history up to communism. The economic foundation of slavery as distinct from the initial killing or even devouring of captured enemies was economically based on the fact that the slave could supply a greater quantum of labor than was necessary for his own individual reproduction. Marx also points out that in slavery—in opposition to serfdom and wage labor—the labor necessary for the self-reproduction of the worker appears to decrease, just as surplus labor, an increment of labor in addition to necessary labor, increases in capitalist wage labor. However, this is a necessary illusion, but nothing more than an illusion. All three economic formations—slavery, serfdom, and wage labor—are objectively based on the appropriation of surplus value through the contemporary ruling classes. The appropriation of surplus value assumes a great variety of historical forms, assumes shapes dictated by the use of immediate brute force or economic compulsion. However, the two most basic presuppositions for the higher development of socioeconomic life are: the constant tendency of the socially necessary labor needed for the reproduction of an individual to decrease, and the corresponding tendency for surplus value to constantly increase. For Marx, it is a fixed law of economic progress that surplus value in general immediately falls prey to the exploitative mechanisms of a society. However, depending upon the different structures of different social formulations, the appropriation of surplus labor can serve the universal social purpose of developing a higher human personality.

The socialization of the means of production rules out the appropriation of surplus labor by means of the possession of private property. However, it in no way transcends the basic categories of economic production; it only establishes a radically new social formation in order to make possible the progressive social use of surplus labor. Marx outlines the economic-cultural essence of the increase in the forces of production in the following manner: "The free development of individuality, and therefore not the reduction of the necessary labor time in order to increase surplus labor but generally the reduction of the necessary work of society to a minimum in order to allow for the artistic and scientific education of individuals as a result of the time and creative means that has become available to all of them."[30] In the *Critique of the Gotha Program*, he takes an appropriately hard line against Lassalle's vulgarized view that socialism only signifies the worker's acquisition of his "full value of labor." In his critique of Lassalle, Marx emphasizes that surplus labor has to cover all the costs that are necessary for the maintenance and further improvement of production itself. It has to pay for the administrative expenses of a society, its general needs such as education, health care, etc. Marx correctly emphasizes that under socialism these social services are better funded than in previous social formations. These general needs include funds for the disabled. According to Marx, these social needs determine the economic framework for individual consumption, for the individual self-reproduction of

the laboring people under socialism. Stalin simply turned Lassalle's fundamentally false conception upside down and he was able to declare the category of surplus labor as nonexistent under socialism. We have already quoted from his arguments. As we have seen, Lassalle was governed by the illusion that socialism signified the transition of the collective products of work into the immediate sphere of the self-production of the individual worker, while Stalin simply equated mediated economic movements into immediate ones; without commodity exchange the worker no longer produced surplus-labor. Both Stalin and Lassalle falsified the fundamental economic constituents of social self-reproduction. They both did this in a diametrically opposite manner, but in both cases this contradiction was based upon a systematic ignorance of the real economic factors of the social reproduction process.

To simplify matters, let us take education as an example. It is certainly not directly included in the process of individual self-reproduction. Under capitalism, the necessity for education only arises from the technological needs of bourgeois society and it is imposed on the working class from above because specific labor processes simply can not be technically performed by illiterate workers. But even though socialism places this question on the social agenda with an intensity unimaginable in any of the previous class societies, it is still neither inclined to nor capable of doing away with the economic penetration and mediation of the educational sphere. But compared to capitalism, socialism introduces, with strong ideological overtones, a qualitatively new idea, that this economic penetration of the sphere of education had to be solved on the initiative of the proletariat themselves. Let us recollect that during the introduction of NEP, Lenin makes the liquidation of illiteracy a crucial political and ideological task.

Naturally, ideology must be understood in the exact Marxist sense. In his introduction to *The Critique of Political Economy,* Marx defines ideological forms as the social medium in which the people themselves become conscious of social conflicts and fight them out. This definition reveals the ambiguity of the inner dialectic of ideology. On the one hand, social conflicts originate in the objectively necessary and deterministic contradiction between the forces of production and the relations of production. On the other hand, and simultaneously, every ideology is a complex instrument that enables the people themselves to become conscious of existing social conflicts and to fight them out in a practical manner. Correspondingly, in Lenin's view the liquidation of illiteracy was a problem that objectively evolved out of Russia's economic backwardness. The solution to illiteracy was the object of Russia's own inherently conscious *praxis* intermediated by the consciousness and activity of the working people. Thus, after the domination of the exploiting class had been broken by the socialization of all the means of production the way was cleared for the proletariat to become capable of solving the collective problems of everyday

life through their own self-activity. Education—to stick to this example—can in this manner be changed from an economically mediated superstructure to a force for the extension and deepening of the life of every individual man. Education can become a social force created by man for himself. Due to its inherent social nature, education can result in the self-genesis of man, the bringing forth of man as his own self-creation and self-completion and to his becoming the producer of his own self. This empowering of man is accomplished through the reduction of the labor time necessary, which Marx once called the "superfluous," for their own self-reproduction, because then more surplus labor time can be applied to the task of man's self-genesis.

Naturally, in the last analysis, the social context is the deciding moment in determining the use of surplus labor. The level of development of production, the reduction of the labor necessary for the self-reproduction of the working class, the ideological struggle over the contents of this superfluous substance are causes that arise from social, objectively determined phenomena. Also, the things that result from this intermixture of socially objective causes must themselves be of a primarily social nature. However, and here this complex of questions connects with the problem of democratization, is there a conflict between the social and the individual? Is the individual absorbed in the social or is there a reciprocal process which reinforces the two poles between the social and the individual? Can individual actions accomplish two reciprocal and simultaneous results: can they produce a social outcome leading to the increase of social productivity and can they develop the individual personality, promote, enrich and deepen a subject's incipient individuality? We have previously mentioned the observation of Marx that the Kingdom of Freedom signifies the unfolding of human powers which is valid as an end in itself. That signifies a mode of *praxis* that surpasses the economic and passes beyond the basic and therefore unsurpassable Kingdom of Necessity. In the *Critique of the Gotha Program,* Marx commented on this transcendence of the domination of the economic, asserting that "labor was not only the means to life but had become the first need of life."

Is the idea of the reciprocity between the social and individual an expression of utopianism? This seems to be the case and indeed is the case, as long as we separate the present from the future, as long as we draw a sharp line between present day actuality and a desired future. Things appear differently if we do not consider the social and the individual as contrasting conditions, but as complementary poles of a unified social process and agree with Lenin that what we call socialist or proletarian democracy is just this concrete process which creatively binds the objective and the subjective to each other. In that case, socialism, the first phase of communism, appears as a particular social formation whose economic structure, whose interpersonal cooperation, can only be adequately developed by means of the reciprocity of the social and the

individual. The social structures that exist outside of and independently of man are purely objective. These social structures are the inherent processes of society that develop in accordance with deterministic laws and lie beyond human control. Human beings live inside these objective social structures. The laws of this social objectivity cannot be suspended, but social development in total unfolds as a mutual process between the objective and subjective conscious human action. Socialist democracy—taking man to be an active creature, which is the true nature of his human species being since he is forced to be active in his everyday *praxis*—transforms the objectified and objective products of human labor into objects that are consciously created by man himself and that fulfill human purposes. Socialist democracy is the political framework that allows objectivity, without violating the inherent law of objectivity, to become a tool in the teleological designs of conscious active men. It is the conquest of consciousness and self-determination over blind objectivity. As the victory of self-determination, socialist democracy transforms the human neighbor, one's fellow man, from acting as a hindrance to one's own *praxis* to an indispensable and affirmative co-worker and co-helper.

Naturally, the intent, intensity, content, and direction of such historical progress is shaped and determined by the economic level of the social formation existing at that time. The proletarian revolution released the totality of socially necessary labor time from its enslavement to capitalism. The amount of surplus labor contained in this totality was clearly a product of the level of Russian industrial development. The Russian Revolution was led into an objective dead end precisely because its backward industrial development required a continuous large outlay of socially necessary labor. The problem of the relationship between necessary and surplus labor could be concealed from the population as long as its victories and the defense of the revolution were still the immediate focus of revolutionary *praxis* and while the insurgent masses were enthusiastically involved in political questions. Within the direct democratic political structures created by the revolution, problems ranging from the most trivial to the most complex issues of world affairs could be debated. These direct democratic political structures not only allowed the Russian masses to participate in tempestuous global affairs, but the issues that confronted Russia were also of interest to the entire world. Let us remember, for example, the international reverberations let loose by the peace negotiation of Brest-Litovsk.

This seemingly overpowering mass spontaneity was even expanded, consolidated and directed toward concrete goals through the organizational work of the Soviets. Originating in the Commune of 1871, spontaneously cropping up anew in 1905, the Soviet movement became the paradigmatic model of socialist democracy in and after 1917. Its dramatic force sprang from the fact that it allowed men, above all in their everyday life, in their work places, their

homes, to organize for direct political action. The Soviets either gradually or abruptly helped the masses rise to a revolutionary consciousness and *praxis* on all critical social questions. During the final phase of the formation of the Soviet movement (1917), the interconnection of everyday life with politics, the question of a rapid conclusion of a peace treaty with Germany, was firmly fused. There emerged a spontaneous interchange between everyday questions and those of the highest political magnitude. Socialist democratization as represented in the Soviets joined the subjective and objective. The context of the times, the Revolution of 1917 and the World War of 1914, facilitated these developments.

The Soviet movement developed spontaneously everywhere and step-by-step rose to a higher and higher level of consciousness. The Stalin era twisted the controversy between Lenin and Luxemburg into a manipulatory demagogical distortion so that what it called conscious behavior stood in exclusive contrast to spontaneity in order to lessen the social significance of spontaneity. Stalin magnified the contrast between Lenin and Luxemburg and made Lenin out to be an opponent of mass spontaneity. Stalin did this in order to strengthen the dominating control of the party over the mass. But Lenin, whom Stalin presented as the authority responsible for this bureaucratic and manipulative attitude, was not hostile to spontaneity and conceived it as the "cell of teleological action."[31] And, indeed, the Revolution sought and often spontaneously found those institutional forms which could constitute the political framework for a real revolutionizing of Russian society, forms which themselves created the opportunity for an expanded level of activity for men. Spontaneous mass movements heighten the sense of human self-determination and show how the knowledge of objective reality can be transformed into an instrument of human teleological action. This can only occur if the connection between the particular interests of the day and the crucial universal questions becomes real for the person involved in the concerns of everyday life. Revolutionary situations differ from the ordinary everyday because such situations spontaneously call for action. It is not sufficient to comprehend revolutionary situations theoretically. Obviously, becoming conscious in this context does not simply mean the reception and understanding of "information," but the inherent transformation of consciousness into a guide for one's own action. This movement of spontaneity towards a teleology of *praxis* will be discussed in detail later on. For now, we have to content ourselves with the observation that the Revolution of 1917—thanks to Lenin's leadership of the Communist party—was capable of synthesizing the everyday with the crucial problems of society and the state, and because of this the Soviet government did not lose its rootedness in the everyday life of the people.

The bitter Civil War raised the accomplishments of the Soviet movement to memorable heights. At the same time, economic factors that stemmed from

the underdevelopment of the Russian Empire worked in a subterranean fashion to undermine the achievements of the Soviets. These economic pitfalls were hidden by the successes of the day. Lenin recognized this dangerous course when he abruptly changed directions, repudiated "war communism" both theoretically and practically and introduced NEP. He saw—and this was the chief danger of bureaucratization—that the spontaneous revolutionary unity of the people, the alliance of proletariat and peasant that brought about their common liberation from the yoke of capitalism, was in danger of being torn apart. In Lenin's day, this revolutionary alliance of workers and peasants was consciously organized and supported by the party. The massive economic problems of Russia that became visible after the Civil War could not be solved by the revolutionary spontaneity of 1917. New problems required new solutions. The need for peaceful consolidation and the higher development of socialist democracy posed completely new qualitative problems for the working masses, which even the most sincere and determined revolutionary enthusiasn was not sufficient to solve. (Lenin made this absolutely clear in his speeches and writings concerning the introduction of NEP.)

These difficult tasks were complicated by the nonclassical genesis of socialism in an underdeveloped country. Seemingly, this was a question of mere quantitative difference: after years of an imperialist war followed by a civil war with all their unavoidable destruction even a highly developed capitalist country must engage in a period of economic restoration. Such a period would have two primary purposes and stood at the center of all social *praxis:* the economic reconstruction of the country and the surpassing of prewar levels of industrial growth. The Soviet Republic was not only concerned with the mere reconstruction of the economy, but with the advance of the economy up to a level, a level that had never been previously attained, which would provide an adequate basis for the building of a socialist society. If we abstractly speak of two durations of time, one a relatively brief period of transition and the other an extended historical epoch, the difference between the transition and the epoch is a mere quantitative one, a variation in the amount of time. However, in terms of social reality, the distinction between transition and epoch is decidedly qualitative, for it concerns not time, but human life. If we speak of a transition in which the reconstitution and advance of the economy can be fulfilled, then we speak of one generation of human beings that can fulfill these tasks. (The transition may amount to a decade.) But if we speak of a historical epoch devoted to the reconstitution and advance of the economy, then we are referring to several generations of human lives which are compelled to concentrate their main purpose and their crucial efforts not so much on the genuine building of socialism as on the material construction of only the economic presupposition of socialism.

The problem outlined above, the development of an objective future eco-

nomic foundation for socialism, was made more difficult for the Soviet people because it was posed imperatively, the people were not given any alternatives. For politically conscious people, the actual historical alternatives could be concretized in the following questions: given the indispensability of an objective economic foundation for the construction of socialism whether and to what degree the industrial advancement of Russia was compatible with socialist democracy? Was the need for industrial improvement and the resulting institutions and social forms compatible with those institutions and social forms prerequisite for a socialist democracy? We have pointed out earlier when referring to the confrontations over economics called forth by the internal struggles among Lenin's successors, that none of the contesting groups realized or posed this alternative. They focused exclusively on economic questions and ignored the issue of democratization. Because they remained oblivious to the claim of democracy, they put into place a system of centralized governmental regulation from above. As we have also suggested, Lenin himself opposed this tendency in the last years of his life in so far as he was theoretically and practically capable of influencing events. The alternative between democracy and bureaucracy formed the core of his later writings which can be referred to as his last *What Is To Be Done?* We have also pointed out what can be seen more clearly from our historical vantage point, that the exclusive preoccupation which economic questions predisposed Lenin's successors to think in exclusively tactical terms. A distorted Marxist methodology which was on the theoretical level the misunderstanding of the economic as a positivist science and which was on the practical level the grasping of the economic as the absolute political priority in Russia, served as the basis for turning the sociopolitical *praxis* of Lenin's successors into more tactical maneuvers. Stalin was also one of those who committed there errors. In terms of the questions we have been discussing, he must not be viewed as a follower of Lenin's method.

The fact that Stalin was a far superior tactician than his opponents does not change anything in relation to the basic problems concerning the direction of later Soviet development. Stalin and his opponents both retreated from Lenin, both allowed politics to be totally controlled by tactical considerations. In this respect, Stalin was also a more gifted figure among those who were struggling for power, for he outmaneuvered his opponents with superior adroitness and shrewdness. He successfully presented himself as the only genuine and worthy successor of Lenin. In the political discussions of the following decades, Stalin's propagandistically proclaimed unanimity with Lenin was hammered deeply into the consciousness of the Communists. It ought to be one of the crucial ideological functions of our contemporary transitional period and of our efforts to reestablish genuine Marxism that this historical legend, which has been systematically built by Stalin and his apparatus, be torn to pieces. Practically nothing has been done about this until now, although the subject is

extraordinarily important. Leninism, in which the spirit of Marx lived, was converted into its diametrical opposite. Stalin accomplished this deformation of Leninism and Marxism, but he was able to create the illusion that complete unanimity existed between Stalin and Marxism-Leninism. It is extremely important that bourgeois anti-Marxism was solidified because it took Stalin at his word and confused Stalinism and Marxism-Leninism. It is far more important that among the ranks of Communists in socialist lands the picture of Marx and Lenin was also distorted owing to this acceptance of Stalin's methodology. This became an extremely effective barrier to self-awareness, especially after the basic facts of the Stalin era became widely known and made the historical revision of Stalinism into a matter of extreme urgency.

This condensed rough draft as it lies before us here is not the appropriate place to undertake this arduous task with the necessary exhaustiveness. In this outline, only methodological suggestions can come under discussion. It will achieve its purpose if it helps bring more detailed research gradually into existence. It is impossible to carry out this kind of research with the presently existing materials, documents, and critical bibliography. Step by step, Stalin had build up a deceptive ideological apparatus. His publications are full of quotes from Marx, Engels, and Lenin that, at times, are not even fundamentally wrong but trivialized. Those statements of Stalin which describe his new method and those which show Stalin in opposition to Marxism-Leninism, need to be collated and gathered in a systematic methodological presentation which would show how the omnipotence of tactics, its domination over theory, was grounded and cemented on this foundation. The first step in the omnipotence of tactics was the simplification, even vulgarization, of the principles of Marx and Lenin. It is only necessary to take a look at the definition of dialectics in the famous fourth chapter of the party history to prove this. In the first years of World War I, in preparation for the forthcoming debates over the war, imperialism and the socialist revolution, Lenin had extraordinarily deepened and differentiated his conception of dialectics in his reading of Hegel's *Logic*. However, in that famous and classical fourth chapter of the party history, we receive nothing but simplifying vulgarization that functioned in the 1930s as a perfect substitute for Marxism and Leninism. The domination of centrally directed tactics can thrive best if scientific investigation and independent reflection are replaced by a reified, although impressive, mobilization of propagandistic methods.

In order to further clarify the problem of democratization, although an exhaustive and penetrating analysis is not possible, I quote Stalin's definition of theory from his lectures on the foundations of Leninism. He said: "Theory is the experience of the worker's movement of all lands taken in its universal form."[32] In order to make the contrast between Stalin and Lenin obvious, it is only necessary to recall the passages of Lenin we quoted earlier in which he

defended Marxism as an incorporation of the major cultural experience of the West. While Stalin limited theory to the experiences of proletariat, Lenin saw Marxism as the culmination of the western experience. Even when Lenin, as we have also seen, approached the theory of the "withering away of the state" it is treated by him as a discovery of a general tendency of the totality of world history the results of which can be utilized by Marxism for the true liberation of humanity. Of course, this liberation must be coincident with socioeconomic possibilities and limitations. If Marxism is divorced from its western cultural heritage, if its philosophical presuppositions are detached from its western precursors then it is separated from its broad humanism and loses its higher purposes. The priority of tactics under Stalin accomplished this purpose and led to the general vulgarization of the methodology of Marxism. Stalinism hid this deformation of Marxism through the clever manipulation of language and gave the impression that he had preserved and even advanced the essence of Marxism. This manifested itself with great clarity in Zhdanov's famous theory concerning the essence of Hegelian philosophy. In order to complete the radical reification of the dialectic, Stalinism found it necessary to rule out the seminal and generative influence of Hegel's dialectic on Marxism. In order to substantiate the divorce between Hegel and Marx "theoretically," Hegelian philosophy was presented by Zhdanov as a reactionary response to the French Revolution. In a purely theoretic manner, this was the epitome of the tendency toward vulgarization: Marxism must be presented as something new without any precursors in the bourgeois world, without any relationship to previous world historic developments.

The Stalinist deformation of Marxism was so obvious that even the very first criticism of it at the twentieth Congress quickly unmasked one of its important theoretical constructs as completely fraudulent. We refer to the thesis concerning the worsening of the class struggle during the period of the proletarian dictatorship. In order to expand this correct critique of Stalinism into a real systematic analysis, in order to extend this attack on one idea into a repudiation of the whole Stalinist system, two methodological observations were required.

First, the thesis regarding the worsening of the class struggle was itself not the initial theoretical foundation of Stalinist *praxis* but only its subsequent justification. The period of the Great Purges, of the physical annihilation of any potential oppositional leader, could be deduced from this highly arbitrary thesis, but the reverse conclusion cuts to the truth: when Stalin, from tactical considerations made the decision for the radical decimation of all opposition, of even individual suspects, the theory of the worsening of the class struggle arose in order to offer propagandistic preparation for and justification of these policies. Secondly, it must be pointed out that this was not an isolated case, but rather illustrated, both objectively and subjectively, Stalin's characteristic and general methods of procedure.

This is graphically shown by the apologistic theories which arose as a consequence of the pact between Hitler and Stalin. The Hitler-Stalin Pact was of a purely politico-tactical character and could be evaluated as such from a variety of viewpoints. (I personally regarded it as a correct tactical diplomatic chess move.) In relation to the matter we are discussing here, it is above all significant that Stalin immediately appended to this purely tactical maneuver a definition of the nature of the Second World War, namely the idea that the emergent conflict was an imperialist war of the same kind as 1914. Those communists who were loyal to Stalin (for instance, in France) were directed to use their major efforts to overthrow their own governments rather than struggle against Hitler. Only when Hitler broke the pact and invaded the Soviet Union did Stalin change his interpretation and designate the Second World War as a struggle against fascism.

The totality of Stalin's *praxis* is replete with such tactically manipulated theoretic decisions. The basis of Stalin's *praxis* was that the existent tactical needs were supported by a generalized theoretic substructure that in many cases bore no resemblance to either the facts or to the general lines of historical development. Rather, the theory was exclusively intended to justify the existing tactical needs. Thus when Stalin felt the tactical need, in the late 1920s, to attack his rivals as enemies of the socialist revolution on the most minimal theoretical differences the "theory" arose that seemingly marginal differences of opinion signified the highest theoretical danger—a devious way of camouflaging the enemy. With the international workers movement, this priority of the tactical received its most important theoretic embodiment when Stalin denounced the social democrats as "twin brothers" of the fascists, and the left wing of social democracy was regarded as the most dangerous ideological current within the labor movement. (The criticism of Stalin's methodology is highly important and of immediate concern. It is as operative in the present almost as frequently as it was during the times of Stalin.)

These examples, which can be multiplied at will, clearly illustrate the inner coherence of Stalin's method: one responds to an existent situation on the basis of tactics. Theory merely has the function of subsequently representing the already made tactical decisions as necessary results of Marxist-Leninist methodology. Within the system, ideology also becomes an object for manipulation. It loses that immense free play, that contradictory multiplicity and asymmetricity that it has in Marx, who looks upon ideology as an instrument to fight out socioeconomic conflicts. Under Stalinism, ideology appeared, on the one hand, as a mechanistic product of a present economic situation. On the other hand, ideology appeared as material without its own content which can for that reason be reshaped according to the will of a person. This corresponds to Stalin's definition of ideology which he gave in his essay on language. In that essay particular emphasis was laid on the mechanical nature of its genesis. Stalin wrote: "The superstructure is the product of one single epoch in the

course of which a given economic basis arises and prevails. For that reason, the superstructure does not last long. It will be removed and disappear with the removal and disappearance of the basis."[33] Even on the stylistic level, the contrast to Marx is striking. For Marx, the disappearance of an ideology is also the outcome of a social process. But Marx did not understand societies as governed by deterministic law. Social developments, for Marx, combines deterministic as well as subjective factors, so the total movement is a relatively non-necessitarian process. In contradiction to Marx, Stalin thought that ideologies were "removed", i.e. they were the simple object of a social activity—namely, Stalin's voluntarism.

The inherent tendency of such manipulation comes to light brilliantly in what is for us the most singular question: Stalin's destruction of the Soviet structure of the socialist state. We have previously tried to show that the essential characteristic of the new Soviet system was the social transcendence of the citizen—idealism of bourgeois society. The historical purpose of socialism is to end the divorce between the man of everyday life and man as a political agent. The citizen, political man, who acts both democratically and practically, should no longer be an ideal essence cut off from real man (the man of the democratic constitution). Within the context of bourgeois society, this real man is taught to function in terms of egoistic and materialistic ends. But under socialism a new social ideal arises, a man who aims at the material concrete realization of his sociability in everyday life so that the immediate questions of the day as well as the universal and great affairs of state are resolved in collective cooperation with his class comrades. We have already pointed out how the revolutionary collapse of capitalism unleashed a broad and deep enthusiasm that penetrated into all areas of everyday life. The first years of the Bolshevik Revolution exerted an international fascination that stemmed from the world historic drama of this huge undertaking and the enthusiasm it launched passed far beyond the ranks of the Communists. The revolution had opened a new historical horizon, the possibility of new human beginnings. From among a multiplicity of voices, it is sufficient to quote Bloch's poem, "The Twelve," in order to show how many people, reacting to the possibilities created by the revolution, now believed that they could achieve a life which combined the worldly, earthly, and material with that of immanent meaning. They believed that the revolution had brought the thousand-year-old dream of the cooperative nature of human species being closer to fulfillment.

The Civil War accomplished two contradictory things: it imparted to this movement the character of inspired heroism and it introduced the bureaucratization of life. At the conclusion of the heroic period, the problem of bureaucratization arose. Emerging in the period after Lenin's death, the problem of bureaucratization was symptomatic of and above all stemmed from the eco-

nomics of the nonclassical genesis of socialism in Russia. Stalin's tactical solution to the existent problems rested in a radical bureaucratic demolition of every tendency that might act as a precondition for socialist democracy. The Soviet system practically ceased to exist. As a mere formality, leaving the one party system in place, the highest democratic organs of the state received a form that brought them extraordinarily close to the impotent parliamentarian system of bourgeois democracy. The lower reaches of the Soviet system were reduced to mere local administrative organs chosen through election. All the efforts of the last years of Lenin's life to ideologically prepare the construction of a real socialist democracy disappeared. At this time, the participant in political or universal social life could only—in the best of cases—justify his actions as mere bourgeois citizen idealism. In the life of the citizen of the state, the ruling tendency was a universal bureaucratization of political as well as administrative *praxis*. I repeat, it is impossible to describe, either extensively or intensively, the entire scope of Stalinist *praxis* in all its theoretical presuppositions and consequences. It appears to me, however, that what has been mentioned so far suffices to make clear how this *praxis* overturned every attempt on the part of Lenin to continue the formation of the objective as well as subjective conditions for a complete construction of a socialist democracy.

It must be stressed that we are speaking of Socialist Democracy and not of socialism in general. One can and must criticize the blurring of these distinctions by all who wish to defend the Leninist heritage. One must admit that Stalin, who assumed the leadership of Russia for decades as a result of the interparty struggles, did accomplish some highly important results. Stalin did create the industrial base for socialism, but not the political base for socialist democracy. These industrial accomplishments did compensate for the weaknesses resulting from the nonclassical origins of the Bolshevik Revolution. It is a commonplace that these questions over the nonclassical nature of the Russian Revolution cannot be considered even today as completely resolved, but it is likewise obvious that the Soviet Union has ceased being the economically backward country that it was in the 1920s. This was Stalin's achievement. Nowadays bourgeois critics tend to forget that they once talked of a forced, partial or total restitution of capitalism at the beginning of NEP. Using strategic terminology, Lenin described the NEP as a "retreat." But the facts say something completely opposite, for capitalism was not restored to Russia and today the Soviet Union has become a major economic power, the second industrial power in the world, despite all its undeniable problems in important areas of economic life. And it has raised itself to this level without having to make the slightest concession in the central principle that the socialization of the means of production is the economic basis of socialism.

This extremely important point is all too often neglected in the current discussions. Especially if one—in addition to many individual factors—criti-

cizes the Stalinist period from the perspective of its political failure to advance socialist democracy, as we do in these pages. At the same time, one must never lose sight of Stalin's success in laying the economic foundations of socialism and the world historic consequences which followed. One can correctly, for example, affirm the guilt of Stalin in the victory of Hitlerism because Stalin divided German Communists from German Social Democrats and prevented a united left front against Hitler. But one would form a completely warped judgement if one did not at the same time note that the world must thank the Soviet Union above all for preventing Europe from becoming a part of the Hitlerian Reich. Munich and its consequences, the style of official French strategy, show that the democratic-capitalist powers of Western Europe neither possessed the will nor the capacity to oppose the Hitlerian plan of world domination. Only in the Soviet Union did Hitler find an enemy, who with the greatest sacrifices, with an unshakable determination, could and did achieve his complete extermination. Even with the victory over Hitler, the services of the Soviet Union to rescue and preserve civilization in our time were still not exhausted. One thinks about the atom bomb and its possible military and political consequences. When it was used against Japan every thinking man knew that its use was not necessary but Hiroshima was the prelude to the world domination of American imperialism. Immediately after dropping the bomb, some apolitical but sophisticated men like Thomas Mann, without being socialists, clearly expressed their opinion that the atom bomb was directed more against the Soviet Union than against Japan itself. The fact that in a surprisingly short space of time the Soviet Union was capable of producing its own atom bomb and the resulting nuclear stalemate did not only portend the prevention of a third world war but also halted the world domination of American imperialism.

Stalin, and other leading political personalities, were not the final causes of world events of such great dimensions. Their individual political activity helped realize those tendencies that necessarily grew out of a given economic structure. The Soviet Union as the protector of world peace, as the impediment to imperialist subjection, can only carry out this function consistently because of its socialist structure. Because the Soviet Union has eliminated private property in the means of production there are no economic groups in this socialist state who stand to profit by an outbreak of hostilities. The eradication of private property has uprooted the economic incentives for war. The socialization of the means of production has indeed created the incentives for a policy of peace. Despite many tactical errors in individual cases, Soviet Russia has successfully fulfilled its role as the defender of world peace. The attitude towards war, even toward a world war with all its economic and social consequences, has completely different dimensions in capitalist countries. The driving force that pushes these countries to conquest and war is undoubtedly that

part of industry, above all heavy industry, that has a direct interest in such adventures. Anyone who has followed the economic development of the imperialist period with even the slightest concern can easily see that the most important advances of modern industrial development are the direct result of the armaments industry and war itself. Even though against the immediate interests of the populace, the success of the capitalist manipulation of public opinion in ideologically mobilizing the broad masses in the cause of patriotic wars need not concern us. In most cases, the power that is gathered behind the war lobby is strong enough to prevail in the unleashing or continuation of war, even against mass opposition.

After the confiscation of the means of production from the hands of individuals or particular groups, there no longer exists in the Soviet Union social groups that find war to be economically profitable. In socialist societies there is no longer any economic base for the social divisiveness engendered by war. Any war can only have purely negative consequences, such as lowering the present or potential standard of living of working people. In all socialist countries, these decisive and automatic economic consequences of the socialization of the means of production are the material conditions for its spontaneous desire for peace.

The ability of socialist society to limit militarism refers exclusively to war itself. The armaments—technological preparation for war is another matter. We must soon delve into the question of how the socialization of the means of production effects the normal functioning of total production. Before we take a closer look at this highly important problem, let us first take note that every socialist economic system, also manipulated by Stalinist methods, was and still is capable of competing both quantitatively and qualitatively with capitalist production, but only in the field of armaments. The reason for this is obvious. Through the mechanism of commodity exchange, capitalism—indeed with specific limitation—can continuously control the quantity and quality of production. It is understandable that it is more difficult for a planned socialist economy to accomplish this, especially in a Stalinist hyperbureaucratized form of planning and the difficulties of its practical execution. Though we cannot consider this crucial problem in detail in this context, we can still point out that in a socialist system it is possible for the armaments industry—and only for it—to create effective organs for the control of the quantity and quality of the goods it produces. The military accomplishes this by placing the army command—and only it—in a position to test those products it needs in the process of their production. The military only permits the actual production of those products that pass the test of properly functioning use—values. Obviously, some errors of judgment are unavoidable even in this context, but the control exerted by the actual consumers which has been raised to the standard of real competence, creates a difference between the quality and quantity

of military production and the quality and quantity of civilian production. This is not just a matter of individual or isolated cases, but a matter that concerns the universal objective structural relations of socialist production itself. Only in the context of the general problem of socialist production can the success or failure of individual cases be discussed.

In pure economic terms, socialism reached two major goals. It created the material basis for a universal policy of peace. At the same time, it developed an industrial-military base that made it an effective force in the power struggle of the imperialist period. But the bureaucratic and ideological manipulation of these attainments seriously reduced the capacity of such policies to internationalize the socialist revolution. Specifically, the purely tactical determination and corresponding manipulation of socialist ideology degraded revolutionary *praxis* to the level of mere national power politics. In the international area as well, the contrasts between Lenin and Stalin are clearly visible. When Lenin supported Kemal Pascha in his national fight for the liberation of Turkey against the dictatorship of the victorious imperialist powers, the principle behind the support was evident to everyone: in terms of every revolt against the imperialist redistribution of the world, the workers' and peasants' state was on the side of the revolutionaries irrespective of the social system in the name of which they rebelled against imperialism. This support was grounded in the principles of socialism, in the philosophically correct theories of Marx and Lenin over the role of the struggle of national liberation in history. Due to his purely tactical approach to all the great questions of history, Stalin was not capable of bestowing such an incontestable spiritual and moral physiognomy to his policies. This was true even against Hitler. When the successors of Stalin, for example, became the protectors of the Arab states against Israel, this decision was modeled on the ideological manipulation of the master. In this void of ideological principle, they were compelled to justify this decision by using the tactical slogan of socialism. Because they embraced Stalin's methodology, their action took on the appearance of an ideologically embellished great power policy, even though it ultimately had a revolutionary and anti-imperialist grounding. There is a difference between revolutionary principle and national power politics. We shall return to the question of the international consequences of this kind of ideological misunderstanding and show the effects such ideological misinterpretation had on socialist world policies since Stalin's time.

7
The Twentieth Congress and Its Consequences

So far, we have attempted to clarify in outline just one group of consequences that evolved from the expropriation of private property in the means of production. This expropriation became the final basis of production, but we are not concerned with the way in which this confiscation was carried out in concrete terms. Naturally, it is out of the question to scientifically discuss this complex of issues intensively as well as extensively. We can only briefly point out some of the essential features of Soviet economic development. For the most part, there were two important stages during Stalin's domination—according to the brilliant analysis of F. Jánossy—the period of economic reconstitution in the thirties and that after the Second Imperialist World War. That means that an inherent tendency exists in the dialectic of economic development not only to reattain the level of production of the period just prior to setbacks stemming from an economic crisis, but also to arrive at a level of production that would have normally been achieved without the intervention of a crisis. Therefore, the accumulations taking place under such a dialectical economic leap will decisively exceed the normal rate of economic development. (In the Federal Republic of Germany, one refers to this developmental advance as an "economic miracle".) According to the same line of reasoning, the system of a centrally directed and planned economy demonstrates a vital advantage over a capitalist system of competition during such periods of economic reconstruction precisely because the calculation of the profitability of individual investments does not exist. A planned economy is able to develop these investments solely in terms of the optimal benefits to society.[34]

Stalinism was incapable of understanding Marx's actual ideas concerning the real presuppositions and driving forces of economic development. The manipulative style of Stalin prevented him from grasping these Marxist concepts, and even blinded him from noticing the consequences of his own *praxis*. In order to warrant Stalin's authoritarian economic policy, the party apparatus created a justificatory ideology: the planned economy of socialism must necessarily develop at a faster rate than capitalist society. When the

tempo of development slowed in the Soviet Union due to objective economic reasons, the Stalinist Soviet mind was perplexed. It could not explain the contradiction between the actual objective performance of the economy and the idealization of official Soviet ideology. Stalin's mandated theory of the more rapid growth of socialism also served political needs. It was used to justify repressive measures, for those who were accused of retarding economic growth were considered to be enemies of the party. Nevertheless, it must be concluded that this overcoming of the nonclassical beginning of the Communist Revolution, which was called "original accumulation" in the 1920s, has neared its completion. In spite of Stalin's ideological and methodological distortion, the Soviet economy before World War II reached its highest level of industrial development and even surpassed that level in the process of rebuilding after the defeat of Hitler. It is therefore self-evident why the process we have described here received the name of "original accumulation," a process that Marx described in his time and whose deterministic laws he laid bare. If we refer to the Marxian categories we purposely do so in order to bring to light the fundamental differences between the capitalist and socialist transition from feudalism. In the developmental history of capitalism, a whole historic period was dominated by brutal and violent measures for the purpose of carrying out a redistribution of the population between agriculture and industry. Capitalism can only become the ruling social formation upon the completion of this demographic revolution. Marx desired "to unravel the eternal laws of the capitalist mode of production."[35] It is only after this economic upheaval, that the normal capitalist process of production and reproduction can be instituted. From then on the worker can leave "the customary passage of things . . . to the natural laws of production."[36]

It does not require a detailed analysis to see that the so-called "original accumulation" in socialism is something qualitatively different than the above described capitalist pattern of growth. What confronts us here is the normal development of capitalism in its classical form. We accept as true Marx's analysis of the history and necessity of the English development. It is also clear that in the building of socialism in an advanced capitalist country the Soviet course of historical transition would not have been chosen. The Russian pattern of development concerns itself with underdevelopment, with raising the economic level to the productive capacity of advanced capitalism so that the economic level can be suitable to function as the foundation of a socialist system. Thus, even force, whose crucial role in history cannot be denied, receives an essentially different function in this context: although it is often a vehicle for the destruction of primitive relations of production (collectivization), its central purpose, however, remains the acceleration of the march to advanced development, the effective construction of the objective-economic quantitative and qualitative conditions of production which make socialism a

possibility. We have here—in contrast to genesis of capitalism—the use of force in which economic motives prevail. But—again in contrast to the capitalist process—after the completion of the economic foundation the specific quality of socialism must be consciously inserted so that this social formation assumes a socialist nature. These specific qualities of socialism are no longer purely economic. Capitalism is composed of a production process which is self-adjusting, whereas socialism means the conscious direction of new and complicated social tasks and possibilities.

In order to penetrate to the specific socialist character of a transition period, we emphasized some of the evolving moments in which the contrast between capitalism and socialism was given graphic expression. Let us add one other important factor. Even in technologically advanced capitalism, what we generally designate as culture is only an epiphenomenon of economic evolution and therefore must display a permanent asymmetry in relation to the economic base. This lack of symmetry manifests itself, in one case, as inadequate public education, even technical education lagging behind the objective needs of production. In recent years, this has been frequently discussed in most of the leading capitalist countries. In another case, the asymmetry becomes apparent in the fact that certain cultural phenomena have become fields for capitalist speculation and investment. Financially controlled by big capital, these cultural phenomena are manipulated and this is the culmination of the tendency to make culture a mere object of commodity exchange. Balzac and the *Communist Manifesto* already diagnosed this process. This development reached its epitome in this contemporary period. In contradiction to this capitalist development, socialist "original accumulation," even in its Stalinist form, has for the most part adhered to the principle of the socialist (not only economically determined) organization of culture. As proof of this assertion, it suffices to point to such important phenomena as the increase in availability of high-quality scientific and artistic works to social groups at the low end of the economic and cultural scale. There are, however, many problems in socialist education, for example, its extreme specialization. But its successes outweigh its failures, and clearly show that neither the capitalist nor socialist forms of "original accumulation" may be compared with each other in any essential respect.

From a historical perspective, the development of capitalism and socialism demonstrated the revolutionary origins of both these social formations. The emergence of capitalism out of feudalism and the emergence of socialism out of capitalism were revolutionary leaps out of the past and atypical of the normal evolutionary paths of social development. This fact they share. But after their sudden appearance out of feudalism and capitalism, the further course of growth of capitalism and socialism took divergent paths. As we indicated with the support of Marx, the transition to a capitalist social formation re-

sulted in the complete determinist hegemony of capitalist economics, the Kingdom of Necessity according to Marx's words. A capitalist social formation is void of conscious teleological direction, and is totally dominated by necessary economic laws. With an inherent driving autonomism, pure economic laws prevail in capitalism and determine the conditions of its future and even produce the next historic social formation within itself. (Even the dominant socially accepted personality types are products of the inner dialectic of the economy.) In terms of human teleological design, socialism distinguishes itself from all previous social formations. The capitalist enslavement to economic determination is no longer valid for the transition of socialism to the higher stage of communism. We have earlier referred to the illusions of Stalin and Khrushchev who believed that every social formation was bound to the same dynamics of development. We have also alluded to the few, but methodologically and theoretically decisive, comments of Marx on this complex of questions.

We must now penetrate to the inner core of these overlapping questions. Marx recognizes the economic (the Kingdom of Necessity) as the indispensable basis for communism (the Kingdom of Freedom). He rejects every form of utopianism, and at the same time designates the Kingdom of Freedom as "the other world" of the Kingdom of Necessity. "The development of human powers, which is valid as an end in itself," can never be considered as a mechanistic-inherent product of economic evolution. And even when Marx gives an account of the economic determinism of a social formation, he never neglects to also take into account the teleological *praxis* of men. For Marx, social evolution cannot be solely accounted for on the basis of the immanent dialectic of economic development. At the stage of the Kingdom of Freedom, we believe that the human species will labor under "conditions most worldly and adequate to its human nature."[37]

Based upon a sound grasp of the social determination of the human labor process, Marx penetrates to a central problem of this history. But in order to approach this problem correctly, one must not be misled by superficial analogies. As the achievements of the human labor process advanced to higher and higher levels, this produced a corresponding increase in mankind's self-pride regarding its own accomplishments. Even class societies experience growth in their self-esteem. This increased self-pride in the accomplishments of human species being, does not allow society to overlook the history of labor from the "instrumentum vocale" of slavery until the wage laborer, who must valorize his own labor power within the framework of the free market. The triumphs of human labor act to draw attention to the history of human labor. Contemporary capitalism has taken steps to improve the way people work, and these include the reduction of socially necessary labor time, the provision of hygienic working conditions and the practical application of industrial psychology to

the factory system. But these are false analogies. Without exception these measures are intended to increase the profitability of work, are aimed at the easiest possible improvement in productivity, have purely economic motives and are not for the enhancement of the powers of man as an end in itself. For that reason, economic profit is always the primary goal and the working person must sacrifice himself to the demands of capitalism. At lower levels of economic development, this sacrifice of the worker was carried through by brute force. Naked power is no longer used today to make the worker adjust, and this has caused a false evaluation of certain capitalist measures. The means have changed, but the end result is still the same. In contemporary capitalism, the economic is still primary, and the worker must still, as in earlier times, sacrifice himself to the objective conditions of production. What Marx has in mind was completely different: not the control of the economic over the human species, but the adjustment of the process of production to the worthy and dignified qualities of human nature. The needs of the species must dictate to the objective. Such a goal and its realization in *praxis* requires placing the needs of humanity above the laws of economics, which does not alter the fact that in order to accomplish this a highly advanced economy is still a presupposition (a basis, as Marx put it).

This same question is dealt with from a slightly different perspective in the *Critique of the Gotha Program*. When Marx speaks here about the nature of a communist society, ("from each according to their abilities, to each according to their needs"), he describes the revolutionary transformation brought about by communism as the fact that "labor is no longer a means to life but itself becomes the first need of life."[38] That is a transcendence of the horizon of the purely economic. Again, all capitalist analogies must be rejected, and its superficial "alleviations" and "acceptability" which are results of higher levels of productivity have nothing to do with the essential point. They still leave the economic in control of the species, whereas Marx wants to invert this process and allow human nature to dictate to the economic.

This is not an example of utopian thinking. Fourier expressed his ideas of the condition of the human species under socialism in a similar manner, that labor itself would be transformed into a kind of game. This dream of the future doubtlessly made a certain impression on Marx. But precisely his scientific study of economic laws allowed him to become aware of his own differences with Fourier's conception, which he now called "very blatantly naive." Marx amplifies his own thoughts on the nature of human labor by approaching this problem from every possible perspective. On the other hand, he defines labor generally as the highest accomplishment of the human species, and does not limit it to merely economic activity: "Really free labor, for example, musical composition is at the same time a cursed serious affair and a

most strenuous effort." And he broadens the definition in relation to the entire domain of labor in an outspoken polemic on Adam Smith with the following words: "To regard labor as a mere sacrifice, and because of that as value positing, as the price to be paid for things and which therefore establishes prices depending upon the amount of labor they cost, is a purely negative definition."[39] And in another place in the same work this definition is more fully explained in the following manner: "The development of individuality, and therefore not the transformation of the reduction of necessary labor time into surplus labor, but the actual reduction of the necessary labor time of a society to a minimum so that it is possible to carry out the artistic and scientific education of each individual through the time that has been saved and become free for all."[40] For that reason, the term "superfluous" when applied to labor can only have meaning in relation to the pure economic sphere. While there can be superfluous labor economically, there can be no superfluous labor when one speaks of the material self-reproduction of society and its constituent individuals. There is never enough labor when it comes to the enhancement of human powers and the improvement of societal productivity. Labor's economic superfluousness in no way makes it superfluous in the societal sense, but on the contrary substantiates its general social utility and indispensability. Furthermore, the early Marx views the division of labor as a social condition to be overturned by communism with the result of liberating laboring humanity from this "slavish oppression." But the later Marx, the Marx who makes a scientific study of economics, reverses himself and comes to look upon the division of labor as a vital presupposition of labor "as the first condition of life." The mature Marx comes to see that the division of labor ultimately heightens human powers because it heightens human productivity which reduces necessary labor time and increases free labor time. But enslavement of work is in no way simply a survival of primitive conditions that the perfection of the modern economy can overturn. Quite the contrary: the continuation of this enslavement is precisely the product of a technologically advanced capitalist society which in various forms lays claim to subjugated labor for its own purposes. Gradually, the subjugation of labor will also extend to the domains of art and science. It is no accident that the greater part of the current capitalist criticism of alienation refers to subjugation of this kind, concerns itself with this kind of slavery, although without seeing the true connection between this form of suppression and an economy based on private property.

One can perceive two interrelated but at the same time contradictory tendencies in these suggestive comments of Marxism which are of enormous importance to our problem. Marx does not content himself with the purely economic. On the contrary, he wants to show that the social preconditions of communism (even of socialism as an economic formation) can only be realized if social structures for the emancipation of labor are established in a tech-

nologically advanced productive society. In order to achieve the emancipation of labor, the liberation of human *praxis,* it is necessary to restructure certain hitherto prevailing conditions of the economy. This reformation will be carried through by means which do not endanger the functioning of this productive totality, but in contract, by advancing it further. We have seen that Marx places special emphasis on two moments: making the most worthy and dignified aspects of human species being the criteria by which to measure the economic process, and what is closely interconnected with that, the transcendence of the enslaving character of the division of labor. It hardly needs to be mentioned that it is impossible in both cases to introduce such changes with a single edict. Changes of this magnitude must be results of a slow societal process in which gradual modifications are initiated. The economic substructure provides the material possibilities for both the subjective and objective development of such tendencies.

Such processes simultaneously transform the nature of man himself. These processes must be objectively extant and take hold of man's active social being. The entire history of humanity shows that the idealistic striving for a mode of life embodying the real human being of men always bears results. The creation of a dream for the perfection of the species being of man, directed towards its goal by human *praxis,* is a powerful instrument for social advancement. Obviously there are exceptions, dead ends and failures in individual cases. In class societies objective economic laws still predominate over human teleology and thus hinder this upward advance. The common goal of the human species can be improved if the average life of the everyday (above all of labor, of economic *praxis*) is applied in an objective manner to the valorization of social being. This tendency to improve the condition of man is not to be denied or curtailed by various kinds of repression, as is and was the case in all previously existing social formations. While man through his own social activity creates the conditions which make him a truly human creature for the first time, this period will be designated—even the socialist social formation—as the precursor to that great decisive moment which Marx characterizes as the end of the prehistory of mankind.

Like Marx, we speak here of labor as the central question of the human being of man. It is, however, evident that the problems previously discussed relate to the totality of human *praxis,* of human life in general. One thinks— in order to take a position closely connected with the economic realm—about the principle of distribution in accordance with need that is to be consummated in a communist society. However, the principles of communism are unattainable as long as the satisfaction of need, exclusively belonging to the ruling classes in former times and in the modern world extended to the broad layers of the productive classes, becomes a consumerism of prestige. In the contemporary world, one does not primarily consume to gratify the basic

needs of life, but rather as a means to achieve victory in the warfare of competition, in order to acquire social prestige and in order to climb up the social ladder. The huge growth of the consumer industry and the service sector has its economic justification exactly in this struggle for social status on the part of the consumer. Without a change in the fundamentals of commercial society, capitalism will be entrapped by increasing stagnation. It will be impossible to redirect the energies of commercial society toward an organized *praxis* leading to the enhancement of human life unless the economic is seen as the object of human teleological design. The force of individuality is limited, for the removal of the enslaving character of the division of labor cannot be overturned by an individual acting alone.

Up to this point, we have spoken continuously about the idea of the everyday life of man, but only in a cursory fashion. The discussion has been incomplete because we were unable to detail the entire spectrum of problems associated with this issue. However, the introduction of this concept enables us to make a more penetrating analysis of the meaning of socialist democracy. Earlier, we made the following statement: in contrast to the citizen-idealism of bourgeois democracy, an ideal which began during the highpoint of the bourgeois revolution, the subject of socialism is the material life of man in everyday existence. Bourgeois society dualistically divided the individual between *homme,* and *citoyen* and the socialist emphasis on the everyday is not intended as the canonization of the material *homme,* one part of that dualism. Socialist democracy has as its task the transcendence of this dualism in the Kingdom of Freedom.

This principle is not a mere speculative construction, and this is shown— as we have already mentioned—by the mass movements which have introduced and accomplished socialist revolutions. We mean, of course, the use of the Soviets in 1871, 1905 and 1917. We have already sketched how this movement aimed at building a social order which was efficient and which corresponded to the elementary class interests of the productive workers, stretching from the everyday real life questions of factory and housing issues to the great political problems of the entire society. After the victorious ending of the Civil War, these goals were replaced by a bureaucratic apparatus and Stalin practically demolished the entire Soviet system and fixed this bureaucratic control in its final form. (As represented in textbooks and in official propaganda publications, the ideological justification of this transformation has no interest at all for those of us who are concerned in the social character of reality). The productive masses lost the role of subjective agency in the evolution of society. They again became objects of an ever stronger and inclusive bureaucratic system that controlled all the problems of their actual lives.

For all practical purposes, the Stalinization of Russia blocked all possibilities for socialism to develop as the Kingdom of Freedom. As we have seen, Lenin never wavered in his opinion that the higher ideals of a socialist democ-

racy always remained a heuristic guide to the immense struggle of Russia in the 1920s. Even while the young and very weak Soviet Republic struggled for self-preservation in the Civil War, Lenin maintained that the principles of the higher forms of socialist life should never be allowed to disappear from the platform of the practical, daily *What Is To Be Done?* He was convinced that Marx and Engels did not hand down a rigid blueprint for the development of socialism, but that its discovery, its correct implementation, was a new task for the present. However, he surmised that there must be an organic connection between activity oriented toward the future and the actual demands of the day. He understood that the future could only be realized through human *praxis*. This connection between teleological action and immediate need was a major characteristic of his thought and behavior, and the movement toward higher ends was never absent from his activity. This methodology of action was present in his continuous admonition to colleagues to concentrate on "the next link in the chain." Nevertheless, there were historical constraints to his own ideas. His own thought processes were conditioned by the historical environment in which he lived. Lenin's definition of habituation which we discussed earlier, did not relate to the complex of questions involved in the interrelationship between teleology and immediacy. His discussion of habituation was concerned with the preconditions necessary for the "withering away of the state." It was not concerned with the linkage between objective and subjective forces that was decisive for the revolutionary transition from capitalism to socialism especially in its advanced stages. So his concept of Soviet democracy, his polemic against Trotsky in the debate over the trade unions, did not pass beyond the historical constraints in which he lived and most importantly the prevailing attitudes within the Bolshevik party.

Lenin has significance for us today in terms of his methodology of action. In his relation to the complex of questions regarding the transition from capitalism to socialism, he is the first to conceptualize a pure Marxist framework and provide a pure Marxist theoretical foundation for daily *praxis*. One finds the universal theoretical foundations for social analysis, and only this, in Marx. Lenin's behavior cannot be used today as an unquestionable model— or as an unchallenged paradigm—for he acted in situations which were qualitatively different from the problems of today. One the one hand, Lenin's statements must be interpreted from the context of the great upheaval of 1917 in which the spontaneously emergent Soviet movement achieved a central position. On the other hand, they must be seen in the context of the critical transition at the time of the introduction of NEP, during which he made the commitment to rescue the most significant democratic socialist accomplishment of the revolution from the threatening process of bureaucratization. Insofar as possible, he wished to transmit to a coming historical period the still-surviving residues of the Soviet movement.

We find ourselves today in a completely different situation than the pe-

riod described above. After the decades long domination of Stalin, the factors that produced authoritarian socialism have practically fallen into total disuse. The historical factors that created Stalinism were both objective and subjective. Today a completely different set of both objective and subjective factors have led to the wide public knowledge and condemnation of the Stalin period. From the point of view of our problem regarding socialist democracy, it is most significant that under Stalin the self-activity of the masses was practically extinguished. Not only did this occur in the great questions of politics, but also in the control of their own daily lives. We emphasize the word practically, for even in the Stalin period, on the formal level, many questions were dealt with according to the procedures of formal democracy such as secret voting and universal suffrage. Nevertheless, Stalin's bureaucratic manipulation and domination were so extensive and powerful that, in general, such voting gave little vent to the actual wishes, aversions and opinions of the masses. Since this is the case, the actual situation of 1917 must be looked upon as having been eradicated a long time ago.

The political and social deformation which Stalin imposed came to be looked upon as the normal condition of socialism. The idea that the class struggle continually intensified during the dictatorship of the proletariat was used by Stalin as the historical justification of his totalitarianism. This idea was often—although never fundamentally—criticized in Stalin's time, but it nevertheless resulted in a reputed theoretic legitimation of his *praxis* of brutal hegemony. He created an atmosphere in which a mental civil war arose. The paranoid search for internal enemies became the standard method of behavior: everyone was a potential traitor even when the actual civil war had come to an end. One must remember that the first critiques of Stalin at the twentieth Party Congress proceeded from the point of view that the Great Purges of the 1930s were politically unnecessary, for the opposition had already been dispersed and rendered politically powerless. The opposition was not a real danger, and a civil war did not exist. Even though merely partial, this essentially correct critique of the Stalinist system, however, had no immediate political consequences. Without interruption, the dogma of the civil war was renewed in the internal policies of the Soviet government even after Khrushchev. Soviet governments after the twentieth Party Congress treated such critiques as overtly or covertly subversive statements which were to be suppressed because they were not in agreement with officially sanctioned views. Starting with the twentieth Party Congress, this promising objective assessment of the Stalinist system was halted by succeeding Kremlin rulers. Even though the twentieth Party Congress was restrained in its attacks on Stalin, successive Soviet administrations reverted back to Stalinism.

The positive accomplishments of the twentieth Party Congress rested in the fact that it started the critique of the Stalinist system. The weakness of the

twentieth Party Congress grew out of the fact that its critique was only partial. Its attack centered on peripheral issues. It did not cut to the systemic core of Stalinism. The denunciation of the personality cult shows the insufficiency of such critiques and reveals why the consequences of the twentieth Party Congress were so limited. The refutation of the personality cult was not in itself incorrect, but only incomplete. This was equally true of the thesis that Stalin's method of domination grew out of his destruction of the rule of law. Nothing false was stated in either case, but both theoretically and practically overlooked the essence of the decisive problems. The brutal manipulation of the masses based on dogmatic presuppositions is not only the product of a skillful, egomaniacal, tyrannical personality. History constantly gave and gives new illustrations in which totalitarian domination is also exercised through collective and persistent repressive practices. In addition, the destruction of the rule of law does not in itself result in totalitarianism. Every modern state possesses sophisticated juridical techniques which equip it to carry out legal manipulation. This is necessary in order to ensure social and political conformity. Just as the personality cult in Russia in open, cynical violation of legality labeled individual behavior in conformity with political dogma as socially normal, and individual behavior in violation of political dogma as socially abnormal so every state possesses the means of legal manipulation so it can dictate its political standards on the population. Stalinism was not reducible to personal totalitarianism or the uprooting of the rule of law.

The core of the Stalinist system rests in other causes. The Stalinist system was rooted in an economic problem, which had profound social consequences. It was the same economic problem that perplexed those who were involved in the struggle for power after Lenin's death. The core question concerned the so-called "original accumulation." Earlier, we tried to show how the positive aspects of the socialization of the means of production were capable of creating the conditions for an effective socialist state. Within the context of "original accumulation," within the context of rapid industrialization, Stalin's system of brutal hegemony had many successes. (Stalin could not see that the successes were based on specific socioeconomic conditions.) Indeed, the economic successes of Stalin increased during the two periods of "reconstruction." However, when a specific level of production was reached, the problem facing the socialist state changed. The new question no longer concerned "original accumulation" but the quality of goods produced and the excellence of services delivered to the people. On the economic level, Stalinism was appropriate for the period of rapid industrialization, but lost its historic effectiveness when the Soviet economy advanced to a higher level.

The Stalinist system failed to adjust to the new socioeconomic order it created. Stalinism tried to govern this new post-World War II socioeconomic order with outmoded political methods. A disjuncture opened between the

politics and society of the Soviet state, and Stalinism tried to govern a post-World War II society with the political structure of the 1920s. This can be seen in the case of the technical specialists. In the period of "original accumulation," the new Soviet state inherited the social strata of technical specialists from prerevolutionary capitalism and the Tzar. The majority of these people were either alienated from socialism or directly hostile to it. The situation today is totally different. These Tzarist technical specialists who were enemies of socialism either died out or retired during the decades' long construction of the socialist base, so this hostile strata disappeared. More importantly, however, and we already mentioned this in other contexts, the socialist education system produced a technological intelligentsia loyal to the Soviet system. The numerous technological intelligentsia were not communist in the sense of adhering to a specific world view, but neither were they enemies or mere uncommitted spectators within the Soviet system. Produced by the educational system of socialism, they were Soviet men, who thought of their work in the process of production as their natural vocation and who, for that reason, justifiably wanted to be recognized and treated as genuine and dignified contributors to the system. This younger generation rebelled against the Stalinist system on objective social grounds. By this time, the methods through which the Stalinist political commissars controlled the technological specialists were already in place. However, the economic and political behavior of this new, indispensable strata of experts, the force for the further advance of the Soviet Union, demanded changed administrative methods in comparison to those practiced under Stalin.

This question of new administrative methods is ultimately connected with the control and purposes of production itself. Economically and politically, it has become increasingly impossible to concentrate the development of production almost exclusively on the construction of heavy industry, in insensitive disregard of consumer needs. In the best cases, and appeal to the masses to adapt an ascetic policy of consumption is only justifiable and defensible during periods of revolutionary idealism. The point is that those methods of bureaucratic concentration and centrally controlled planning that functioned successfully for the purposes of constructing a relatively advanced technological industrial apparatus during the 1930s, must be condemned as totally inefficient at present. The more rigid the centralized bureaucratic planning mechanisms, the more difficult it is to both quantitatively and qualitatively meet the needs of popular consumption. This deficiency already shows itself in the manufacture of the means of production devoted to the making of consumer goods. At this point, we do not consider the applicability of the model of a correctly functioning war economy, because it is impossible for the inflexible control of wartime production to be a criteria for civilian everyday life.

We believe that socioeconomic pressures in the communist world have brought about a period of reconstruction and simultaneously the time has arrived for a revival of speculations on renewed attempts to call socialist democracy into life. Two false alternatives, which we treated at the beginning of this book, step to the foreground within the communist world: the attempt at the partial improvement of this crisis through the preservation of the essentials of the Stalinist method, or the introduction of those methods that dominate in the West. The reasons for this conflict are easy to understand. On the one hand, the centralized planning bureaucracy does not want to renounce its absolute leading role, even though every close investigation shows how little its applied criteria, tasks, or means of control have succeeded in satisfying the genuine actual needs of men. The Old Guard proposes that the present apparatus be provided with cybernetic machines in order to carry through its calculations with more exactitude, as if a fundamentally flawed mechanism could really be improved through such means. From the side of the reformers, on the other hand, the model of western industrial organization is proposed. The reformers proceed from the false presupposition that the market competition practiced under capitalism (with its advantages and disadvantages) can only fulfill its dream in a socialist society, for without the existence of competing capitalists society can adjust perfectly to market forces. Reformers and Stalinists engage in preliminary experiments. But these are based upon inseparable and indecisive compromises that leave the still-powerful central planning mechanism unshatterable and intact.

It is not our purpose to enter upon an exhaustive discussion of these economic problems. It is more important to see the interconnection between the economic and the political. The fact that economic reform is on the agenda for socialist societies means that the question of socialist democracy has also become an immediate issue. We have again and again pointed to the Soviet movement as the historically specific, uniquely democratic form of socialist society. We must, however, acknowledge, if we are not to deal with the question of democratization in an abstract manner but in a relevant socially-historical form, that we face a radically new situation. Lenin faced such a situation when he theoretically struggled with this complex of problems at the time he introduced NEP. The basic question is: are the Soviets still relevant to the problems of democratization as it exists in socialist societies today? The Soviet movement, the pressure of the broad masses, was that social dynamism that immediately connected the everyday affairs of men with the great questions of high politics. This movement of mass initiative, appears to have been brought to a complete stop. As we have already indicated, when social institutions lose their validity and become atrophied, the masses develop a deep disinterest in them. When the political structure of a society is no longer legitimate, does not correspond to democratic interests, the masses slip into

apathy. Today the people participate in meetings, discussions and votes since it meets their immediate self-interest not to appear to the official apparatus as members of an opposition. Nevertheless, they remain preponderately passive or their participation limits itself to the routinized approval of official proposals. The participants are deeply convinced that taking part in such discussions has practically no significance for the issues themselves, or can frequently cause the participants personal harm. On the average, these facts are generally well-known, although the official reports paint a totally different picture and this becomes part of the public record. Political participation is reduced to mere automatonism.

On the other hand, vibrant and free public opinion exists, but in an underground and subterranean form. This covert "public opinion" does not express itself in an open or formal manner. Within Eastern European society, and dealing with all aspects of social life, this public opinion is primarily a matter of private conversation, of immediate and spontaneous discussions between two people. The real influence of such a secretive world is extraordinarily various. However, it would be wrong to underestimate it, or to judge it as completely ineffectual. I mention only in passing that it has been my personal experience for decades that success in the cultural areas is determined by this subterranean public opinion. Whether a work has artistic merit or is superficial, whether a novel has been successfully adapted into film, are questions decided upon more by this secretive world than by the published critics (above all, by the official writers).

It is much more difficult to assess the impact that this secretive world has in the economic field. One must never forget that this system of regulation, this manipulation of the entire social process from above, is much too alienated from reality to be able to fulfill its original purpose of stifling all free thought and action. There is less bureaucratic domination under capitalism than is the case under Stalinist socialism. For example, under capitalism there are still wild-cat railroad strikes which arise when workers spontaneously stop obeying their employers and consequently bring all commerce to a *de facto* standstill. Worker protest exists under capitalism and calls into being a compromise between capital and labor. These kinds of industrial adjustments, a compromise between capital and labor, normally occur by means of private negotiations between management and the proletariat. For the most part, these adjustments, in which both labor and capital gain, concern issues of the conditions of labor in factories and the means of transportation. In present-day socialism, there is more social alienation than under capitalism. Because Stalinist socialism is more abstract, mechanical, and bureaucratic then capitalism, the phenomena of labor strikes is just as frequent under socialism as in the world of private property. Labor unrest still exists in the world of the so-called workers' paradise.

This mute, subterranean public opinion is the opening wedge to a democratization of existing socialism. It is a social force, and its mobilization into a systematic public-*praxis* appears to me to be the first step toward a socialist democracy. The democratization of socialism is impossible through the old methods. It cannot be achieved by a spontaneous revolutionary upheaval. It cannot be achieved by attempting to resurrect the Soviet movement, which was characterized by the extension of direct democracy in all areas of social life during the period of revolution. None of the objective or subjective conditions for such a return to the past exist. Anyone who dreams of a rebirth of a spontaneously generated Soviet movement condemns themselves to live in empty fantasy. Such illusions spring from private enthusiasm for and deep commitment to the heroism of the past, but it is hopeless to expect that a movement equal in breadth and intensity to that of the years 1871 or 1905 will ever occur again. The Stalinist period broke the continuity of this Soviet movement with authoritarian measures, at the same time that the movement itself was already internally dominated by reactionary tendencies. Just as it is impossible on the theoretical level to have an immediate, total, methodologically and substantively correct renaissance of Marxism, so it is impossible to have a direct renewal of this great tradition from the past. The Soviet movement was historically generated, it was the product of a decade of social development and this cannot be recreated by individual or party resolutions. To think that the Soviet movement can be brought back into existence voluntaristically, is to remain imprisoned in the dangerous closed circle of the bureaucratic priority of tactics. Bureaucratic tactics can indeed retard or slacken the course of history, or direct it on a wrong path. But bureaucratic tactics are incapable of mobilizing the masses, in the form in which they exist, for a radical and extended process of reform.

The awakening of this subterranean movement cannot imitate the passionate, spontaneous forms of the earlier Soviet movement. Learning from experience, the growth of this mute, covert tendency into a mode of relating to society as a self-conscious force of criticism cannot copy earlier institutional models. But this does not mean that a different kind of renewal is impossible. Indeed, we believe that the overturning of the mechanistic, centralized and hyperbureaucratic practice of the present system of planning cannot be carried through without an effective appeal to this subterranean popular force that has been suppressed into anonymity. Critics of centralized planning have already spoken out on the necessity of decentralization. Propaganda and deceit, the old methods of Stalinist parties, will not accomplish this debureaucratization. This redirection of a socialist economy must be experienced by the masses on a daily basis as a complete break with the Stalinist tradition. The masses must be reeducated, reactivated, and once again feel their potency. For that reason, it is insufficient to merely remove the psychological-social barriers to the free

expression of individual opinion. In its fear of faction-building organizations, the Stalinist period had not only repressed individual opinion, but systematically persecuted and uprooted every type of worker association devoted to the critique and improvement of the system or to the elimination of specific dysfunctions. The destruction of the bureaucracy is impossible without the active involvement of the masses, without spontaneous, often ephemeral, temporary and frequently formless associations. Through the conscious mobilization of this subterranean movement, the masses must once again gain a sense of empowerment that they can improve their everyday lives.

The long duration of the Stalinist system had ruinous effects on the creativity of the masses. They lost faith in themselves, in the belief in the possibilities of their own personal-social *praxis*. Since it was appropriate under such circumstances, under the 1917 Revolution's explosive and spontaneously developed Soviet movement, the masses accustomed themselves to participatory behavior in the conduct of public affairs. During the period of Stalin, not active but passive behavior became the rule, because this was appropriate under such authoritarian circumstances. Because it has a double meaning, emphasizing the significance of the concept of habituation in Lenin's thought is both truthful and instructive. It contains two alternatives: it can signify radical change, however useful or harmful; or, according to its inherent quality, it can signify social accommodation. During the time of the Stalinist priority of tactics, when an entire society became inclusively and thoroughly manipulated by the bureaucracy, both the active participants and noncommitted passive individuals had to habituate themselves to the type of life they wished to adopt within such a system.

We shall speak now about the social formation of types of human *praxis*, about the social genesis of models of human personality. But the heroic days of the French and Russian revolutions are over, and rather than greatness we have the average. The contemporary world makes for the small, and we must be satisfied to be pale reflections of more noble prototypes from the past. Within the socialist world, there is the active-idealist type. Eastern European critics see the political activist as a contemporary caricature of the *citoyen* model. The political activist possesses idealism (in the sense of Marx), but with the important nuance that this contemporary type can neither be a self-sacrificing idealist organized into a revolutionary movement by a dominant personality, as in the time of the Jacobin movement, nor a formal, empty, superficial individual as represented in the present by bourgeois democrats. Socialist activists must limit themselves to the dedicated execution of party resolutions and believe that they are truly serving the cause of the proletarian revolution. (In order to prevent any misunderstanding, we wish to make clear that the point of this remark is not directed against discipline in general. The point is related to the important question of the social formation of a human

type, or a mode of *praxis*. The decisive difference, the contrast, concerns the question of criticism and transcendence. There is a discipline that does not allow criticism and improvement, and this is only slavish obedience. But there is a discipline that incorporates participation, engagement, self-correction, and abolition, and this is indispensable for any political movement.)

In addition to the forms of human *praxis* already mentioned, there emerges a contrasting type which uses its social position in order to raise its personal standard of living. It does this with either acceptable, surreptitious, or even illegal means. Its psychology and morality are extremely proximate to that of the *homme* of bourgeois society, but it is still qualitatively distinct from bourgeois behavior because no human exploitation arises from this manipulative activity. Naturally, we do not mean that the increase of one's own standard of living through one's own work is an illegitimate form of behavior. What we question is a *praxis* that manipulates the law, legal loopholes, traditional and emerging patterns of habituation, for the egoistic end of its own self-aggrandizement. At this point a qualification must be introduced: there can be no comparison between socialist production, particularly in its massive, centralized, and bureaucratic forms, and bourgeois society. This is true because the whole structure of socialist society makes any accumulation derived from the exploitation of the work of other human beings impossible from the first. The kinds of jobs created by socialist society are nonexploitative. The overwhelming majority of laboring people in socialism are included in this category. They perform their work with more of less personal conscientiousness. However, there is a disparity between the laboring people's aggressive desire to improve their standards of living and their political apathy. They are interested in economic advancement, but they surrender their right to make corrective critical interventions into the existing political structure.

These remarks are not intended to offer an exhaustive examination of the totality of human behavioral types under socialism and the problems arising from them. Accordingly, it is solely necessary to indicate those subjective societal tendencies that necessarily evolve out of the order of production initiated by Stalin. Our main purpose is to distinguish every form of socialist critique of the Stalinist system from every form of bourgeois criticism. Ever since the introduction of NEP, capitalist anticommunism has argued that socialist society would develop in a fashion similar to that of capitalism, or that a single industrial society would evolve on a global scale in which the differences between capitalism and socialism would disappear. On the contrary, and this has been alluded to many times in these pages, the economic being of all socialist states shows that the socialization of the means of production necessarily created objective relationships that must remain qualitatively different than in a class society. In addition, however, a penetrating and pro-

found analysis of the presently existing socialist societies shows that it indeed objectively demolished and made impossible any exploitation of man by man, but developed in such an economic and social manner that its political structure was not capable—not yet—of calling socialist democracy into being. Socialist society has not politically empowered socialist man. The laboring masses do not have the means to transform themselves into active subjects. They do not know how to make the socialization of the means of production the basis from which they can emerge as free men in a communist social formation. The imputation that already existing socialism lacks an objective socialist character belongs to the armory of bourgeois slanders and demagoguery. On the contrary, the construction and extension of the subjective character of socialist society remains the great present and future task of all who sincerely affirm that socialism is the only worthwhile alternative to the contradictions of capitalism.

Considered from an objective standpoint, we are dealing with the fact that the economic and social order instituted by Stalin was capable of overcoming the immanent and inclusive economic underdevelopment of Russia, and coupled with the unexpectedly rapid growth of the forces of production did lay the basis for the Kingdom of Freedom. This statement does not relate to the question of socialist democracy, nor to the fact that socialism was unable to destroy the bountifulness of the capitalist economic formation. The Kingdom of Freedom was an adequate basis for the uniquely human self-creation of man. Paradoxically, the Stalinist system not only created the basis for human self-genesis, but also created objective and insurmountable barriers to the realization of this process of human becoming. We have already touched on this paradox in our analysis of bourgeois democracy. Marx tries to explain how in the fundamental constitutions of the French Revolution, which established the doctrine of human rights, men also placed limits on the freedom of men. He states: "However, human rights, freedom based not on the association of man with men, but much more on the separation of men from humanity. It is the right of separation, the right of limitation by limited individuals themselves." Bourgeois society "allows every man to find in his fellow men not the realization but the barrier to his own freedom."[41]

The texts that Marx interprets accurately depicts social reality, although their authors were infused with the heroic illusions of revolutionary transformation. If one wishes to gain a correct understanding of these texts, one must regard them as offering a true portrayal of the actual conditions of bourgeois society. Their great precursor is Hobbes, who describes the condition of man under capitalism as "a war of all against all." The work of the Marquis de Sade also reflects the nature of the human condition under capitalism, and the contemporary bourgeoisie has newly discovered de Sade as a serious thinker. The sexual act becomes a mirror for human relationships under capitalism.

The Pure Alternative: Stalinism or Socialist Democracy / 155

The Marquis de Sade does not describe the sexual act as a common activity shared by two people, as a partnership between two equals, but rather as an act in which the man exploits the woman as nothing but an object of lust, a dominated object whose participation, feelings, and reactions are of complete indifference to the male. By showing the extremes to which the idea of possession can be carried, Kant's famous definition of marriage details the inherent social reality of capitalism. Kant fuses the cynical egoism of de Sade with the language of free commodity exchange of a capitalist social formation. Kant says: "Marriage is the agreement between two people of the opposite sexes to the life-long exclusive possession of each other's sexual organs."

As frequently happens today, this last statement should not shift the objective focus of our discussion from the sex act as a characterization of capitalist reality to sex in and for itself. It should only point out that Marx's universal characterization of the fundamental structure of capitalist reality must also be true in the particular, must also accurately describe every type of human *praxis* under capitalism. Marx had already expressed this capitalist universal human relationship in the *Communist Manifesto*. The following sentences are contained in that work concerning the *praxis* of the bourgeoisie as the ruling class, behavior necessarily induced by a capitalist economy. "It has dissolved personal dignity in exchange-value . . . it transformed the doctor, the jurist, the pastor, the poet, the man of science into its paid wage-workers."[42] The question that is placed on the historical agenda concerns the process of the humanization of humanity. The socialist revolution concerns the transition of a lower social formation to a higher one, and the emergence of a new human social existence based on this higher social formation. Through the production of a new social environment, this new being of humanity, this socialist being, will be able to create new forms of human interdependence and cooperation by means of the spontaneous *praxis* of socialist humanity.

It is necessary to understand the distinctions between the transition from feudalism to capitalism and the transition from capitalism to socialism. History has witnessed many revolutionary transformations of society, but they each have their unique qualities. The transition from feudalism to capitalism was concerned with the rise of radical capitalist economic relationships. If one compares the division of labor in the period of manufacturers in the eighteenth and nineteenth centuries with that of the guilds in feudalism, this radical change in the relationship of each worker to his own labor process becomes immediately apparent. As a consequence of this transition, the attitude of the workers—they are compelled to adopt either an affirmative or negative attitude toward this new situation—will be dictated to the worker by the social division of labor.

The transition from capitalism to socialism has an extremely different nature. The transition from feudalism to capitalism concerned itself with the

change from one exploitative class society to another, although an exploitation corresponding to a higher level of the unfolding of the productive forces. In the transition from capitalism to socialism, on the contrary, the process concerns the transcendence of exploitation *sui generis*. The transition from feudalism to capitalism brought forth radical alterations in all modes of material production. (It is sufficient to indicate, as we have already done, the differences in the division of labor under the guild system and capitalist manufacture.) Whereas changes in the mode of production and the elimination of exploitation are social changes, technological change is quite different. As distinct from social change, technological developments did not differentiate between capitalism and socialism, but have an independent inherent tendency of their own. (A factory built for capitalist production can also, for the most part and without great modifications, function under socialism and vice versa.) But the transition from capitalism to socialism or the socialization of the means of production, totally transforms society. The socialization of the means of production can reshape the mode of work and, because of that, the mode of activity in the everyday life of man. When the forces of production are governed by society in general, this brings about a radical transformation of man and his relation to his labor and to his fellow men. These are the exact social presuppositions that prepare the transition from socialism to communism. In his war essays, Lenin clearly stated that socialism was indeed founded on an economic basis, but the economic in no way formed the entire context of socialism.[43] Some will doubt that man will be transformed through a transformation of social relationships. But this does not mean we must adopt the opposite view that man will be transformed solely through ideological transformations. Ideology, as a theoretic-practical moment of social development, as a means for the fighting out of social conflicts that are created by the process of material production, is indeed an important, even indispensable, component of every society's superstructure. However, it is still only a reflection, an image by which men try to comprehend the objective transformation of production. Ideology must have a material foundation so that its practical influence as a force in society is not annulled. To be effective, ideology must be intensively and extensively grounded within the objective social existant.

    Social change is always the result of objective and subjective forces. Historical transitions are pushed forward by both automatic-economic and conscious-ideological forces. Material production must bring forth—naturally not without the mediation of the ideological response—changes in men, their transformation into conscious agents who will teleologically plan the future social formation. The immanent, automatic functioning of the economy cannot bring such a human transformation into existence from its own spontaneous dialectic. The economy—as the basis of the coming-to-be—must be

directed by human design. The objective must be structured by human intelligence so that it can create those social conditions that call forth in men the ability to engage in cooperative relationships with his fellow man. The objective must react on men so they become capable of realizing themselves as the genuine being of the species.

Our comparison of the transition to capitalism and socialism has shown us that the revolutionary change to socialism has no comparison in history. Because socialism is so unique, there are no parallel historical examples by which to judge it. For that reason, as one attempts to prognosticate the nature of a future socialist order, one must be circumspect and cautious about applying lessons drawn from previous historical social formations. Marx, in the *Communist Manifesto,* had good reason for calling capitalism the last social formation in history to rest on the means of exploitation. In so doing, he not only referred to economic exploitation but to all the consequences that such expropriation inserted in intersubjective relationships. Both Lassalle and Stalin put forth fallacious definitions of socialism, for they both reduced it to the mere economic. For Lassalle, socialism was synonymous with the right of "full compensation for labor." Stalin also evaded the essential point when he also gave an economist's definition of socialism by equating it with the abolition of surplus labor completely forgetting that surplus labor was indispensable for societal development. The new definition of socialism concerns the internal and external transformation of human life by means of surplus labor, which is simultaneously objectively economic and subjectively human. To repeat earlier statements: the bourgeoisie likes to refer to the humanization of human labor, which they claim is also taking place under capitalism. However, in capitalism, it is man, the subjective, who is compelled to adjust to the economic, the objective. Under capitalism, the so-called humanization of labor signifies the creation of means by which humans can be made to adapt to the existing or newly introduced modes of labor. The improvements of the conditions of labor are a means by which to improve productivity, and by increasing productivity to also increase the rate of exploitation of surplus labor. The humanization of labor has a completely different meaning under socialism. There it is the economic, the objective, that must bend and accommodate man, the subjective. Under socialism, the subjective rules the objective. Under socialism, the mode of human labor must correspond to the species being of man, and the being of man is made the criteria and guiding principle for the organization of the condition of labor.

With the elimination of the dominance of the economic, it is clear that the reshaping of the process of production can itself be a material force toward the socialist purpose of creating a higher humanity. It is readily clear that only a socialist-planned economy can have as its goal the production of a higher humanity. The socialization of the means of production is a necessary precondi-

158 / The Process of Democratization

tion for the bringing forth of a human teleological design for the achievement of the socialist ideal. However, it is just as clear that human teleological activity cannot in itself produce socialism. The subjective requires the objective. Human *praxis* can achieve a great deal, but the full emancipation and humanization of labor also requires the requisite economic-objective level of productivity.

One must speak of a reciprocal process between the subjective and the objective. The fulfillment of the species being of man must be brought into correspondence with the possibilities of production in order to be realizable in the practical world. But the humanization of labor cannot be totally derived from the sphere of production alone; it must be introduced, as Lenin took pains to say, from outside, from a source external to those who are involved in the immediate processes of production. It must be cosponsored by the political-subjective. That is exactly the specific function of socialist democracy. The specificity of socialist democracy is determined by this particular politicosocial task, to bring an external theoretic-humanizing perspective into the economic domain. This task also determines the specific difference between socialist democracy and every previous democratic formation resting on private possession, exploitation, and estrangement, especially in its capitalist mode. This political-societal task of socialist democracy, shaped by the socialist revolution of 1917, received a direct, mass expression in the repeatedly mentioned great, enthusiastic, spontaneous Soviet movement. We have no firm guidelines on how socialist democracy can be made an organic component of socialist society. The lessons of the present or past offer us no generalized blueprint. The revolutions of 1871 and 1905 were repressed before the problems of socialist democracy as an immediate social possibility could be addressed. In Lenin's last years of life, the Soviet movement was overtaken by atrophy and fragmentation. We have commented on Lenin's futile efforts to preserve the Soviets as the political content of socialism, as the living force of democracy struggling against the ever irresistible advance of bureaucracy.

We know that these endeavors were shattered. Today, the crucial question within the socialist world is: how can Marxism be reconstructed? What are the social forces from which a renaissance of Marxism will spring? Realistically, the attempt to resurrect the Soviet movement is impossible. There is no theoretic basis for any hope of Soviet reconstruction. In addition, the revolutionary conditions of 1917 which gave rise to their spontaneous growth cannot be recaptured, and no one desires to return to the period of their debility which started in the 1920s. The present task of Marxism, the revival of Marxism after its long petrification under Stalin, cannot be directly connected to any existing societal movement. This is also true for the mute, subterranean movement about which we have already spoken, for it is incapable of providing any theoretical foundation for such a rebirth. On the contrary, the attempt

at renewal must be initiated on the basis of theory. A Marxist analysis of the contemporary crisis of socialism must be undertaken, for only when we understand the reasons for such a crisis can we begin to redefine socialism and establish the principle for a conscious renaissance of Marxism. Only on the basis of a reconstructed Marxist theory can we also set forth a tactic which corresponds to the actual conditions of the moment, a proper individual *praxis*. When one is involved in a theoretical reformulation, one is embarked upon a consciously inspired, consciously directed, extended, and contradictory process. One may never lose sight of the fertile dialectic involved in redefining socialism, the conflict between objective and subjective factors, which should be built into our understanding of this higher social order. On the one hand, there is human *praxis,* which is the direct opposite of the economic, which does not limit economic development but on the contrary organizes the purely economic to better satisfy social needs. On the other hand, the process of building a socialist democracy is an undertaking of long duration, and the precondition for its growth will be set when social *praxis* is brought into unison with pure economic necessity. Theoretic, learned insights into the content of socialist democracy grow in a continuous, uninterrupted manner from day to day, indicating that there must be harmony between the political and the deterministic objective. The fusion of the subjective and the objective is the future direction for a new Marxist analysis of socialist economics, and our speculations here are only intended as a sketch that merely seeks to discover the most general principles for such an enterprise. Therefore, it is impossible to attempt to enter into any more detailed analysis. For that reason, it is all the more important to create clarity over theoretic foundations. In his famous and correct distinction between spontaneity and consciousness (Marxist consciousness, pure class consciousness), Lenin said that "consciousness could only be brought to the worker . . . that means from an area outside the economic fight . . . a domain from which all this knowledge can be created."[44] Lenin spoke of a matrix of forces, an interrelationship of all social forces, meaning the totality of society in its historic dynamic. Lenin, who made these remarks under the influence of the conditions of 1903 and who we believe was correct, did not merely relate to the realities of his own historical circumstances but referred to something more universal in principle. It is imperative to return to Lenin's method, which is an exact continuation of the method of Marx. The renaissance of Marxism can only emerge out of a return to the method and theory of Marx, for a correct *praxis* in our contemporary situation is a direct result of a correct Marxist analysis of that contemporary situation.

Is it possible today to simply apply the ruling theories of the last decade? We have already indicated the theoretical axis of Stalin's method: the inversion of the hierarchical relation between theory, method, and strategy. Stalin displaced the Marxist hierarchy, prioritized tactics, and deformed the entire

method of Marx. This mutilation of Marxism has still not been overcome today, and if this crippling of Marxism is to be undone it will require specific studies of every particular case that was falsified due to Stalin's deformed general method. For that reason, if we limit ourselves to the most specific types we can illustrate the essential issue with the following example: since Lenin's *Imperialism* (1916), there has not been a scientific investigation into the specificity of the new characteristics of contemporary capitalism, nor have there been any investigations regarding the specific determinations of socialist development. Our knowledge of the present is inadequate because it is the result of outmoded methods that were even erroneous when they were created. We have, in other contexts, quickly glanced at Stalin's economic speculations, and this discussion has shown that the theoretic domination of tactics led to a distortion of Marx's method and results in this area as well. Another case of historical falsification was the deletion of the concept of the "Asiatic mode of production" from the Marxist interpretation of the evolution of social formations. This deletion was made in order to prove that a Chinese feudalism, which in fact did not exist, had occurred in China. This falsification of history was necessary in order for Stalin to substantiate his tactical decisions in relation to China in the 1920s and 1930s. The elimination of the concept of the "Asiatic mode of production" set back the Marxist scholarship of China for a decade, for without this interpretive paradigm it was impossible to carry out a true Marxist analysis of the genuine facts and their necessary interrelationship in this important area of the world. The idea that the class struggle intensified during the period of the dictatorship of the proletariat was another case of historical falsification. Indeed, this instance was perhaps the most striking illustration of how the methodological priority of tactics led to the distortion of the Marxist-Leninist method. Prioritizing the idea of the aggravation of the class struggle served to exclude every factual theoretical discussion over the true nature of the political situation under Stalin. Russia was considered to be in a state of permanent civil war, government decisions were made on purely tactical grounds, and those who did not give their agreement were branded as open or hidden enemies of the state. It was not sufficient to logically refute such enemies, but they had to be morally defamed and socially stigmatized as "detrimental." The maintenance of the Stalinist system can easily lead to a renewal of the thesis of the aggravation of the class struggle and its attendant secret police state. If the powerful bureaucracy remains in place, and if this bureaucracy feels itself threatened, regardless of the falseness of the aggravation thesis, it can be renewed as a way of maintaining the power of the bureaucracy. The twentieth Party Congress rejected the aggravation thesis, but if the Stalinist structure of government remains intact it is possible that it can again be used.

These cases of the distortions of the Marxist-Leninist method can be extended limitlessly, but such an extended enumeration cannot be carried

through in this context. Because it is so deeply connected with the question of socialist democracy, because it stands in such contrast to Stalinist tactical manipulation, we may allude at this point to Lenin's idea of the self-determination of nations which was a direct continuation of Marx's thoughts on the problem of nationalism. In 1917, Lenin demanded the unlimited right of every people to declare their independence and just as energetically rejected every attempt to make exceptions to this right.[45] Even during the imperialist war, he called it a betrayal of socialism to want to deny this right of self-determination. There is no bureaucratic sophistry which can annul the central importance of this thesis for Marxism-Leninism. During the last days of his life, Lenin vehemently protested against its destruction.[48] No tactical manipulation can overlook the fact that Lenin, just as Marx, looked upon the right of the self-determination of nations as a crucial, indispensable component of the proletarian revolution, of socialist construction.

The practical development of socialist democracy presupposes the reconstruction of Marx's method. This is not intended as a mere abstract, philosophical statement. On the contrary. The reconstruction of Marxism is a question of the survival of the communist movement. The cleansing of the historical record will neither be immediate nor final, for it is impossible at this point to have a concrete grasp of all the problems and cases to be faced because so much of the present is still hidden in the unexamined Stalinist past. Because the past is still shrouded in darkness, it is impossible to have a correct grasp of the true problems of the present or to formulate an appropriate immediate *praxis*. The cleansing of history is never possible through a single, all-inclusive illumination. Decades of omissions, confusions, distortions can only be put aside through many years of investigative work, through factual discussions concerning fundamental issues of theory and history. Indeed, this cleansing of history will create its own distortions. Both the party apparatus and the independent critic speak of the need for a plurality of perspectives as a way of avoiding distortions. This is a deception. Pluralism can also be the foundation for a neo-positivist manipulation of thought. The priority of the Marxist method must be maintained over that of pluralism. Of course, the results of the Marxist method are not arrived at arbitrarily or voluntaristically. The results are the outcome of factual investigation, analysis, *et cetera,* and must be tested through critical discussions. Because the process of verification is so lengthy, it takes a long time before a truth can be scientifically legitimated. However, if the communist movement wants to have firm ground under its feet, it must choose the way of self-correction. Although it is a painful process, the renaissance of Marxism will arise out of this self-cleansing and self-criticism. But it is a course which must be chosen and embarked upon, because only by freeing itself from the errors of the past can Marxism regain its stature as a viable theoretic and political instrument.

The renaissance of Marxism requires the solution of all these problems.

The awakening of socialist democracy will give this movement a spirited impetus. But when we approach the question of socialist democracy we find ourselves on new, totally unexplored terrain. What Lenin said upon the introduction of NEP is also thoroughly valid here; we have no guidelines to lead us into the future. The classical theoreticians of Marxism all died without providing us with a clear outline of the nature of socialist democracy. Even though we are sailing in unchartered waters, whatever we do know about socialist democracy indicates that in the present situation its spontaneous emergence is out of the question. On the contrary, difficult and purposeful efforts will be unconditionally necessary to bring about its reawakening, to place socialist democracy on the road to becoming. That is easily understandable to anyone who has taken seriously what we have already discussed regarding Lenin's definition of political consciousness. According to Lenin's expression, the movement toward the democratization of socialism is only capable of being stimulated from outside, for it is not capable of rising spontaneously in the consciousness of the population. Indeed, we have already emphasized earlier that the present, extremely widespread apathy of the laboring masses can only develop itself to such socialist democratic activity through goals provided it by an outside force. For a Marxist, it is clear from these few but also fundamental facts that the natural leader and driving force in the establishment of this goal orientation must be the Communist party. The problem touched upon here is that of mobilization, of taking the currently private, intersubjective, and subterranean movements and organizing them in practical life as emancipator, as goal-oriented behavior. The reawakening of Marxism requires a conscious commitment to the validity of the great, general social tasks which beckon. The *Communist Manifesto* already identifies the special mission of communists in the fact that they "represented the general interests of the entire proletariat—continuously represented the interests of the entire movement."[47] A half century later, Lenin continues to execute and concretize these thoughts of Marx. With a correct definition of class consciousness, Lenin recognizes that the party possessed a clearer insight into the totality of social dynamics, that the party represents the cause of the great, enduring interests of the proletariat, critically if necessary, in the struggle to transcend the present. Lenin never doubts the leading role of the party, and today the party must make contact with and articulate the desires of this subterranean world of private culture.

During the practice of the Stalin period, the Communist party also succumbed to the bureaucracy of the tactical. On the question of the party, we can only in this brief space discuss the major points in relation to the tasks and possibilities that face us. Above all, the successful activity of the party, its continued life, is dependent upon the renaissance of Marxism. In terms of reinvigorating the party, one factor is exceptionally important: innerparty de-

mocracy. In the Eastern European world, there are some ideologies that seek the internal reform of existing socialism by means of a bourgeois multiparty system. We offered a criticism of bourgeois democracy at the beginning of this text. Without being able to enter more deeply into this complex issue, it need only be remarked that we mean an effective innerparty democracy within the socialist world. We are thoroughly aware that in the democratic multiparty system of capitalism no political party practices a real innerparty democracy.

From the standpoint of the problem of the party, the most critical task to be undertaken is a realistic division of labor between the state and the party. The great new task of socialist democracy is the practical purification of everyday life from the existing and operative survivals of class society. Existing socialist society still suffers with the residues of class society specifically in the form of prestige consumption. The normal improvements in the economy, not developments specifically aimed at socialism, will increase the standard of living and this will heighten the problem of prestige consumption. This blatant consumerism can neither be made extinct through bureaucratic command nor by new propaganda. At this point, socialist democracy must connect with Lenin's profound definition of habituation. The practice of habituation can only become effective if men become accustomed to putting aside forms of behavior that fall below the dignity of species being, that often incorporate self-destructive and counter-human drives. Habituation must create a social being that discards any aggressive attitudes toward fellow human beings or their own lives (both are inherently inseparable). The creation of a being that is social in content is the end result of the gradual process of habituation. Such an inner transformation of man cannot be carried out without a restructuring of the external world of everyday life. Regardless of whether material production have developed itself to a high level, a communist society can never arise unless everyday life becomes not only an arena of political decision making but also the basis of social being.

In the last decades, much has been said about the survival of capitalism. People have criticized it, denounced it and even proclaimed its collapse. Considered from a sociological perspective, these condemnations of capitalism are overly simplistic. Every society is a composite of individual exceptions, precursors of the future, an amalgam of contradictory and asymmetrical forces moving in both positive and negative directions. Assuming great differentials in the gradations of importance, every man can overcome his estrangement from the being of humanity only by himself, only through the exertion of his own powers. In most cases, this process always starts from a critique or self-critique of a specific form of such estrangement. However, true human liberation can only begin from a change in social conditions in the objective surroundings on men. From this point of view of social being, which always

originates in society, the typical attitude of men can be considered as actually transcended when new conditions of life develop which are capable of radically separating past ideas from present conscious behavior. (Cannibalism and vendettas are examples of how the social habituates human behavior.) In periods of great social transition, individual attempts at transformation on ideological or moral grounds naturally play a significant role. Regardless of the intent, these kinds of individual acts can never achieve a real societal universality in the above mentioned sense. To change man it is first necessary to change society. We are concerned here with a fundamental transformation of the entire man in all his manifestations of life, not merely with the transcendence of a specific, concrete, individual vice inside a particular, singular life condition. The author has no desire to undervalue this kind of individual transformation. On the contrary, he is deeply convinced that both individual and social protest in the past epochs of human history created the possibilities of social transcendence. If this individual or collective protest had not existed in the past, had not struggled against the inhumanity of its time, against the denial of human dignity, there would be no hope in history. Even though these struggles were fought with a false consciousness, even though they may have been pure utopian experiments, they helped create historical possibility and future.

The author also does not believe that it is possible to judge these attempts at transcending the human indignities of our existence solely in terms of their immediate, practico-social consequences. The prior history of human development—with profound logic Marx calls it the prehistory of humanity—provides only scattered, often contradictory claims in the formation of those subjective attitudes that contribute to these social transformations. All these attempts must be evaluated judiciously and man must learn from these examinations that the becoming of humanity is a result of its own activity, its own social activity. However, transcendence can never take place in a vacuum, but must always accord with the existent real possibilities and the objective process of social reproduction will always set the conditions and limits of such transformation. Socialist democracy is called upon to transcend the last, most highly developed form of antihumanity (the other human being as limit, as mere object, as possible opponent or enemy to one's own self-developing *praxis*). Socialist democracy is called upon to complete this task because it alone is capable of producing a social-human foundation for this decisive transformation.

The great Soviet movement of the immediate revolutionary past was filled with the instinctive tendency to place this complex of problems on the schedule of history. The real conditions of the emergence of the Soviets corresponded to the existent objective, concrete universal problems within Russia. In an inextinguishable fashion, the memory of the Soviets survives in the

broad masses of the people. Falsely grounded in an idealist-utopian hope, these masses believe that the simple renewal of this movement can open a new horizon for humanity. They believe that the inherent tendencies of the Soviet movement are toward renewal and revitalization. But the Soviet movement cannot be the only force for the renewal of socialism in the post-Stalinist world. It is an imperative task of the present that all socialist states embark upon a fundamental restructuring of their economies. In this context, the Soviets appear as the only true alternative to both the Stalinist hyperbureaucratization of socialism and the positivist manipulation of bourgeois democracy. The Soviets have achieved a new historical potential at the beginning of a new epoch. From these facts one cannot draw the conclusion that the Soviets can again possess something of the electrifying spontaneity of the earlier, volcanic upheaval. One can only draw the conclusion that new forms of democratization must come forth from the social-historical. Although it is still not existent, the present world economy provides increasing signs of a coming crisis, and a Marxist interpretation of the crisis—unfortunately still inadequate—suggests a revival of the democratization process. For decades, both capitalist and socialist worlds have given an impression of unshatterable continuity. But they are filled with general contradictions, divisions, unsolvable conflicts and these are being pushed to the surface. Nevertheless, both capitalist and socialist worlds may continue in existence in their present forms through compromise, or through the continuance of routine manipulatory agreements. Bourgeois governments are experimenting with the tactics of co-option, since they are eager to incorporate the still chaotic spontaneous protest movement into the establishment and thereby pacify it.

A sociopolitical crisis of worldwide proportions is visible. The task of these sketchy observations cannot be to advance a detailed program of politico-economic renewal. From out of the crisis, a new epoch of Marxism has begun. Based on a renaissance of the methodology of Marx, the radical new task confronting Marxists is to discover new ways to fight against capitalist imperialism and to commence the inner rejuvenation of socialism. We cannot here discuss the relationship between the old and new, the dead Marxist past and the new epoch of the living Marxist future. There must be both continuity and discontinuity: the viable heritage of the Marxist past must be continued, while the deformation must be discontinued. Concerning the relationship between past and future, we can and must state that the reconstruction of socialist production is not merely an economic endeavor. It should be looked upon as laying the basis for the transformation of man, for his habituation to a dignified human existence in everyday life and the permeation of this dignity to all his manifestations of life. The practical application of these principles of economic development to the transformation of humanity is an extremely complicated matter. On the immediate level, the transformation is simply an

economic reform aiming at the quantitative increase and qualitative improvement of the mechanism of production and distribution. The problems of the socialist economy, although its intimate connection to the increase of consumption has become a life and death question for it, are not capable of being solved by the simple introduction of the capitalist "model." Those economic tasks that the market can accomplish under capitalism in an essentially spontaneous manner must be broadened under socialism to include multidimensional, pluralistic forms for the democratization of the process of production, from the planning stage up to its practical application. In the first instance, this is necessarily a pure economic problem. However, even at this level, the labor union question, for example, immediately emerges. This leads to a contemporary revival of the Leninist standpoint, and to the urgent driving out of the ideology of Trotskytism as it existed during the 1921 debate over the labor unions. The genuine activation of the masses, the surmounting of its apathy is impossible without a renaissance of the Leninist position. This process of economic reform will surely last a long time, and will call forth the creation of new economic forms, new modes of economic organization. As we have already indicated, at every stage of this process there will emerge pioneering experiments for the awakening and formation of the subjective attitudes necessary for a socialist society. Without wishing to indulge in a mechanistic division of labor, it is certain that the democratized institutions of the state and mass organizations (labor unions) will be called upon to play the leading role in the first stage of this social reconstruction. In the second stage, a democratically renewed Communist party carries an extremely important task within itself. By continuing the advances of the democratized state and labor unions, the party must perform the decisively important role of acting as a permanent critic of the policies of reconstruction. Naturally, we must never lose sight of the crucial, additional impetus to be given to this process of reform by the spontaneous direct initiative of the masses themselves. But it is impossible to predict beforehand how important and what kind of role the reemergent and newly constituted Soviet movement will play. Our speculations can, indeed—maximally—only claim to raise highly speculative outlines of future possibilities.

From a superficial point of view, the world appears to be immobile. But this is a deception. The conjuncture of all present historical tendencies shows that the globe is driven forward by an unbreakable dynamic. Within a specific historical framework, reality is dominated by the inherent and continuous unfolding of social stages. There is a crisis in the capitalist system of manipulation, and the process of decolonization has opened new perspectives before mankind. These are important symptoms of the transformation currently underway. However, what for us is the most essential point, is the internal tendency of the communist movement toward a renaissance of Marxism, in

which the renewal of its genuine, theoretic-practical leading role in the revolutionary renewal of society is coincident with the wishes of humanity. Any process of social rejuvenation is necessarily connected with unrest and uncertainty, and it is all too natural that the party will be frightened away from such a challenge and concentrate its efforts on preserving wherever possible in an unchanged form the seemingly static, narrow continuity of the last decades. From the perspective of the current historical crisis, these efforts at conservation appear, in the last analysis, to be futile. Regarding the general social-historical basis for periods of transition, Marx wrote: "Humanity only sets itself those tasks which it can solve, for exactly stated humanity will continuously find that the tasks themselves only arise where the material conditions for their situation are already present or at least in the process of becoming." Any ideas of conserving the Stalinist order are just as hopeless as the illusion of a spectacular, in contemporary jargon, a happening, an immediate radical-revolutionary overthrow. Today, a considerable number of young people and the left intelligentsia feel a strong pull toward this kind of romantic revolutionism. In relating to this worldwide crisis, we are dealing with—in various modes in the various parts of the world—an extended, indeed internal as well as external conflict-ridden process of self-understanding over concrete perspectives and goals, over concrete means to further its inherent development.

Socialism is ripe for a break with the past. It is factually incorrect to have any anxiety over the radical severance of socialism from its Stalinist heritage. Lenin called for a "breathing space" only infrequently and only under great duress. He only did this when the Soviets faced a permanent threat to their existence. In the immediate past, the great political acts of socialism (the victory over Hitler, the achievement of nuclear parity) offered by far the most solid ground for a breathing space, which was devoted to domestic reconstruction. Naturally, the imperialists will remain imperialists. On the other hand, one cannot overlook the change that has taken place within the imperialist world. The social background of the imperialists, their restless and limitless drive for power, is different than it was in 1914 or in the immediate post-1945 period. The time is propitious for an internal reconstruction of socialism because the imperialist world is less a threat to socialism than in Lenin's time. We must bear in mind that we live in a favorable moment in which to start the long process of internal reformation. The danger of armed intervention by the imperialist world was greater in Lenin's time than it is today. In order to express an extremely unpleasant truth, we must simultaneously admit that the spontaneous sympathy of the masses and of the intelligentsia of the capitalist countries was far stronger in 1917 than they are today. The cause of this is easily found. In 1917 and in the years immediately following, many people in the capitalist world felt—from Anatole France to the simple working men and women—that everything happening in the Soviet Union contributed to their own human

liberation, that everything that transpired in Russia was a struggle connected to their own affairs, connected to their own human salvation. Stalin's passage to the absolute domination of tactics in all questions of theory and *praxis* was the knife that cut, to a great degree, this thread of connection between events in Russia and the western conscience. The events of the Moscow Trials of the 1930s naturally played an extremely important role in this estrangement of the western conscience from Russian communism. However, the impact of disgraceful individual acts was capable of being overcome were it not that a firm ideological line of separation arose between Russian communism and the West. The developmental patterns of the Soviet Union and the Western world diverged, for the mentality of capitalism drove people to a seemingly unquenchable desire for instant gratification and personal hedonism. Under capitalism, the general influence of the rise of the economic level and of the standard of living, and particular accomplishments in the fields of technology, with all the self-indulgence these successes created, prevented any return to the community of feeling that existed at the beginning in 1917. However, the possibility for such a recrudescence of good feelings is contained in every capitalist society. It is only in socialist society that the enticing drama of human becoming is potentially played out. With all the power of an insensitive propaganda apparatus, at the end of the war socialist society attempted to invent an image or slogan that had as much advertising attraction as the phrase the "American way of life." However, the lack of a real human substance can also cause the most extensive, best-organized advertising apparatus to fail. Commitment to and respect for human species being cannot be acquired with financial investments. Only socialism is capable of participating in this drama of human becoming. The spirit of capitalism is opposed to this spiritual quest. Nevertheless, if socialism and capitalism were summoned to this purpose, a new eruption of the sympathies of 1917 is still possible.

Since the twentieth Party Congress, this is generally the situation throughout the entire world. Obviously, it must be repeated again and again that imperialism is imperialism and it will remain as such as long as it is not toppled by a revolution and its foundations radically destroyed. So long as it can breath, capitalism will obviously seek to bring about the collapse of socialism. But the attainment of nuclear parity has made a third world war, or an outright attack by capitalism on socialism extremely risky and potentially self-destructive. For that reason, as the real chances of a third world war being unleashed steadily decrease, so the international ideological struggle gains greater importance. Therefore, immediately after the twentieth Party Congress, the author of these lines characterized coexistence, a child of nuclear parity, as a new form of class struggle. In this new form of class struggle, in Lenin's words the principle Who? against Whom? achieves validity. There are those who hope to retrieve the Stalinist system. There are those who seek

only temporary, formal modifications, who want to slow down the process of reform, but these forces are not in the ascendent. Nevertheless, such hopes are still alive and the signs of crisis within the imperialist system of manipulation gives them an impetus. They wish to wait for the collapse of capitalism, feeling that such an upheaval will vindicate their conservatism. On the other hand, there exists in the present throughout the entire world new forces of progress and hope. Even though they are weak and still confused, these forces seek a reapproximation of Marxism. There is a dynamic toward the rebirth of Marxism. Objectively, such movements can only be allies of socialism. The Leninist tradition embodies the possibility of a unified fight against a common enemy and the prevention of the deformation of Marxism by means of precise logical distinctions and a critique based on principle. Stalinism is the mentality of the permanent revolution. It brands every dissenting viewpoint as an enemy of the people. Anyone who does not agree with the official, tactically determined party decisions is judged as a subversive, or the direct tool of the agents of imperialism. An effort is made to destroy them with the organized means of the government apparatus. That was the method of the Great Purge Trials. But the struggles between Leninism and Stalinism is today—without being concretely organized—the foundation of the official ideological struggle inside as well as outside the socialist world.

The preservation of Stalinism is the greatest barrier to the rise of socialist democratization inside the domains of socialism. It is equally the major barrier to international cooperation and the integrating of all people striving for a renaissance of the genuine method of Marx. Marxism offers enlightenment to all that transpires in the world today, and it can help all those who seek to overtake the future just as it did when it was most effective during the days of Marx, Engels and Lenin. In addition, the understanding of the transition to socialist democratization, to socialism as the way to communism, to the end of the prehistory of humanity, appears today as something different than it appeared during Marx's lifetime. The Marxist picture was painted more than a hundred years ago and showed the different paths of development of the bourgeois and socialist revolutions. The foundation of these revolutions was the class struggle which moved them forward and these revolutions were the womb of future societal possibilities: "Bourgeois revolutions, like those of the eighteenth century, sweep on rapidly from success to success, surpassing one another in dramatic effects; men and things seem set in sparkling diamonds, ecstasy is the spirit of every day; but they are short-lived, soon reaching their climax, and a long hangover afflicts society until it learns soberly to assimilate the results of its periods of storm and of the nineteenth century, constantly criticize themselves, continually interrupt their own progress, return to what seemed completed in order to start all over again, make a terrible and total mock of the half-measures, weaknesses and meanness of their just

attempts; they seem to overthrow their opponent only that he may drain new powers from the earth and rise up against them more gigantic than before, they recoil repeatedly from the indeterminate enormity of their own aims, till a situation is created from which retreat is impossible, and circumstances themselves cry: Hic Rhodus, Hic Salta. Here is the rose, dance here."[48]

Today, Rhodus still lies in a distant future. However, everything shows that only the way that Marx prescribes can lead us to that future. The degree to which that future is reached, rests on the insights and courage of the communist movement.

Notes

1. Karl Marx, Friedrich Engels, *Manifest der Kommunistischen Partei* (The Manifesto of the Communist Party), in Marx-Engels Werke (MEW), Berlin 1956, Bd. 4, S. 462.

2. Marx, *Der achtzehnte Brumaire des Louis Bonaparte* (The 18th Brumaire of Louis Bonaparte), in MEW Bd. 8, S. 111–207.

3. Marx, *Grundrisse der Kritik der politischen Ökonomie* (The Foundation of a Critique of Political Economy), (1857–58) Berlin 1953, S. 379.

4. Ebenda, S. 156.

5. Marx, *Zur Judenfrage* (On the Jewish Question) in MEW Bd. 1, S. 368.

6. Ebenda, S. 369.

7. Ebenda, S. 365.

8. Ebenda, S. 354.

9. Marx, *Der achtzehnte Brumaire des Louis Bonaparte* (The 18th Brumaire of Louis Bonaparte), S. 116.

10. Marx, Engels, *Die Deutsche Ideologie* (The German Ideology), in MEW Bd. 3, S. 163.

11. Marx, *Thesen über Feuerbach* (Theses on Feuerbach), in MEW Bd. 3, S. 6.

12. Marx, *Ökonomisch-philosophische Manuskripte aus dem Jahr 1844* (The Economic-philosophic Manuscripts of 1844), in MEW EB1, S. 538.

13. Marx, *Zur Judenfrage* (On the Jewish Question), S. 364.

14. Kant, Immanual, *Die Metaphysik der Sitten* (The Metaphysics of Morals), in Werke in 12 Bänden, hg. v. W. Weischedel, Bd. 8, Frankfurt/ Main 1968, S. 390.

15. Marx, *Ökonomisch-philosophische Manuskripte aus dem Jahr 1844* (The Economic-philosophic Manuscripts of 1844), S. 540.

16. Lenin, W.I. *Der linke Radikalismus, die Kinderkrankheit im Kommunismus* (Left-Wing Communism: An Infantile Disorder), in Lenin-Werke, Band 31, S. 5.

17. Lenin, *Politischer Bericht des Zentralkomitees der KPR(B)* (Political Report to the Central Committee of the Russian Communist Party), 27. Marz 1922, in LW Bd. 33, S. 256.

18. Ebenda, S. 256.

19. Marx, *Das Kapital* (Capital), Bd. III, in MEW Bd. 25, S. 828.

20. Lenin, *Über die Gewerkschaften, die gegenwärtige Lage und die Fehler Trotskis* (Concerning the Labor Unions, the Present Situation and the Errors of Trotsky), in LW Bd. 32, S. 7.

21. Lenin, *Staat und Revolution* (State and Revolution), in LW Bd. 25, S. 476.

22. Lenin, *Referat über die Subbotniks* (Concerning the Subbotniks), in LW Bd. 30, S. 308.

23. Lenin, *Über proletarische Kultur* (On Proletarian Culture), in LW Bd. 31, S. 308.

24. Already in 1925, long before it came to a break between Bukharin and Stalin, I protested against this conception. (Compare Georg Lukács, *Bucharin: Theorie des historischen Materialismus* (Bukharini: The Theory of Historical Materialism), in Archiv für die Geschichte des Sozialismus und der Arbeiterbewegung, Elfter Jahrgang, Leipzig, 1925, S. 216–224.)

25. Marx to Engels, 25.9.1857, in MEW Bd. 29, S. 192.

26. Stalin, J.W. *Ökonomische Probleme des Sozialismus in der UdSSR* (The Economic Problems of Socialism in the USSR), Berlin 1952, S. 20.

27. Ebenda, S. 23.

28. Marx, *Das Kapital* (Capital), Bd. 1, in MEW Bd. 23, S. 93.

29. Stalin, *Ökonomische Probleme des Sozialismus in der UdSSR* (The Economic Problems of Socialism in the USSR), S. 18.

30. Marx, *Grundrisse der Kritik der politischen Ökonomie* (Foundations of a Critique of Political Economy), S. 593.

31. Lenin, *Was Tun?* (What Is To Be Done?), in LW Bd. 5, S. 385.

32. Stalin, *Über die Grundlagen des Leninismus* (The Foundations of Leninism), in: ders., *Fragen des Leninismus* (The Problems of Leninism), Berlin 1951, S. 24.

33. Stalin, *Der Marxismus und die Fragen der Sprachwissenschaft* (Marxism and the Question of Linguistics), Berlin 1954, S. 10.

34. Jánossy, Ferenc, *Das Ende der Wirtschaftswunder* (The End of the Economic Miracle), Frankfurt/Main 1966.

35. Marx, *Das Kapital* (Capital), Bd. 1, S. 787.

36. Ebenda, S. 765.

37. Marx, *Das Kapital* (Capital), Bd. III, S. 828.

38. Marx, *Randglossen zum Programm der Deutschen Arbeiterpartie* (Kritik des Gothaer Programms), (Critique of the Gotha Program), in MEW Bd. 19, S. 21.

39. Marx, *Grundrisse der Kritik der politischen Ökonomie* (Foundations of a Critique of Political Economy), S. 505.

40. Ebenda, S. 593.

41. Marx, Zur Judenfrage (On the Jewish Question), Bd. 1, S. 360.

42. Marx and Engels, *Das Manifest der Kommunistischen Partei* (The Manifesto of the Communist Party), S. 465.

43. Lenin, *Die Ergebnisse der Diskussion über Selbstbestimmung* (The Results of the Discussion over Self-Determination), in LW Bd. 22, S. 326.

44. Lenin, *Was Tun?* (What Is To Be Done?), S. 436.

45. Lenin, *Die Aufgaben des Proletariats in unserer Revolution* (The Tasks of the Proletariat in Our Revolution), in LW Bd. 24, S. 58.

46. Lenin, *Zur Frage der Nationalitäten oder der, Autonomisierung'* (The Nationalities Question or "Autonomization"), in LW Bd. 36, S. 590–596.

47. Marx and Engels, *Das Manifest der Kommunistischen Partei* (The Manifesto of the Communist Party), S. 474.

48. Marx, *Der achtzehnte Brumaire des Louis Bonaparte* (The Eighteenth Brumaire of Louis Bonaparte), S. 118.

Index

Abundance, 22, 27, 35
Administrative-managerial paradigm, 11, 12, 32
Alienation, 84, 132, 163
Anarchism, 8, 15
Anarchy, 7, 16, 17, 19, 24, 52, 53, 54
Anthropology, 13, 14, 25, 41, 42, 44, 54
Aristotle, 67
Asiatic mode of production, 160
Atom bomb, 134
Authority, 15; party authoritarianism, 12; social authoritarianism, 23

Babeuf, Gracchus, 44
Bahro, Rudolf, *The Alternative in Eastern Europe*, 27
Base-superstructure, 35, 71–78, 81, 98, 117, 139, 141, 156–157; base, 98, 156–157; superstructure, 81, 98, 124
Behavioralism, 34, 35, 53
Bentham, Jeremy, 34
Bernstein, Eduard, 109, 110
Bolshevism, 24, 29, 108, 110 Bolshevist historiography, 29, 31, 32, 33, 34; Bolshevist revolution (1917), 29; Bolshevist theory of politics, 24, 29, 32; classical Bolshevism, 31, 32, 33, 34, 35; Leninist Bolshevism, 33, 34, 36, 44, 46; Stalinist Bolshevism, 33, 34
Bourgeois: bourgeois anthropology, 42; bourgeois citizen-ideal, 45, 132, 133; bourgeois class, 15; bourgeois definition of freedom, 48; bourgeois democracy, 18, 19, 39, 45, 52, 53, 71–89, 93, 102, 133, 144, 163; bourgeois humanism, 26, 40; bourgeois representative, institutions, 78; bourgeois materialism, 86; bourgeois revolution, 144; bourgeois society, 71–89, 102, 103, 133, 144, 153, 154, 155, 165, 168; bourgeois state, 15; bourgeois state, smashing of, 33; bourgeois theory of the state, 42; bourgeois world, 40
Bukharin, Nicolai, 108, 111, 114, 117, 118, 119
Bureaucracy, 23, 48, 100, 101, 103, 128, 132, 133, 144; bureaucratic totalitarianism, 26, 33, 117, 118, 128, 132, 148, 149, 151; party bureaucracy, 23

Capitalism, 9–10, 13, 14, 40, 47, 48, 71–75, 81–89, 94–95, 138–144, 149, 151–157; capitalism and war, 134–135; capitalist anti-communism, 153; transition to capitalism, 138, 139, 155–157
Central Intelligence Agency, 87, 88, 89
Citizen, 72, 74, 86, 132, 133, 144
Class, 8, 13, 14, 15, 16, 20, 21, 29, 32, 41, 48, 52; bourgeois class, 15; classlessness, 9, 19, 32, 52, 53, 54; class politics, 20; class power, 24, 52; class property, 17; class reductionism, 8, 17; class struggle, 20, 77, 82–83; proletarian class, 15
Cold War, 85, 88–89, 104
Commodity-exchange, 120, 121, 123
Communism, 8–9, 10, 15, 16, 18, 19, 21, 22, 31, 32, 33, 103, 104, 114,

Communism (*continued*)
140, 143; communism-as-heuristic, 31; communism-as-immanent, 31; communist society, 103; communist revolution, 16
Communist party, 19, 23, 34, 49, 50, 51, 52, 113, 162; and communist movement, 161, 162; as conspiratorial party, 51; and "democratic centralism," 51; democratization of party, 166; internal democratization, 51, 163, 166; separation of state and party, 163; totalitarianism of, 133, 149, 151; twentieth Party Congress, 29, 93, 114, 146–147, 160, 168; and world revolution, 112–113, 136
Consciousness, 97, 99, 100, 103, 123–124, 125, 126, 141–144, 154–158
Consumerism, 143, 144, 163
Consumption, 11, 12
Cromwell, Oliver, 78, 81
Czechoslovakian Revolution, 4–5, 31

Democracy, 18, 19, 20, 21, 24, 25, 27, 28, 30, 32, 34, 36, 37, 39, 40, 45, 46, 52, 53, 54, 67–89, 93, 102, 104, 113, 114; bourgeois democracy, 40, 52, 67–89, 102; democracy-as-bourgeois, 52; democracy-as-plebeianism, 52, 81; democratic populism, 79; direct democracy, 18, 19, 46; Greek democracy, 37; plebeian democracy, 27, 78; proletarian democracy, 101, 124; representative democracy, 18; socialist democracy, 102, 125–127; Soviet democracy, 125–128
Democratization, 26, 27, 32, 33, 34, 36, 46, 68, 81–89, 93, 104, 108, 124, 128, 129, 149, 150, 151, 162, 165, 166, 169
Determinism, 67, 68, 97, 98, 99, 103, 117, 125, 132, 140–144
Dialectics, 129–131
Dialectical materialism, 38, 117–123, 127–132

Dictatorship of the proletariat, 25, 33, 146
Disunity between Lenin and Stalin, 169
Disunity between Marx and Stalin, 169
Division of labor, 22, 142, 143, 144
Dubcek, Alexander, 4, 5, 31

Eastern Europe: contemporary, 149–152, 163
Economic formations, 72, 73, 77, 122, 125, 152, 153, 154, 155
Economics, 44, 46, 98, 99, 113–114, 117–125, 128, 139–141, 144, 147, 149, 156–157; economic reductionism, 117, 127–132
Economism, 22, 35, 113
Egalitarian paradigm, 9–10, 11, 27
Egalitarianism, 10–11, 12, 23, 24, 44; administrative-managerial egalitarianism, 18; democratic egalitarianism, 18; economic egalitarianism, 10–11, 21, 22, 24; functional egalitarianism, 12, 13; income egalitarianism, 18; job egalitarianism, 12; salary egalitarianism, 18; social egalitarianism, 21; 22, 44; talent egalitarianism, 10–11; time egalitarianism, 25
Egoism, 74–78, 86, 102
Emancipation, 43; of human labor, 143; of human *praxis*, 143
Engels, Friedrich, 73, 99, 110; *Origins of the Family, Private Property and the State*, 7–8; *Ludwig Feuerbach and the End of Classical German Philosophy*, 40
English Revolution, 78
Equality, 73, 78–79, 86, 87
Equalization: equalization of consumption, 10–11; equalization of distribution, 10–11; equalization of function, 12, 20; equalization of jobs, 12; equalization of talent, 11
European social democracy, 109, 110, 117
Everyday life, 28, 45, 46, 100, 101, 124, 125–127, 132, 143, 144, 146, 148, 163, 165

Fascism, 40, 131
Fehér, Ferenc, 5; *The Frozen Revolution*, 44
Feudalism, 72–73, 78, 95, 138, 139, 155–156
Feuerbach, Ludwig, 41, 42, 83
Freedom, 48, 73, 78–79, 86, 87, 97
French Revolution, 73, 74, 78, 81, 87

German Humanism, 40, 45, 46, 47
German Enlightenment, 26–27, 45, 46
Gorbachev, Mikhail, 5
Greek ideal, 35, 39, 43, 46, 71–77; Athens, 46, 72; Greek democracy, 37, 71–77; Greek humanism, 39

Habituation, 23, 24, 26, 53, 102, 103, 104–105, 145, 163, 165
Hegel, G.W.F., 26, 36, 37, 40, 129, 130; *Phenomenology of Mind*, 47; *Logic*, 129
Heller, Agnes, 5
Historical materialism, 33
Historicism, 33, 36, 37, 47, 48, 53, 54
Hitler, Adolf, 40, 85, 95, 134, 167
Homogenization, 21, 22, 28; social homogenization, 22, 28, 32, 44
Human activity, 25, 36, 37, 42, 45
Hungarian Revolution, 4–6, 30, 31

Ideology, 123, 131–132; de-ideologization, 86–87; Stalinist ideology, 137–138
Imperialism, 134, 136, 167, 168
Individual liberty, 39
Individualism, 43, 73–78, 83, 86
Industrialization, 108
Interest, 9; self-interest, 10, 11, 34, 35, 73–78, 86

Jacobinism, 27, 44, 152

Kautsky, Karl, 9, 16, 110
Khruschev, Nikita, 114, 146

Kingdom of Freedom, 43, 97, 98, 99, 101, 103, 124, 140, 144, 154–158
Kingdom of Necessity, 98, 99, 124, 140
Kingdom of Reason, 73
Kolakowski, Lesek: Main Currents of Marxism, 26

Labor, 25, 38, 39, 42, 142; emancipation of labor, 142–143, 157–158; human labor, 38, 39, 42, 141, 142; labor process, 140; labor time, 120, 124; mental labor, 22, 23; necessary labor, 43, 46, 121–125, 140; physical labor, 22, 23; social labor, 26, 45, 140; surplus labor, 43, 121–125; wage-labor, 140
Liberalism, 79
Lenin, Nicolai, 49–50, 98, 99, 100–116, 145, 158, 161, 166, 167, 169; and conspiratorial party, 51; and definition of socialism, 100, 145; and democracy, 133; and "democratic centralism," 51; and "democratic dictatorship of workers and peasants," 27, 51; *Dictatorship of the Proletariat*, 16; *Imperialism: The Highest Stage of Capitalism*, 160; Kronstadt Rebellion, 29; Last Will and Testament, 107–108; Leninism, 7–9, 15–25, 26, 36, 128–129, 133; Leninist Bolshevism, 5, 33, 34, 36, 49, 50, 52; Leninist opposition, 4–6, 33, 51; Leninist party, 49, 51; and methodology, 104–105, 106, 108, 109, 113, 129, 145; and national self-determination, 161; New Economic Policy, 25, 27, 36, 49, 50, 100, 111, 123, 127, 133, 145, 149, 162; *Proletarian Revolution and the Renegade Kautsky*, 16; *State and Revolution*, 4, 7, 13, 14, 15–25, 26, 28, 29, 31, 34, 52, 53, 54, 101, 102; strategy-tactics, 108; *The Development of Capitalism in Russia*, 17; *The Infantile Disorders of Communism*, 94; "The Reorganization of the Party," 51; and theory of politics, 19,

Lenin, Nicolai (*continued*)
24, 53; and theory of the state, 53; *Two Tactics of Social Democracy in the Democratic Revolution*, 29; unity of Lenin and Marx, 128–130, 136; *What Is To Be Done?*, 128

Lukács, Georg, 25–55, 67–170; and anti-bourgeois attitudes, 39, 40; and anti-Stalinism, 26, 27, 33, 48, 51; *Blum Theses*, 27, 29, 30, 50; "democratic dictatorship of workers and peasants," 51; *Die Eigenart des Asthetischen*, 3, 27; Hungarian Communist Party, 30; Lenin, 25–26, 33, 50; "Letter to Alberto Carocci," 26; and methodology, 104–105; and "new democracy," 50; and "Popular Front," 29; *Record of a Life*, 50; and redefinition of socialism, 47, 48, 139; and renaissance of Marxism, 28–29; *The Destruction of Reason*, 40; "The International Significance of Russian Democratic Literary Criticism," 27; "The Moral Mission of the Communist Party," 104; *The Process of Democratization*, 3–5, 15, 24, 25–55, 67–170; and theory of democracy, 46; and theory of politics, 28, 29, 32–33, 36, 39, 40, 42, 44, 46; and theory of the state, 32–33, 44; *Theses on Feuerbach*, 42, 43; worker-peasant alliance, 5; *Zur Ontologie des gesellschaftlichen Seins*, 3, 27

Market forces, 149
Marx, Karl, 6, 11, 13, 14, 17, 20, 84–86, 97–98, 110, 154, 155, 169, 170; *Communist Manifesto*, 103, 129–130, 157, 159–161, 162; *Critique of the Gotha Program*, 122, 124, 141; *Das Kapital*, 43, 120; definition of communism, 141, 142; definition of socialism, 141, 142; depoliticization of a theory of politics, 20, 21; division of labor, 142; *Economic-Philosophic Manuscripts of 1844*, 37, 38, 42, 83; *Eighteenth Brumaire of Louis Bonaparte*, 68; labor theory of value, 47–81; Marxism, 4, 7–8, 67–68, 71–89, 109, 128–130; Marxism of the Second International, 7; Marxist critique, 104; and methodology, 104–105, 106, 113, 120–125; and proletarian revolution, 94–95; renaissance of Marxism, 28, 36, 158–161, 165, 166, 169; repoliticization of a theory of politics, 41, 44, 54; role of the economic base, 117, 118; tactics of revolution, 20; theory of historical development, 137–140, 143; theory of politics, 6–7, 9, 13, 15, 20, 21, 24–25, 36, 39, 40, 41, 42, 44, 54; theory of the state, 6–7, 25, 28, 29, 36, 39, 40, 41, 42, 44, 54; *Theses on Feuerbach*, 38, 41, 42, 83; unity of Marx and Lenin, 128–130, 136

Means of production, 77, 123; nationalization of, 122; socialization of, 133, 147, 154, 156, 157
Mechanical materialism, 38, 97, 117, 118, 127–132
Methodology, 67–68, 104–105, 106, 127–132
Militarism, 134–136
Multi-party system, 51, 52, 163

Natural Rights, 39, 42, 74, 154
Need, 9, 10, 11, 34, 35, 41, 42, 45, 143, 144

Objectivism, 38, 117, 127–132, 157–158
Opportunism, 15
Original accumulation, 147, 148

Paris Commune, 17, 18, 20
Parliamentarianism, 16, 17, 18, 19, 27, 52, 77, 78, 81, 133
Peace, 134
Peasants, 50, 95, 96
Philosophy, 36

Philosophy of identity, 26
Plebeianism, 78-79; plebeian-democracy, 79, 81
polis, 34, 35, 39, 40, 45, 46, 71-77, 102
Politics, 7-8, 9, 13, 14, 17, 24, 28, 29, 41, 42, 44, 46, 52, 53, 54, 125-127, 149, 152, 153; "end of politics," 7-8, 24, 34, 35, 52, 53, 54; political authority, 14; political man, 132; politicslessness, 19, 24, 34, 35, 54; repoliticization of politics, 41
Positivism, 117, 118, 127-132
Practico-critical activity, 38, 39, 46
praxis, 4, 25, 38, 39, 42, 43, 44, 45, 68, 72, 97, 98, 102, 108, 109, 110, 124, 125, 133, 143, 145, 146; mode of *praxis,* 152, 153
Private life, 72, 74, 77
Process, 37, 68, 84
Productivist paradigm, 9-10, 11, 22, 27
Proletariat, 8; dictatorship of proletariat, 18, 19; proletarian class, 15; proletarian democracy, 18, 20, 25; proletarian humanism, 26, 46; proletarian revolution, 8, 20, 31, 125; proletarian state, 15, 17, 18, 19, 20, 33
Property, 8, 11, 15, 17; class property, 17; nationalization of, 37, 44, 50, 122, 133, 134; personal property, 8; productive property, 8; property reductionism, 17; propertylessness, 9; reprivitization of, 50; socialization of, 37, 44, 133
Public and private man, 39, 40, 41, 45-47, 86, 132, 152-153; citizen, 152; political activist, 152, 153; private man, 153

Rapid industrialization, 147
Reproduction, 123-124; self-reproduction, 124; social reproduction, 142
Revolution, 151, 157; bourgeois revolution, 144; communist revolution, 125; economic revolution, 139; proletarian revolution, 125; revolution and transcendence, 132; revolutionary consciousness, 126; revolutionary spontaneity, 126-127; Russian Revolution, 94-95, 125; socialist revolution, 144
Robespierre, Maximilien, 39, 81
Rome, 72
Rousseau, Jean-Jacques, 39, 67, 81
Russia, 95, 96, 147
Russian Revolution, 94-95, 125; Brest-Litovsk, 125; Civil War, 96, 101, 126-127, 132, 144; Great Purges Trials, 130, 146, 168; non-classical nature of, 98, 99, 106, 112, 113, 127; October 1917, 96

Scarcity, 10, 27
Second International, 6-7, 9, 10, 11, 12, 13, 14, 17, 21, 22, 24, 25, 27, 34, 35, 44
Self-activity, 100, 103, 124-125, 141-144, 145, 146, 154-158
Self-determination, 43, 46, 47, 97, 99, 100, 103, 123-124, 125, 126, 141-144, 145, 146, 154-158
Separation of party and state, 34, 49-50
Social: socialized life, 84; socialized man, 84
Social atomism, 84
Social being, 143, 163
Social formations, 72, 73, 77, 81, 97, 99, 104, 118, 122, 125, 139, 140, 143, 152, 153, 154, 157
Social epiphenomenology, 36, 71-78, 117, 139
Social ontology, 26, 31, 36, 37, 38, 40, 41-44, 54, 77, 78, 98, 99, 102, 123, 124, 125, 143, 154, 155, 163
Social phenomenology, 36, 37, 41-44, 54, 123, 124, 125, 143, 154, 155
Social science, 36
Social totality, 83, 97, 118
Socialism, 26, 27, 32, 34, 35, 37, 39, 40, 43, 45, 46, 47, 48, 54, 100, 114,

Socialism (*continued*)
125, 132, 139, 140, 141, 143, 144, 153, 154, 157, 158, 167, 168; crisis of socialism, 159–162; economic preconditions for, 128, 133, 138; socialism and war, 134–135; socialist culture, 139; socialist definition of freedom, 49; socialist democracy, 26, 54, 93, 97–100, 102–104, 108, 114, 125–127, 132, 133, 144–146, 149, 151, 154, 158, 159–162, 163, 164, 166; socialist democratization, 169; socialist economics, 166; socialist humanity, 155–158; socialist man, 132, 153, 154; socialist revolution, 100–101, 144; socialist society, 104, 132, 154, 158; socialist transformation, 99; transition to socialism, 96, 98, 99, 105, 128, 138, 139, 155–157
Socialism in one country, 112, 113
Society, 13, 14, 41, 42, 84; civil society, 4, 13–14, 17, 28, 29, 41, 42, 49, 73; depoliticize society, 13; repoliticize society, 14, 28
Soviet Union, 133, 134, 164
Soviets, 6, 19, 20, 25, 28, 33, 34, 36, 45, 46, 49, 52, 54, 96, 104, 113, 125–127, 132, 133, 144, 146, 149, 151, 152, 158, 164, 165, 166, 168; Soviet democracy, 125–128
Species being, 4, 13, 14, 28, 41, 42, 73, 83, 84, 103, 143; human species, 141
Stalin, Joseph, 23, 26, 93, 107, 109, 110–123, 128–136, 137–138, 146–152, 154, 157, 159, 167, 168, 169; anti-Stalinism, 26, 27, 33; death of, 30; deformation of Lenin, 126, 129–133, 136; deformation of Marx, 120–121, 128, 129–132, 159–161, 169; deformation of Socialism, 121; Hitler-Stalin Pact, 131; methodology of, 109, 114, 117–125, 129; "personality cult," 114, 147, "The Economic Problem of Socialism in the U.S.S.R.," 119, 120, 121; Stalinism, 4–5, 26, 40, 47, 48, 104, 105, 128–132, 144; worsening of the class struggle, 130–131, 146, 160
State, 7–8, 9, 13, 14, 15, 19, 21, 24, 28, 34, 41, 42, 52, 53, 54, 73, 77; bourgeois state, 15, 16, 17, 19; class reductionist view of state, 28; class view of state, 7–8; commune-state, 18, 20, 33; depoliticize, state, 13, 14, 17; proletarian state, 8, 15, 17, 18, 19, 20, 33, 113; separation of state and party, 163; "smashing" of the bourgeois state, 33; state-as-domination, 7; statelessness, 7–8, 9, 19, 34, 35, 52, 53–54; "withering away of the state," 7–8, 19, 22, 25, 101, 104
Strategy-tactics, 108–115, 117, 118, 128–132, 152, 162
Stratification: social stratification, 12, 32; talent stratification, 12, 23
Subject-object unity, 37, 38, 39, 41, 99, 117–118, 124; object, 38, 39; objective, 124–125; subject, 38, 39; subjective intervention, 124–125, 132, 141–144, 145, 146, 154–158
Sziklai, László, 4

Talent, stratification of talent, 11, 12
Technological intelligentsia, 148
Teleological action, 4, 38, 39, 42, 100, 102, 103, 124–125; teleology, 84, 94, 98, 99, 141–144, 145, 146, 154–158
Theory-practice, 109
Theory of value, 25, 47, 48, 81, 119–125; surplus value, 121, 122, 123; under capitalism, 47; under socialism, 47
Totalitarianism, 67; left totalitarianism, 40, 44, 146, 148–151; right totalitarianism, 40
Trade Unions, 49, 50, 101, 104, 166
Transcendence: of division of labor, 143; of subjugated labor, 143; transcendence of bourgeois order, 168

Transition, 145, 155–157; to capitalism, 138, 139; to socialism, 138, 139
Trotsky, Leon, 101, 104, 108, 110, 111, 113, 114

Underdevelopment, 94, 98, 99, 104, 112, 133, 138, 147, 154
Uneven development, 108, 112
United States, 87–88, 134, 136
Unity of Lukács, Marx, and Lenin, 169
Unity of Marx and Lenin, 169
Utilitarianism, 34, 35

Valorization, 25, 44, 54, 140, 143
"Vulgar sociology," 35

Wants, 11, 34, 35
World Wars: Imperial wars, 126, 131; WW I, 126; WW II, 131, 134
World-wide crisis; of capitalism, 165, 166, 168; of communism, 165, 166, 168
Worker-peasant alliance, 29, 51, 111, 127
Worker self-management, 6

THE PROCESS OF DEMOCRATIZATION
Georg Lukács
Translated by Susanne Bernhardt and Norman Levine
Introduction by Norman Levine

Georg Lukács's *The Process of Democratization* provides indispensable reading for an understanding of the revolution that swept Russia and Eastern Europe during 1989–1990. Lukács, a spokesman for anti-Bolshevik communism, was the advance guard of anti-Stalinist reform. Written in the aftermath of the Prague Spring, his book was a precursor to many of the Gorbachev reforms.

Lukács was the leading communist intellectual in the world until his death. During his last 15 years, he embarked upon a massive effort to revive Marxism as philosophy, as aesthetics, and as politics. *The Process of Democratization* was part of this attempt at a Marxist renaissance. He would probably be surprised to find that the Second Russian Revolution of 1989–1990 moved far beyond his reformism, overthrowing even the anti-Stalinist communism that he fought to retain.

Susanne Bernhardt is a translator and author residing in Berlin, Germany. **Norman Levine** is Professor of History at the Consortium for Atlantic Studies at Arizona State University, Tempe. He has written *The Tragic Deception: Marx Contra Engels* and *Dialogue Within the Dialectic*.

*A volume in the SUNY series in
Contemporary Continental Philosophy
Dennis J. Schmidt, editor*

STATE UNIVERSITY OF NEW YORK PRESS

ISBN 0-7914-0762-4